"At last, a Genesis commentary wi
gaps in Genesis interpretation by
book. She also draws from her wo
the integrity of all life in the divii
and clear, and she uses scholarship wiun....
Beginning will be terrific for use in classrooms, for study groups, anu ~,
serious readers of Genesis. Bergant's book is a cause for celebration."

—Kathleen M. O'Connor
William Marcellus McPheeters Professor of
Old Testament, Emerita
Columbia Theological Seminary
Decatur, Georgia

"In many programs of Bible study for adults, the tendency to want to reduce
the biblical text to a simple and familiar message looms large. In her book
Genesis: In The Beginning, Dianne Bergant does what she does so well: she
keeps before the reader the many and varied elements that must be employed
when approaching the Bible for understanding. Although not intended as a
book for adult Bible study, the point is made that if one wishes to advance
beyond a simple reading, the serious learner must come to realize the text
cannot be separated from the world that produced it. The reader must take
into account how that 'world behind the text' and the 'world of the text'
provide the necessary context for being able to discover meaning in this living
word of God that has relevance for us today. This contemporary application
is the 'world in front of the text,' our world! Bergant explains this process and
the variety of questions we might ask the text as we confront many uncertain
passages. She then applies the method. Such a fresh presentation keeps us
aware that the word of God cannot be reduced to a simple read."

—Barbara Shanahan
Director of the Catholic Biblical School
Buffalo, New York

Genesis

In the Beginning

Dianne Bergant, CSA

A Michael Glazier Book

LITURGICAL PRESS
Collegeville, Minnesota

www.litpress.org

A Michael Glazier Book published by Liturgical Press

Cover design by Ann Blattner. Illustration: *God as the Creator of the World*. Bibles moralisées, Paris, first half of the 13th century. Cod. 2554, fol. 1v (Genesis).

Scripture translations are the author's own.

1   2   3   4   5   6   7   8   9

Library of Congress Cataloging-in-Publication Data

Bergant, Dianne.
    Genesis : in the beginning / Dianne Bergant, CSA.
        pages   cm
    "A Michael Glazier Book."
    Includes bibliographical references and index.
    ISBN 978-0-8146-8250-0 — ISBN 978-0-8146-8275-3 (ebook)
    1. Bible. Genesis—Commentaries.   I. Title.

BS1235.53.B473 2013
222.1107—dc23   2013015818

Contents

Introduction

The Bible opens with בְּרֵאשִׁית usually translated as "In the beginning
. . . ." But in the beginning of what? Is this a temporal clause indicating in the beginning of time? Or does it refer to the beginning of God's
creative activity with no specific reference to the time? What appears to
be a subtle and, perhaps to some, a minor distinction is really quite significant. One might appeal to this passage for evidence that the universe
is constantly unfolding into more and more complexity, as contemporary
science claims. Or one might appeal to it as evidence of specific acts of
creation out of nothing (*ex nihilo*), as many traditional believers hold.
Since such a distinction is a contemporary concern, not one of ancient
believers, we would do well not to look to an ancient story for an endorse-
ment of any current cosmological understanding.

Yet another possible way of understanding the phrase might be considered. It concerns the origins of ancient Israel. Scholars agree that this
account of creation was placed in front of a much earlier story of the history of the nation, a story that included its own version of creation (Gen
2:4a-25). The additional and later version of primordial divine activity
(1:1-31) now provides a lens through which the entire tradition of the
foundation and development of Israel as a nation can be read and understood. In other words, it is now clear that from the creation of the universe
the God of the people of Israel was always present, bringing order out of
chaos, whether that chaos was primordial, social, or political. Though the
Hebrew form of that first word does not allow for the translation "From
beginning . . . ," the theological sense of the entire history of the people
does suggest such an understanding: From the beginning, God has been
creating order out of chaos and continues to do so even to our own day.

Literary Structure and Genre(s)

The book of Genesis has been divided into two major parts: Genesis 1–11 is referred to as the Primeval History; Genesis 12–50 as the Ancestral History. Though distinct in themselves, these two parts are linked by means of a *genealogy*. A genealogy can be structured in one of two ways. It can move backward in time in a linear fashion, noting successive ancestors and their relation with each other until one arrives at the original ancestor. A second way begins with the ancestor and traces descendants, noting how they branch out from generation to generation. In biblical genealogies, the names of women were only included when, because of the practice of polygamy, it was necessary to know which wife was the mother of the son through whom descent was traced. It is obvious that these women were indispensable for the sake of legitimate descent,[1] yet their indispensability did not seem to earn them lasting importance.

Throughout Genesis, genealogies provide ancestral information and link various stories. Each genealogy is introduced by the word תּוֹלְדוֹת (*tôlēdôt*, generations), a word derived from the verb יָלַד (*yālad*, to beget or to bring forth). It is usually translated "descendants," "generations," or "family history." This word serves as a structuring device throughout the entire book of Genesis:

2:4	the generations of heaven and Earth
5:1	the generations of Adam
6:9	the generations of Noah
10:1	the generations of the sons of Noah
11:10	the generations of Shem
11:27	the generations of Terah
25:12	the generations of Ishmael
25:19	the generations of Isaac
36:1, 9	the generations of Esau
37:2	the generations of Jacob

---

1. The essential role played by these women exemplifies what contemporary readers criticize as "biology determines destiny."

While some cultures trace lineage through their mothers (matrilineal), ancient Israel's practice was patrilineal, concerned with the male line. Usually tracing lineage has less to do with gender preference than with determining lines of inheritance. Though in most contemporary societies people can inherit from both parents, traces of patrilineal preference can be found in the almost universal custom of offspring carrying the father's surname and women generally assuming the surname of their husbands.

The book of Genesis is characterized as the unfolding of an ongoing narrative, made up of various types of stories. The first to be encountered is the *myth*. Contrary to popular understanding that myths lack truth, they actually address fundamental issues such as life and death, origins and ends, matters that are too comprehensive to be confined to the specificity required of history or science. The major characters in myths are gods or other supernatural beings. The events described take place in sacred time, time-out-of-time, a form of time often referred to as primordial time. Because they describe what took place in sacred time, myths are frequently associated with religious ritual. Although most of the mythic stories in Genesis are restricted to the Primeval History, mythic elements are frequently found in the Ancestral History as well: God speaking directly to Abram (12:1-3) or in a dream to Hagar (16:7-14).

A second type of narrative found in Genesis is the *legend*. Many scholars do not differentiate between the between legend and saga. Unlike the otherworldly character of the myth, the legend recounts human actions that occurred in human history at a place accessible to human beings. Many of them memorialize cultural champions such as Rachel, who tricked her father when he deprived her of her share of inheritance (31:14-19). Other legends are linked with places such as the spring where Hagar rested (16:14). A particular kind of legendary narrative is the etiology, a story that provides an explanation for unusual natural phenomena, such as the pillar of salt (19:12-29). Though their historical accuracy might be questioned, legends are generally considered believable.

Some readers might regard parts of Genesis as *historical narrative*, but there are no genuine historical narratives in the book. Genesis does supply us with a great deal of historical information and provides a sketch of some of the historical periods that served as backdrops for the narratives. It acquaints us with several social, economic, and political practices that were current during the times assigned to main characters. Nevertheless, according to modern standards, the historical accuracy of the Genesis accounts is doubtful and the material found here should not be used in any attempt at historical reconstruction.

The *genealogy* plays a very important role in the book of Genesis. Though not rigidly historical, it is a social map that provides a sketch of a person's place within the lineage system. Besides identifying that person's place within the kinship structure, it indicates who is an eligible marriage partner and who is not. The genealogies in Genesis are all patrilineal (traced through the father's line).

Aesthetics of the Text

The narrative character of the book of Genesis is enhanced by creative literary techniques. The *metaphor* is a figure of speech that ascribes to one object attributes that really belong to another. For example, a vast harvest is described as "grain in quantities like the sands of the sea" (41:49). The most striking metaphoric language is found in the characterization of God. Using anthropomorphic (human-form) language, God is depicted as a potter (2:7), a sculptor (2:22), a savior (7:1), an executioner (19:24), a match-maker (24:27), and a wrestler (32:28). Metaphoric language is not descriptive identification; God is not a potter, sculptor, savior, executioner, match-maker, or wrestler. Metaphors are chosen because some dominant characteristic of each of them is ascribed to God. The gender bias of the ancient Israelites is evident in their primary male characterization of God in Genesis.

A second literary technique found in Genesis is the *pun* or play on the sound of words. This manner of speaking is commonly found in oral cultures but frequently lost in translation. Examples of this feature are found in the creation narrative where the man, אָדָם (*'ādām*), is made from the ground, אֲדָמָה (*'ădāmâ*, 2:7), and the woman, אִשָּׁה (*'ishshâ*), is made from the man, אִישׁ (*'îsh*, 2:23); Isaac, יִצְחָק (*yiṣḥāq*), is derived from the verb for laugh, צָחַק (*ṣāḥaq*, 18:13), and Israel, יִשְׂרָאֵל (*yiśrā'el*), from the verb for contend, שָׂרָה (*śārâ*, 32:28).

The poetic sections of the Genesis narratives regularly include examples of *parallelism*, a form consisting of a couplet or triplet in which the first line is either repeated or contrasted in the succeeding line(s). Parallelism provides a way of emphasizing the thought in the first line of the couplet or triplet. An example is found in the creation narrative (1:27):

God created	*adam*	in his image
he created	them	in the image of God
he created	them	male and female[2]

The artistry in the narrative of the flood can be seen in the very struc-ture of the account (6:9–8:22). The story unfolds in the form of a *chiasm*, in which a sequence of ideas is repeated or contrasted in reverse order, and the midpoint is the principal idea:

A Noah is described as righteous
 B God instructs Noah to build and enter the ark
  C The flood commences
   D The waters rise
    E God remembers Noah
   D¹ The waters recede
  C¹ The waters dry up
 B¹ God instructs Noah to leave the ark
A¹ Noah offers sacrifice

Authorship

The origin of the material found in the book of Genesis is shrouded in mystery. Many of the accounts, such as ancestral stories, originated as oral folktales that were cherished by various tribes, handed down from generation to generation, and finally compiled into a cohesive narrative. Other stories, such as the creation and flood accounts, were borrowed from neighboring ancient Near Eastern civilizations, recast so as to reflect the experience and religious understanding of the Isra-elites, and incorporated into their own national history. In the case of Genesis, the question is less one of authorship than of composition and editorial activity.

2. Literary analysis of this parallel pattern led Phyllis Trible to interpret the image of God as male and female. See *God and the Rhetoric of Sexuality*, Overtures to Biblical Theology (Philadelphia: Fortress Press, 1978), 15–21.

Though the exact authorship of material in Genesis cannot be established, conclusions can be drawn regarding the character of the groups that shaped and transmitted the stories. The pervasive androcentric focus of the material indicates that the biblical stories originated and developed in male circles. That is not to say that women did not originate or develop stories that reflect women's experience and women's concerns. Because women did not exercise authority outside of their own tents, however, they did not normally have a voice in deciding which traditions were preserved; they did not function in significant roles in cultic ceremonies where tribal and clan traditions were recited and reshaped; they did not reinterpret the basic stories when circumstances signaled the need for new perspectives. Along with the rest of the community, women did hand down the traditions to the next generation. Nevertheless, they exercised little or no influence in its formation or re-formation.

The Genesis narratives not only reflect an androcentric focus but also reveal a particular social situation. All the major characters are relatively independent, self-sufficient male heads of their respective households. They may have faced extraordinary obstacles, but they always overcame them and emerged triumphant and prosperous. With few exceptions, these stories originated from positions of privilege. This privilege was exercised within the patriarchal household as well, where the power of life and death rested in the hands of the patriarch. Characteristics such as these are reflected in the biblical stories and contribute to the notion of male authorship.

Sources, Date, and Place of Composition

A complex of recognizable vocabulary and narrative styles has led scholars to believe that Genesis, like the Pentateuch in its entirety, was the result of the combination of four discrete literary traditions. An explanation of the combination of these traditions is known as the Documentary Hypothesis. Though the initial particulars of this hypothesis have been modified over the years, its basic premise continues to be accepted by most scholars.[3] Two of these sources were identified by the specific name for God most frequently used in that literary complex. Yahwist is the name

---

3. Antony F. Campbell and Mark A. O'Brien, *Sources of the Pentateuch: Texts, Introductions, Annotations* (Minneapolis, MN: Fortress Press, 1993).

given to the tradition that prefers יהוה (YHWH), the personal name of the God of Israel; Elohist is the name given to the tradition that favors אֱלֹהִים (ʾĕlōhîm), the generic word for gods. A third tradition, called Priestly, is also found in the pages of Genesis. These traditions, along with a fourth known as Deuteronomic, which is not found in Genesis, can be traced throughout the entire Pentateuch.

The Yahwist, designated J from the German spelling *Jahve*, is the oldest tradition, usually dated some time during the tenth century BCE. In addition to its accounts of creation, it traces Israel's history from its ancestral origins to the preparation of its entry into Canaan. Its stories are dynamic; it portrays its characters as flawed human beings, and it describes God in highly anthropomorphic (human-form) language. Because the stories in this tradition exhibit particular interest in the tribes located in the southern territory of Judah, scholars believe that it may have functioned as the national epic of the Davidic/Solomonic monarchy that ruled in the south of the land.

Though it usually dates sometime in the ninth century BCE, the Elohist (E) includes stories reflecting the same period of history as does J. Its stories possess a Mosaic character, however, often focusing on the covenant. Many scholars today reject the idea that E was ever an independent literary document, arguing that it was really a northern reinterpretation of the southern Davidic version of the national history. Whether it existed in its own right or was simply a reinterpretation of J, E shows more interest in the northern tribes of Israel than those of Judah and in the Levitical priests of Shiloh than in the Aaronite priests in Jerusalem.

Most contemporary scholars maintain that the last source added in the development of Genesis is the Priestly tradition (P). Its name testifies to its cultic focus. While many of the social and religious regulations found in this tradition predated the Babylonian Exile (ca. 586–538 BCE), the literary tradition itself has long been considered postexilic, probably from the sixth century BCE. Whether or not all these traditions were actual literary documents, and whatever their precise dating might have been, scholars agree that Genesis, or the entire Pentateuch for that matter, is a composite of different theological traditions woven together to create one coherent story.

Social Setting[4]

The primary social institution found in Genesis is the ancient household. It is patriarchal (father-headed) in structure, patrilineal (descending through the male line) in identification, and patrilocal (located in the household of the husband) in residence. The households are usually multigenerational, including both family members and those under the care of the patriarch, such as slaves, debt servants, and resident aliens. These households are economically, culturally, and religiously self-sufficient, and members are dependent on them for their survival. The needs of the household influence the decision as to whether marriage will be endogamous (within the tribe or clan) or exogamous (outside the tribe or clan). The former practice tends to strengthen family bonds and ensure continuity; the latter enriches the family and expands it.

The women in patriarchal households function in two very important ways. Wives are expected to give birth to many children, both sons and daughters. Besides the firstborn son, the successor of the patriarch as heir and head of the household, sons enhance the honor of the patriarch and are seen as evidence of his virility. Daughters are needed for marriage exchange. Daughters of one household are exchanged in marriage for the daughters of another. In that way, their productive and reproductive potential, which is lost to their family of origin through marriage, is compensated by the productive and reproductive potential of the daughters who marry into the household.

Some commentators refer to the wives of the male ancestors as matriarchs. This is not an accurate designation. The word "matriarch" means "mother-head," or "female ruler." Though married to a patriarch, the wife does not thereby govern but is subservient to the men who rule in her patriarchal household. Therefore, the wives of biblical ancestors were not true matriarchs. Though not as the heads of their households, women did exercise authority within them. This was particularly true of the chief wife of the patriarch. Ancient Israelite women raised the children, tended

---

4. For an extensive treatment of women in ancient Israelite society, see Carol Meyers, *Discovering Eve: Ancient Israelite Women in Context* (New York: Oxford University Press, 1988), or "The Family in Early Israel" in *Families in Ancient Israel*, ed. Leo G. Perdue, Joseph Blenkinsopp, John J. Collins, and Carol Meyers, *The Family, Religion, and Culture* (Minneapolis, MN: Westminster/John Knox Press, 1997), 1–47.

the fire, provided food and clothing for the members of the household, drew the water for the family and the livestock, and cared for the small animals. Women of lower economic classes often worked along with the men, farming crops and herding flocks.

The Bible portrays Canaan, the land of promise, as "a land flowing with milk and honey" (Exod 3:8, 17). The ancestors appear initially as nomadic herders. The stories suggest, however, that they also did some farming. Most likely their livelihood was a combination of herding and seasonal farming. Sheep were raised primarily for their wool, but they also provided meat and hides. The family's diet probably consisted of grains, vegetables, and fruits. Though slaughtered for sacrifice, an animal's meat was eaten only on rare occasions, chiefly when hospitality required that such honor be shown a guest. Then a young male animal was chosen, because the female was necessary for breeding and for the milk that it could produce.

Theological Perspectives

Genesis is above all a book of theology, not an account of history. Besides the various Pentateuchal traditions (J, E, D, P), which are really theological perspectives, Genesis is rich with many important theological themes. Prominent here are the various images of God found within the stories. In the Primeval History, God is depicted as the sole creator of and ruler over the heavens and Earth and all that is within them. The exclusive sovereignty of God's power is remarkable in the ancient Near Eastern world, which revered many gods. In the Ancestral History, God is portrayed as the divine patron of the main ancestors, which, in the patriarchal character of the Bible, meant the male ancestors. In other words, God is identified with men, not women (the God of Abraham, the God of Isaac, the God of Jacob). As patron deity, God calls the ancestors, promises them descendants and land, and protects them from enemies. Israel's response to God as creator and patron is worship that expresses gratitude and praise.

The second important theological theme is the integrity of creation. The natural world is not the source of temptation or evil, as some ancient cultures and earlier theological perspectives have claimed. Nor is it simply the storehouse of riches made available for human consumption and exploitation, as some contemporary people maintain. Rather, creation's fundamental goodness is affirmed by the Bible itself. The first creation account states that "God looked at everything . . . and . . . found it very good" (Gen 1:31). Furthermore, elements of natural creation are frequently the vehicles of divine revelation and communication. Genesis states that humans have been given responsibility for this creation; it also insists that they are accountable to God for its growth and well-being. The responsibility that is theirs exemplifies the dignity bestowed on human beings at the time of their creation; a corresponding responsibility implies ethical standards which, if lived out, lead to living in harmony with the rest of creation as well as with each other.

The fecund character of much of natural creation led the ancient Israelites to associate it closely with women and the mystery of life that they carry within themselves. This similarity led to a reverence for the creative and procreative powers of both natural creation and women. It also resulted, however, in men's apparent desire to possess and control these powers. Thus, both nature and women were brought under the domination of the men of the society.

A third theme points to the literary pattern of sin–punishment–second chance, which can be traced throughout the book of Genesis. This pattern reflects three theological issues. First, sin presumes that there is a moral imperative either explicitly stated, such as the prohibition of eating from the tree of the knowledge of good and evil (2:17), or implicitly recognized, as in Cain's need to respect the life of his brother (4:1-16). Second, the notion of retribution maintains that good behavior should be rewarded and evil behavior punished: Noah follows God's directives in building the ark and is rewarded with survival (8:1); Sodom is punished for its sinfulness (19:24). The third issue, offering a second chance, characterizes the God of Israel in a unique way. Though justice is certainly required, the God of Israel is merciful. God's reaction to human failing does not rest with punishment. A chance to start anew is always offered, beginning with the Adam and Eve (3:23) to the transformation of Joseph's brothers (45:5).

The special relationship between God and the people is sometimes characterized as a covenant, which was a solemn legal pact that bound two parties together. This pact included grave responsibilities on the part of one or both of the parties. Genesis records two such covenants. In each instance, it is God who initiates the covenant and, though it is made through the agency of an individual, the bond established is never with that individual alone. Though made through Noah, the first covenant was really established with "all living creatures that are on earth" (9:17). Genesis contains two versions of the second covenant made through Abram/Abraham (15:1-21 and 17:1-27). This covenant includes all those who belong to his family. Biblical covenants are evidence of God's desire to relate with human beings in a personal and intimate manner.

Contemporary Reading

It is clear from this introduction that Genesis was written from a male perspective, attentive primarily to male concerns. How is a contemporary reader to treat such literature? First, regardless of how offensive the passage might seem, it is important that the reader first respect the integrity of the passage and read it carefully to discover what it actually says. Scholars refer to this first step as discovering the world within the text. Biases within the passage that we today might recognize should be acknowledged so that the cultural limitations of the people portrayed in the passage are not seen as a standard by which contemporary life is to be judged. Next, the cultural and religious world of the author should be examined. This examination should uncover the world behind the text. Insights into this historical world aid in understanding aspects of the biblical passage itself. Here too the cultural differences between the ancient world and the contemporary world must be noted so that the limitations of that world not be considered a standard either.

Some maintain that at times these literary and/or historical limitations deprive biblical passages of revelatory value for today. The contemporary reader must be very careful not to draw this conclusion too quickly, for it might stem from the reader's own inclination to view such cultural limitations as standards, which they are not, and to reject them as standards rather than acknowledge them as cultural limitations.

As important as these two steps are, they merely place the reader first in the story itself and then in ancient history. An additional step is needed to provide insight into how the message of the passage might have religious value for the reader situated in the contemporary world. This third perspective, attentive to the concerns of this reader, is known as the world in front of the text. It takes the meaning of the passage, not simply details of the story, and brings it into the world or social location of the reader. This social location always includes the concerns that the reader brings to the passage. The primary concerns highlighted in this commentary include issues of gender, social status, economic class, and integrity of creation. Such issues will serve as the lens through which both the biblical passage and the author and history behind it will be critiqued and contemporary reinterpretation will be suggested.

Part 1

"In the Beginning"
(Gen 1:1–11:36)

Often referred to as the Primeval History, the first eleven chapters of Genesis are a combination of myths and genealogies (see "Literary Structure and Genre[s]" in the introduction). The stories describe beginnings: the beginning of the world, the beginning of humankind and fundamental social practices, the beginning of clans and cities, the beginning of agriculture and invention. They also recount the beginning of rebellion, murder, licentiousness, and other forms of dissolute living. The stories in these first chapters reach deep into the human psyche and describe some of the struggles that every human being faces, regardless of generation or culture.

Chapter 1

"And God Saw That It Was Good"
(Gen 1:1–3:24)

Very few biblical passages have influenced Western thinking as deeply as have the first three chapters of Genesis. Our view of humankind's place in the world of nature and the character of the interactions that this entails as well as our perception of gender relations are often grounded in our view of these stories. Creation in all of its splendor, diversity, and goodness is described as having come directly from God. At the time of their creation, the first human couple enjoys gender parity and jointly exercises limited jurisdiction over the rest of the created world. This initial harmony crumbles, however, with the entrance of sin. Enmity between humans and animals threatens, earth rebels against human mismanagement, and the man dominates the woman. It is clear from the stories that the subsequent state of alienation was not the initial intention of the creator. It is, however, the state of the world. While the first chapter of this commentary opens with stories of creation and the promise that this newness brings, it leaves us at the end in a world of conflict and hostility.

A Cosmology (Gen 1:1–2:4a)

Initial attention turns to the Hebrew word אֱלֹהִים (*ʾĕlōhîm*). This is not a formal name but the masculine plural form of the generic term, "god." Like the other Near Eastern societies, ancient Israel possessed an androcentric (man-centered) perspective and perceived its world accordingly.

Though women sometimes exercised authority and wielded a certain amount of power, men were considered superior, and thus the principal gods were generally characterized as male. This male characterization is a metaphor, not a definition. God is no more male than God is a rock.[1]

The Hebrew plural form of the word "god" is no reference to trinitarian belief, as has been asserted in some interpretations of the passage throughout the centuries. Rather, it betrays Israel's henotheistic perspective, a perspective that recognized the possibility of other gods for other nations but only one God for Israel (see Josh 24:15). It was not until after the exile that Israel insisted that only one God exists. The move to monotheism is generally seen as enlightened.[2] This move eliminated the respect and loyalty previously accorded female deities,[3] however, and thus strengthened the patriarchal character of Israelite religion. Divine power was eventually considered exclusively male.

Earth is described as תֹהוּ (*tōhû*, formless) and בֹהוּ (*bōhû*, void). Depending on how the first word of Genesis is understood (see the introduction), this account states that either God created a formless void and then filled it or a formless void existed before God began creating.[4] Besides formless and void, there is חֹשֶׁךְ (*ḥōshek*, darkness) and תְהוֹם (*tᵉhôm*, deep). The latter word is a reference to the chaotic cosmic sea on which Earth rests. "Formless," "void," and "deep" call to mind Mesopotamian gods of chaos. Some interpreters maintain "deep" is akin to Tiamat, a dragon of chaos characterized as unruly waters and defeated in the primordial cosmic battle. In the ancient Akkadian myth *Enuma Elish*, this disruptive and dangerous female force was conquered by an orderly and controlling male power, thus adding support to the bias against female divine power.

Besides providing an account of primordial events, this account refutes the polytheistic ideology undergirding the Mesopotamian ver-

---

1. God is referred to as a rock in several psalms: Pss 18:3, 32, 48; 19:15; 28:1; 31:3; 42:10; 62:3, 7, 8; 78:35; 89:27; 92:16; 94:22; 144:1.

2. For a study that uncovers some of the "violent, exclusionary, negatively defining" features of monotheism, see Regina M. Schwartz, *The Curse of Cain: The Violent Legacy of Monotheism* (Chicago, IL: The University of Chicago Press, 1997).

3. It is clear that at times some Israelites worshiped female deities: Asherah (1 Kgs 15:13; 23:4) and "the queen of heaven" (Jer 44:17-19).

4. Down through the centuries, cosmologists have wrestled with the question of the origin of the universe. Even Stephen Hawking addresses it in *A Brief History of Time*, rev. ed. (New York: Bantam Books, 1998), 7–9.

sion, demonstrating that it is Israel's God and that God alone orders the universe. Moreover, this ordering is accomplished by divine decree, not through any cosmic battle, as the Mesopotamian story recounts. This divine decree more closely resembles the creative method of the Egyptian god Ptah, who, according to an inscription found in a temple in Memphis, also created by divine word. It is clear that ancient Israel was influenced by Egyptian myths as well as those from Mesopotamia.

The cosmogony, or creation of the cosmos, begins with the creation and adornment first of the heavens and then of Earth. The divine activity that unfolds throughout the six days of creation follows the same order found in *Enuma Elish*. Though the ancient perspective was anthropocentric (human-centered), the ancient people recognized the extraordinary power and majesty of the natural world of which they were a part. This creation account pays special attention to the world's orderly design and the interdependence of its various entities. Literary patterns exemplify this ordering: Creation of the universe took place during the first three days; its adornment was called forth on the next three days:

Day 1: light	Day 4: luminaries
Day 2: sky and waters	Day 5: birds and fish
Day 3: land and plants	Day 6: animals and humans

The repetition of evening and morning measures time. The inherent goodness of the natural world is stated again and again: "And God saw that it was good" (vv. 10, 12, 18, 21, 25).[5]

The report of the creation of animals follows a definite structure: God decides to create; God creates; God blesses (vv. 20-28). While most elements of the created world appear because God said, "Let there be," and vegetation springs forth because God includes Earth in the creative process, it is not merely that the plants have life within them. Earth itself is fertile and able to bring forth plants that are self-perpetuating. This mysterious power within Earth has fascinated human beings from the beginning. The planet is called Mother Earth precisely because it

---

5. See Luise Schottroff, "The Creation Narrative: Genesis 1:1–2:4a," in *A Feminist Companion to Genesis*, ed. Athalya Brenner (Sheffield, UK: Sheffield Academic Press, 1997), 24–38.

corresponds to a woman's ability to bring forth life. This mysterious power of Earth has also been a source of serious temptation. Ancient people often perceived the bounty of Earth's produce as a sign of its divine character, and they worshiped Earth. Modern people see the same bounty and too often exploit it for their own ends.

The account of the creation of the animals contains the blessing of self-propagation and the promise of a multitude of offspring. Like vegetation, animals participate in the creative process, having been made with the ability to perpetuate their species. There are, however, noticeable differences in the account of the creation of humankind. The verb form is cohortative, denoting deliberation ("Let us make"; v. 26), rather than jussive, which denotes direction ("Let the water . . . the earth bring forth"; vv. 20, 24). Furthermore, while the animals are made "of every kind" (vv. 21, 24-25), humankind is made "in our image, after our likeness" (v. 26). Finally, human beings not only receive a blessing but also are given a twofold commission, "subdue. . . . Have dominion" (v. 28). These differences in the story call attention to the uniqueness of the human creature.

Image and likeness are sometimes employed as synonyms. Nevertheless, "image" refers to something concrete, like a statue, while "likeness" is less concrete. The dual expression is a form of emphasis. The word referring to humankind is אָדָם (*'ādām*). Since no definite article appears here (v. 26), the reference is not to a specific person. The word is singular and here has a collective meaning. Thus it is translated "humankind." Although it is a masculine form, it is clear from the passage that there is no gender exclusivity here; nor is there gender preference. Furthermore, both the man and the woman are made in the image of God. This can be seen in the poetic construction of the text:

God created	*adam*	in his image
he created	them	in the image of God
he created	them	male and female

Over the centuries, many explanations of the phrase "image of God" have been advanced. The original meaning reflects the practice of setting up an image or symbol that signifies sovereignty, something similar to a national flag. As images of God, the human beings represented the locale where God rules supreme. In the ancient world, royalty were perceived in this way.[6] They were either considered divine themselves or they represented the deity to their people. The twofold commission given the human couple in this story, "subdue. . . . Have dominion," is also royal language. Thus, one can say that this is a royal couple that exercises authority over the rest of the created world. Still, their authority is limited. The woman and man are not gods; they are images of God, representatives responsible for God's world and accountable to God in carrying out this responsibility.

Although royalty implies hierarchy, the nature of the mythical story tends to minimize the disparity in such social reality. The characterization of the couple might be royal, but the woman and man here represent the entire human race, not simply the monarchy. The myth actually democratizes their privilege of jurisdiction and oversight. Every woman and every man is made in God's image and has been commissioned to stand as God's representative in the management of the natural world.[7]

In many ways the creation of the human beings parallels the creation of the animals, yet humans also enjoy a unique characteristic. Despite the fact that they share the same habitat with some of these creatures, they are given limited jurisdiction over the rest of creation. This is an invitation not to exploit or cause harm to the natural world but to oversee its growth and to manage its productivity, for they are representatives of God, meant to govern as God would govern. It should be noted that this privilege is accorded both the woman and the man. There is no distinction here; there is no gender bias.

The last act of God is the establishment of the Sabbath (2:3). Its placement as the final divine act implies that observance of the Sabbath is grounded in the very structure of the created universe. There is no gender bias here either; both the woman and the man are obligated to observe the

6. For an extensive treatment of this theme, see Phyllis Bird, "Male and Female He Created Them," in *Missing Persons and Mistaken Identities: Women and Gender in Ancient Israel*, Overtures to Biblical Theology (Minneapolis, MN: Fortress Press, 1997), 123–54.

7. For very different interpretations of images of God derived from literary analysis, see Phyllis Trible, *God and the Rhetoric of Sexuality*, Overtures to Biblical Theology (Philadelphia: Fortress Press, 1978), 15–21; Phyllis A. Bird, " 'Male and Female He Created Them': Gen 1:27b in the Context of the Priestly Account of Creation," *Harvard Theological Review* 74 (1981): 129–59.

Sabbath and are entitled to enjoy its blessings. Furthermore, this gender inclusivity is somehow grounded in creation itself.

The Garden (Gen 2:4b-25)

The very first words of this second creation account alert us to the different point of view: "In the day that YHWH God made the earth and the heavens" (2:4b). First, YHWH (יהוה),[8] the personal name of the God of Israel, is added to the general designation, God. Second, the primary focus of this account is Earth. This narrative is not a cosmology, describing the creation of the cosmos, as is the first account. There is no mention of the creation of celestial bodies, and Earth has already been created when the story begins. The first creation account opens with "In the beginning . . ." (1:1). This second account opens with "In that day . . ." (2:4b), indicating that time has already begun. Earth is the stage on which the events described here unfold.

The two accounts of creation differ in several other ways. In the first story, Earth was a formless void; here, it is barren. In the first account, water was fraught with danger; here, it is indispensable for life. One of the reasons given for the barrenness of Earth is the lack of rain; the other reason is the absence of a human worker. In other words, Earth's fertility is dependent on cooperation between God who sends rain and human beings who work the soil. The relationship between human beings and Earth is a very important theme here. Finally, work itself is not an evil but integral to being human.

The characterizations of God also differ. In the first account, God appears distant, able to create simply by declaration. Here, God is very involved, actually getting down onto the ground and, like a potter, shaping the ground into the form of a man. Furthermore, God appears to be personally involved in the life of this man, conversing with him, providing him a verdant place to live and a companion with whom he can

---

8. Rather than use the sacred name of God, most English versions of the Bible prefer the substitution LORD. This substitution might accord respect to the sacred name, but it reverts to the use of masculine language (LORD) for God. For this reason, YHWH will be used in this commentary when the sacred name of God is found in the text. Furthermore, out of respect for this name, both Jews and Christians refrain from using it in their liturgies.

share his life. God is here portrayed anthropomorphically, that is, with human traits.

The actual report of the creation of the first human being is described in a single verse (2:7). Some contemporary feminist interpreters maintain that there is no sexual specificity to this first creature. According to this view, sexual differentiation occurs only when a rib is taken from this creature's side and fashioned into a woman.[9] Such a position might address contemporary concerns of gender parity, but it moves beyond what the actual biblical narrative reports. Throughout this account, הָאָדָם (*hā'ādām*) appears with the definite article (the man), meaning that a specific male individual is intended, not the generic humankind. This man is a creature of Earth, yet he possesses a vital force that transcends the substance of Earth. אָדָם, (*'ādām*, man) is made from אֲדָמָה, (*'ādāmâ*, ground). When the story is told orally, the play on words is obvious.

As intimate as might be this Earth-creature's relationship with Earth, he does not become a living being until the breath of life is breathed into him, a detail not found in the accounts of the creation of the other creatures of Earth. The second creative act is this biblical author's way of setting the man apart from the other creatures. This is not the breath of God but the breath of life. Nor is it a soul as some much later interpretations suggest, for the ancient Hebrew language had no word for soul. Still, they did realize that there was something more to the human being than merely material substance. The creation of this first human being is reminiscent of human creation in the *Enuma Elish* (a Babylonian creation account) where the victorious god shapes a human being out of the ground that has been mixed with the blood of a god.[10]

---

9. Trible, *God and the Rhetoric of Sexuality*, 94–105. This interpretation conforms to a Jewish tradition claiming that the first man was androgynous. See Gen. Rab. 8:1; Jacob Neuser, *Genesis Rabbah: The Jewish Commentary to the Book of Genesis*, vol. 1 (Atlanta, GA: Scholars Press, 1985); A. T. Reisenberger, "The Creation of Adam as Hermaphrodite—and Its Implications for Feminist Theology," *Judaica* 42 (1993): 447–52; Mieke Bal, *Lethal Love: Feminist Literary Readings of Biblical Love Stories* (Bloomington: Indiana University Press, 1987), 114–19.

10. This perception of the human makeup is not far from the position held today by contemporary science, which contends that humankind emerged from the stuff of the earth and possesses characteristics like consciousness and self-reflection that seem to transcend the confines of material substance.

The description of the garden into which God placed this man (vv. 8-17) has fascinated people from the time the story was first told. The garden was planted in the midst of a barren land, reminiscent of an oasis so familiar to people in the ancient Near East. עֵדֶן (*ʿēden*, Eden) is also translated "luxury" (2 Sam 1:24) or "delight" (Ps 36:8). Thus, the name itself denotes pleasure, explaining why the place is frequently referred to as the Garden of Paradise. Down through the centuries, the search for this mythical garden has been the life project of many. Eden is, however, a metaphor for perfect harmony, not an identifiable geographic place.

Taking the same ground from which the man was created, God made trees to grow that provide the man with both food and delight. Initially, only the tree of life is in the midst of the garden; the tree of the knowledge of good and evil seems to be an afterthought. The tree of life represents humankind's perennial quest for everlasting life. Stories of a search for a plant that can grant humans this life abound in ancient literature. The fact that people believed that there was such a plant indicates that they realized that, though they crave immortality, human beings are mortal by nature. The second tree, the tree of the knowledge of good and evil, may have been inserted into the story when the account of the sin (Gen 3) was added. Both trees now belong to this part of the narrative.

A river wells up to irrigate the mythical garden, dividing into four main branches that flow into the four corners of Earth. Thus, the garden becomes the source of life and fertility for the entire world. These branches represent the major rivers of the world. The Tigris and the Euphrates are well-known rivers that define the borders of Mesopotamia. Presumably, the Pishon is some place in Arabia and the Gihon is in what is today Ethiopia.

God places the man in the garden and gives him a twofold task to perform: to serve the garden[11] and to keep it. The man is placed in the garden with serious responsibility for its fruitfulness. All but one tree, the tree of the knowledge of good and evil, is accessible to him. Many explanations of this knowledge have been advanced over the years. Some maintain that it is simply the practical knowledge that comes from obeying or disobeying. Others consider it moral discernment or even sexual experiential knowledge. It probably refers to knowledge that by right belongs to God alone.

---

11. The word usually translated "till" is derived from the Hebrew word עָבַד (*ʿābad*, to serve) and שָׁמַר (*shāmar*, to keep) and means "to exercise great care for." These renderings better emphasize the custodial character of the man's responsibilities.

This latter explanation is confirmed later by the serpent's remark and the fact that, after the human couple eat the fruit of the tree, they are forbidden to eat of the tree of life that was originally accessible to them. Many ancient people believed that the two most important traits of the gods were divine wisdom and everlasting life. The gods often shared one of these traits but not both of them. To share both would render the recipient divine (see 3:22). This idea, known as "the envy of the gods,"[12] was widespread in the ancient world at this time and might explain why eating the fruit of the tree was forbidden.

The prohibition is delivered in apodictic form: You shall . . . You shall not . . . Unlike the casuistic law form, which includes conditions that lessen the seriousness of the offense and the severity of the punishment (see Exod 21:12-14), law articulated in this form is unconditional. Nothing mitigates its seriousness, and frequently the penalty of violation is death. Certainly the desire to obtain knowledge that is the prerogative of God is an offense serious enough to warrant apodictic expression and its accompanying threat of death. Eating of the tree of life promises everlasting life; eating of the tree of the knowledge of good and evil threatens death.

God recognizes the isolation of this lone Earth creature and decides to remedy it by creating a suitable partner for him.[13] The creation of the animals parallels the earlier creation of the man. God takes the same ground and, like a potter, forms various animals. The intimate link between the

---

12. For an extensive explanation of this motif, see Claus Westermann, *Genesis 1–11: A Commentary* (Minneapolis, MN: Augsburg Publishing House, 1984), 273. It is still a significant theme in many traditional African religions; see Modupẹ Oduyọye, *The Sons of the Gods and the Daughters of Men: An Afro-Asiatic Interpretation of Genesis 1–11* (Maryknoll, NY: Orbis Books, 1984), 25.

13. עֵזֶר כְּנֶגֶר (*'ezer kᵉneged*) is often translated as "suitable helper." Until recently, the focus of this translation has been on the noun עֵזֶר ("helper"), thereby placing the man's companion in a subservient position. Following this, כְּנֶגֶר ("suitable") has been understood according to the way various cultures understand helpers. This could mean a menial helper or an efficient helper. The Hebrew meaning of "suitable" really has the connotation of prominence or complementarity. The word translated "helper" has also frequently been misunderstood. When it appears in other places in the Bible, it connotes strength, frequently military aid. When used in the psalms, it often refers to God (Pss 10:14; 30:10; 54:4; 72:12). The word certainly does not imply subservience. Therefore, in this passage, the companion that God intends to provide is a strong helper who corresponds to the man.

man and the animals cannot be denied. They are all truly creatures of Earth. Nevertheless, a distinction remains. The animals do not correspond to the man; there is no suitable partner here. Instead, the man demonstrates his authority over these animals by naming them.

The creation of the woman (vv. 21-24) is as poetically expressed as was the creation of the man. The story of building a woman from the man's rib is more than picturesque; its mythic roots can be traced back to a wordplay found in an ancient Sumerian creation tradition. There the sound of the word for "rib" is similar to that of "life."[14] Though this play on words was lost when the story was translated into Hebrew, the intended connection between rib and life survived. The initial link between the lady of the rib and lady of life is reinforced in the Genesis account when Eve, the woman of the rib, is referred to as the mother of all the living (3:20). Another play on words reinforces this connection: חַוָּה (ḥawwāh, Eve) is derived from חָיָה (ḥayyāh, to live).

Some people maintain that being fashioned from the rib of the man makes the woman derivative and, therefore, inferior to him. This biased interpretation forgets that the man was made from the ground, and this has never been seen as a sign of his inferiority to Earth. Actually, the creations of the man and the woman are both depicted artistically, and both carry deep anthropological meaning. The man's origin from the ground suggests that he is embedded in the very stuff of material creation. Made of the substance of the man, the woman is like him and, therefore, a suitable partner for him. The man recognizes her suitability, and he declares that she is "bone of my bones and flesh of my flesh" (v. 23). Flesh and bone are what anthropologists call binary opposites. They identify the opposite poles of some aspect of reality and include everything that lies between them. Such a figure of speech is also known as a merismus, in which a part or parts stand for the whole. "Bone and flesh," just like the more familiar "flesh and blood," refers to the entire person. As used here, the phrase not only indicates that the woman is made from the material substance of the man but also indicates natural kinship (see 29:14). As a figurative idiom, bone implies strength and flesh implies weakness. This interpretation suggests that the man sees her as the strength of his strength and weakness of his weakness. She is definitely like him and,

---

14. Samuel Noah Kramer, *The Sumerians: Their History, Culture and Character* (Chicago, IL: University of Chicago Press, 1963), 149.

therefore, a suitable partner. This declaration ends with yet another play on words: אִשָּׁה (*'ishā*, woman) and אִישׁ (*'îsh*, man).[15] As *'ādām* is derived from the ground, so woman is fashioned from the man.

Many maintain that the author's mention of the union that exists between the man and the woman is a reference to marriage (v. 24). Such an understanding is far too narrow. The verse opens with the word "therefore," meaning that what follows is the consequence of what preceded, namely, a description of the intimate relationship between the man and the woman. This relationship is both physical and emotional. Most scholars believe that this verse is an etiological explanation of the powerful attraction between the sexes. Leaving the parents does not mean starting a separate new household, because most patriarchal societies were patrilocal (father-locale; married children lived in the household of the husband's father). Leaving parents and clinging to another refers to a transfer of attachment, loyalty, and obligation. Marriage may be the external expression of this new bonding, but the union of which the bonding is a consequence is much deeper than the social institution.

The very last verse of this chapter (v. 25) reverts to the use of אָדָם (*'ādām*, man). In this verse אִשָּׁה (*'ishshâ*, woman) is used with the masculine possessive modifier "his." Whether the word is translated "woman" or "wife," both of which are options for the Hebrew term, she still belongs to him. No reciprocal feminine possessive modifier indicates that he is hers. Nor does the author choose אִישׁ (*'îsh*), the corresponding relational word for "husband," to refer to the man; he is a man and she is his wife. Mutuality has been replaced by male control. The gender bias in this choice of words is obvious and not in keeping with the perspective of the creation account. The fact that this verse probably came from a later hand in no way mitigates the gender disparity. Rather, it alerts us to the imbalanced relationship between women and men in marital unions found in the ancestral narratives that follow.

The Sin (Gen 3:1-24)

The spotlight now shifts from the actions of God to those of the human couple, and the narrative becomes a drama. First on the stage

---

15. Though אִשָּׁה (*'ishshâ*; woman) and אִישׁ (*'îsh*; man) come from different roots, the similarity of sound is unmistakable.

is the serpent, described as crafty and a wild animal. The play on the sounds of עָרוּם ('*ārûm*, crafty) and עֲרוּמִּים ('*ārûmmîm*, naked) links this chapter with the previous one (2:25). This serpent is a mythic creature, not Satan or the devil. Perhaps it is cast in this questionable role because of its association with Canaanite fertility cults, religious practices that often employed images of serpents. Or it might simply be the serpent's craftiness that suggested it as one who could test the couple's acceptance of their human condition.

Even more puzzling is the choice of the woman rather than the man as the serpent's conversation partner. There is no clear explanation for this in the passage itself, but gender-biased reasons abound. Some claim that women are more gullible than men and a woman would be more easily taken in by the crafty serpent.[16] Others advance the opposite position.[17] They maintain that this woman was much more appealing, more intelligent, and more assertive than the man who seems to remain in the shadows during this conversation.[18] Perhaps the reason for the choice of the woman is really found in Israel's opposition to the Canaanite fertility cults where the snake is found closely associated with a goddess of fertility.[19] In its opposition to these cults, Israel portrayed both the serpent and the woman negatively.

The woman has often been decried as being not only covetous but also a temptress.[20] She wants the forbidden fruit for herself, and she entices her husband to partake of it as well. Several interpreters today see a similarity between this story and one in the ancient Sumerian *Gilgamesh Epic*. There, Enkidu, a man of the wild, is tempted by a seductress who leads him out of savagery into civilization. Some interpreters try to rehabilitate the reputation of the Genesis woman by drawing a comparison between

16. This bias is found in the Bible itself (Sir 25:24; 1 Tim 2:13).

17. For an interpretation of the woman as a knower and actor, an interpreter, and a moral decision maker, see Beverly J. Stratton, *Out of Eden: Reading, Rhetoric, and Ideology in Genesis 2–3* (Sheffield, UK: Sheffield Academic Press, 1995), 85–91.

18. Much Renaissance art contrasts the couple in this way.

19. See William Park, "Why Eve?," *St. Vladimir's Theological Quarterly* 35 (1991): 130.

20. For an overview of such a reading, see Jean Higgins, "The Myth of Eve: The Temptress," *Journal of the American Academy of Religion* 44, no. 4 (1976): 639–47.

these two narratives,[21] thus claiming that, in her desire for wisdom, she initiates the man out of the mythical paradise into the real world. Such attempts at explanation overlook a very important phrase describing the man as one "who was with her" (v. 6). Though silent, the man is not absent. Furthermore, his silence need not imply passivity, as some have contended, but rather consent. They are both guilty.

Upon eating the fruit, the couple's eyes are opened, a reference to attaining insight; they now have firsthand knowledge of evil.[22] They also realize that they are naked, and they become ashamed. The shame of nakedness has led some to conclude that the sin was somehow associated with sexual consciousness. This shame refers to something else, however, for earlier the creation account stated that the couple "become one body" and that "they were naked and not ashamed" (2:24-25). The passage itself gives very little information concerning this matter. All it says is that they were ashamed of their nakedness and so they covered themselves.

The scene of God walking in the garden in the cool of the evening is both charming and theologically revealing. The fact that God addresses only the man does not mean that God is more interested in him than in the woman, or that the man is the spokesperson for both. This may simply be a matter of literary consistency. Since in the previous account of creation it was the man who received the prohibition, it follows that he is the one questioned about it. As soon as the man's shame in nakedness demonstrates his guilt, the recriminations begin. He blames the woman,[23] and she blames the serpent. Neither of them takes responsibility for the free choice each made.

The sentences of the three guilty creatures are all etiological explanations of some aspect of each respective life. They answer questions such as the following: Why does the serpent crawl on its belly and inspire such

21. See Lyn Bechtel, "Rethinking the Interpretation of Genesis 2:4b–3:24," in *A Feminist Companion to Genesis*, ed. Athalya Brenner (Sheffield, UK: Sheffield Academic Press, 1997), 78–117.

22. This sin has traditionally been referred to as the Fall. That designation stems from a much later Christian context, however, that understood the first sin as a fall from grace. Since the ancient Israelites had no concept of grace as Christian theology would later develop it, the designation is out of place in any interpretation of this Genesis account.

23. Adam even seems to blame God: "The woman whom *you gave* to be with me . . ." (v. 12).

dread in the human heart? Why does the woman suffer such excruciating pain in childbearing and yet desire her husband? Why is the land so unwilling to yield its fruit despite the man's backbreaking labor?

Once again there is a pun. The serpent once described as עָרוּם (*'ārûm,* crafty) is now אָרוּר (*'ārûr,* cursed).[24] Some serpents hold the front part of their bodies erect when threatening to attack. Many ancient mythic representations picture them in this pose. As a result of God's curse, the proud serpent is now humbled, doomed to crawl on its belly. Adding to this humiliation, it is destined to eat dust, a symbol of death. The curse also includes a perennial state of enmity between the serpent and the woman and between its offspring and hers. The woman is cited here rather than the man, probably because both she and the serpent are closely associated with life. She is regarded as the source of life, because she bears the children; the serpent was often considered a symbol of everlasting life, because it sheds its skin and seems to start life over again.

The ongoing enmity will be between the offspring of these original adversaries. Because of its abased circumstances, the serpent will be able to attack only the human being's heel.[25] Still, that attack could prove deadly because of its poisonous venom. Likewise, human beings will constantly strike at the head of snakes in an attempt to kill them.

The punishments meted out to the woman and the man are etiological explanations of the hardships they face, conflicts in their relationships with the sources of their origin. Taken from the man, the woman will suffer in her relationship with him; taken from the ground, the man will suffer in his relationship with it. The same word describes this hardship: עִצָּבוֹן (*'iṣṣābôn,* pain [v. 16] and toil [v. 17]). Both she and he will bring forth life only through great effort and suffering. The question of the woman's desire for her husband, which is not reciprocated, has been highly disputed. Some maintain that it implies that the woman's desire to

---

24. Though the words come from very different verbal roots, they are similar in sound.

25. The familiar depiction of Mary under the title of Immaculate Conception portrays her with her heel on the head of the serpent. The biblical passage reads: "*he* will strike your head and you will strike *his* heel" (Gen 3:15). This depiction of Mary stems from a confusion of two Hebrew letters ו and ' resulting in the misreading of the Hebrew.

control the man is countered by his control of her.[26] However the word is translated, its meaning is overshadowed by the subsequent mention of the man's domination over the woman.

The text says that the ground, which is guilty of no offense, is also cursed. This ground is, however, neither barren nor toxic terrain. It is soil that does produce but that is now difficult to cultivate, and its fruits are not always nourishing for human beings. The curse does not really totally affect the ground itself but seems to be limited to its relationship with those who work it. So the curse relates to the man's relation with the ground.

Much has been made of the inevitability of death: "you are dust and to dust you shall return" (3:19). Being made of dust implies that the human creature was really never considered immortal. Eating of the tree of life was the way everlasting life might be attained. Thus, death would be inevitable if the human creature lost access to that tree. The structure of this passage does not suggest that death is the penalty of sin. It says that the man will suffer greatly until he returns to the ground. Death is not itself the punishment. Rather, it marks the end of the suffering, which is the real punishment.

God is now cast in the role of a tailor (3:21), an activity that was usually performed by women. The garments that God provides are made of skins, not leaves, the loincloths with which the couple first clothed themselves (see 3:7). Skins imply a more sophisticated level of civilization. They also imply that death has already entered the scene, namely, the death of animals.

Having eaten of the tree of the knowledge of good and evil, the couple is now kept from the tree of life, lest they possess both wisdom and knowledge that presumably would make them divine (the envy of the gods motif). Only the man is mentioned in this closing unit. This exclusive attention to the man reflects the androcentric (male-centered) practice of including within the reference "man" all those subject to him ("he shall

---

26. The word תְּשׁוּקָה (*t*shûqâ*, desire) clearly denotes sexual desire in Song 7:11. In Genesis 4:7, however, it refers to sin's desire to conquer. See Gordon J. Wenham, *Genesis 1–15*, Word Biblical Commentary (Waco, TX: Word Books Publication, 1987), 81–82; Kenneth A. Mathews, *Genesis 1–11:26*, The New American Commentary: An Exegetical and Theological Exposition of Holy Scripture, vol. 1A (Nashville, TN: Broadman & Holman Publishers, 1996), 248–52; Kristen E. Kvam, Linda S. Schearing, and Valarie H. Ziegler, eds., *Eve & Adam: Jewish, Christian, and Muslim Readings on Genesis and Gender* (Bloomington: Indiana University Press, 1999), 34–36.

rule over you"; 3:16). Having been cast out of the garden of delights and barred from reentry, the human couple must now embark on a new kind of life in a new kind of world.

Contemporary Reading: Banished from the Garden

Adam and Even were not the only ones banished from the garden. All of us who followed them have had to fend off the thorns and thistles of life. Often women have been shackled by both readings and misreadings of the stories treated in this chapter. Their intrinsic human worth and the relationships that flow from it have too often been determined by stories of what happened after the sin, when the harmony between the woman and the man was shattered. Stories that portray them before the sin, however, describe the woman as both on a par with the man and unique in her own right. The stories portraying woman's presumed inferiority and man's presumed dominance should be seen as evidence of a shattered world, not of the world as it was first created. The characterization that stems from the original sinfulness is distorted. Furthermore, the different roles the woman and the man play—bringing forth the next generation and bringing forth the next harvest—should be regarded as both honorable and indispensable for the survival of the human race.

The prevailing male characterization of God is also problematic. This should be understood for what it is, namely, characterization that stems from a culture that erroneously presumes inherent male superiority. Furthermore, characterizations of God (potter, sculptor, and tailor) are simply metaphors, not definitions. They highlight a single aspect in our understanding of God. Images or perceptions of God need not be reduced to one such metaphor, regardless of how prominent that metaphor might be in the Bible.

Contemporary readers should realize that only when mutual respect among women and men is fostered will harmony once more prevail. These stories further remind such readers that, as images of God, both women and men have the awesome responsibility of overseeing the reestablishment of this harmony within all of creation.

Chapter 2

"Sin Is a Demon Lurking at the Door"
(Gen 4:1–6:4)

Born into a world of insubordination, recrimination, and struggle, the next generations of human beings carry on patterns of betrayal set by their ancestors. Here we find the ultimate example of sibling rivalry, which reflects the deadly enmity that often exists between two very different ways of life that may have both claimed the exclusive use of land. There are also reports of blood vengeance and mythic accounts of crossing the boundary that separates humans from the divine. Despite all these transgressions, the human family seems to advance from one stage of cultural development to another.

The androcentric point of view from which these stories are told paints a distorted picture of this human family. There are no stories about the daughters of the first couple, nor are daughters even mentioned in the stories about the sons, this despite the indispensable role played by women in bringing forth the next generation, contributing to the maintenance of the family, and furthering the survival and development of the clan. The prominent ways of life (herding and farming) are accorded male characterization (Abel and Cain), suggesting that the presence of women is simply presumed. This further suggests that whatever women do to support or enhance either way of life is taken for granted and is insignificant. The genealogies that trace descent and mark various developments of the culture are patrilineal (father-line) and women are mentioned only when it is necessary to identify the sons through whom the lineage is traced.

When women do appear, they are depicted as the source of temptation and as weak victims of the desire of others. The gender imbalance that is attributed to the sin of the first couple is felt throughout this entire unit.

The Sons of Eve (Gen 4:1-16)

The first offspring of Adam and Eve are Cain and Abel. At the birth of Cain, Eve explains: "I have produced a man with the help of God" (v. 1). Though procreation was usually credited to the man, Eve claims to have cocreated with God, as if she is the one who has furthered the family and, indeed, the entire human race. There is a play on the sound of קַיִן (*qayin*; Cain) and the verb קָנָה (*qānâ*; produced), as well as קִנֵּא (*qānāʾ*; jealous), which describes Cain's disposition. Abel (הֶבֶל; *hebel*) means "ephemeral" or "short-lived," a portent of what is to come.

The story reflects a common ancient theme (the hostile brothers) and is reminiscent of a Sumerian myth, *Dumuzi and Enkimdu: The Dispute between the Shepherd-God and the Farmer-God*, which describes the conflict between a farmer and a herder, a conflict that is clearly cultural rather than strictly familial. The fact that various ways of life, tribes, and nations are accorded male characterizations points to a definite gender bias. In such situations, women and children are considered merely members of the patriarchal household or tribe, and the importance of people, objects, or events is determined from an androcentric perspective.

The choice of the shepherd (Abel) over the farmer (Cain) may reflect Israel's opposition to the Canaanites' agricultural fertility cults that posed a constant threat to the exclusive worship of Israel's God.[1] Abel conformed to the prescription governing animal husbandry, offering "the firstlings of his flock" (Gen 4:4; see Exod 13:2). Cain, on the other hand, simply brings "an offering of the fruit of the ground" (4:3), not necessarily the firstfruits as the law prescribes (Exod 23:19). The difference in the character of the sacrifices might explain God's preference of one over the other.

---

1. Fertility rituals were practices of sympathetic magic in which the participants attempted to control life forces. Both women and men functioned as sacred prostitutes in these practices. The theology of ancient Israel strongly condemned them (see Deut 23:17).

Cain succumbs to his anger and kills his brother. The pattern of his sin is remarkably similar to that found in Genesis 3:

Crime:	she ate . . . he ate (3:6)
	rose up . . . and killed him (4:8)
Inquiry:	"Where are you?" (3:9)
	"Where is your brother?" (4:9)
Excuse:	"the woman gave me fruit . . . the serpent tricked me" (3:12, 13)
	"Am I my brother's keeper?" (4:9)
Penalty:	"in toil you shall eat of it . . . and send forth" (3:17, 23)
	"it will no longer yield . . . a fugitive" (4:12)

The deed is done, and though Cain tries to hide his guilt, he cannot. In Israel's close-knit tribal society, his question, "Am I my brother's keeper?" would be answered with a resounding: "Yes! You are your brother's keeper!" Or, your sister's or your cousin's keeper. In Israel's sociocentric society, tribal loyalties were fierce regardless of the gender of the one aggrieved.[2] Here the one meant to be his brother's keeper tragically has become his brother's killer. Cain has both violated a social bond by disregarding the sanctity of human life and put at risk his relationship with the land.

Like many traditional cultures, the ancient Israelites recognized the importance and sacredness of blood. They believed that "the blood is the life" (Deut 12:23). The shedding of blood outside a strictly regulated ritual experience resulted in cultic pollution. If this blood was soaked up by the land, the land was thereby polluted as well (see Num 35:33). Abel's innocent blood not only pollutes the land but also cries out to God for vindication and for proper burial. Cain is guilty of bloodguilt and deserving of the punishment of blood-vengeance. He is cursed from the ground, which features prominently in his story, for, like Adam, he is a "tiller of the ground" (Gen 4:2). Cain suffers the same punishment meted out to Adam: the ground will refuse to yield its fruits to him, and he will be banished from its cultivated areas.

The inherent relation between human beings and the ground is apparent in the way the consequences of Cain's sin spread to the ground and

---

2. An example of such loyalty is seen in the vehement response of the sons of Jacob at the violation of their sister Dinah (Gen 34).

then, through the ground, return back to him. He murders his brother, and this violent act results in the death-blood polluting the ground; the polluted ground then fails to produce the fruits that constitute Cain's livelihood. Innocent of transgression, nature appears to suffer because of this crime. As was the case with Adam, however, the ground is not really made barren and useless. The bond between the ground and the human being has been severed, and it now refuses to supply the sinner with what is needed to sustain human life.

Guilty of fratricide, Cain fears for his own life. There is no way of knowing the nature of the mark that God placed on him. One thing is clear: it not only accuses him as a criminal but also protects him. If vengeance is exacted, retribution would be sevenfold. In other words, seven members of his family would pay with their lives. Cain is then confined to Nod (נוֹד; *nôd*), a word derived from the Hebrew verb נוד (*nûd*; to wander).

This first biblical narrative reveals a prominent theme, namely, preference for the younger son. It is the reverse of what one might expect in a society with patrilineal practices that privileged the eldest son. This preference could reflect the author's (someone living much later than the story itself suggests) support of Davidic ascendency, despite the fact that David was not in line to succeed Saul, the first king. Found woven through the national history of Israel, this particular religious tradition demonstrated that God's choice of leaders was not restrained by the patriarchal primogenital firstborn custom. This insight into divine freedom did not, however, carry over into other narrow patriarchal perspectives, such as gender bias. It only opened a broader political horizon because of the insistence of those who supported David. No one seemed interested in remedying the limitations imposed on women.

Generation after Generation (Gen 4:17-26)

The account of Cain's sin and punishment is followed by a short patrilineal genealogy that traces his family through his male descendants. This genealogy is more than a simple family tree sketching kinship structure. Some of the names identify individuals; others designate tribes or clans; still others are the names of cities. The entire genealogy is etiological in nature, providing plausible explanations for some of the human inventions that constitute cultural history. It is blatantly androcentric, disregarding women's contributions to cultural advancements.

The information provided for some of the names suggests that the genealogy is tracing the advance in civilization rather than the history of one
particular family. Since Lamech practiced polygamy, the names of his
wives are necessary to distinguish his sons: Adah gave birth to Jabal, the
ancestor of those who embraced the nomadic Bedouin life of herding,
and to Jubal, the ancestor of those known for their dexterity in playing
musical instruments. Zillah bore Tubal-cain, the ancestor of blacksmiths,
and a daughter named Naamah. A daughter is usually only included if
she becomes a significant member of another genealogy. Details about
Naamah might have survived in the oral memory of the people, but no
literary evidence has survived in the biblical record.

Lamech's association with Cain is found in his boasting song of revenge (4:23-24). Like Cain, he is guilty of murder. The one he killed was
not innocent, however, as Abel had been. Lamech suffered some kind of
personal injury at that person's hand, and so he struck back. Knowing that
his own action could initiate a blood feud with the family of the deceased,
he took upon himself a vow of blood vengeance. If the one who might
strike the guilty Cain was threatened with the death of seven people from
his clan, anyone who would strike the avenging Lamech could expect the
deaths of seventy times seven. Lamech's boasting song is directed toward
his wives. This could reflect the custom of women publicly celebrating
the remarkable feats of men.[3] The story of Cain begins with uncontrolled
violence and his genealogy ends with even greater violence.

The void created by the death of Abel must be filled or the future of the
human race would reside in the blood line of the murderer. Consequently,
Eve "bore a son and named him Seth" (4:25), who in turn became the
father of Enosh. Much has been made about the naming and the names.
By naming, one exercises power over the one named. Seth, like Cain, is
named by his mother, while Enosh is named by his father. There is nothing in the passage that throws light on this variation. It seems that in such
familial situations, the woman often did exercise a degree of authority.

Names have meaning. Eve provided an explanation for the name Cain
(4:1); she provides a similar explanation for Seth. The actual meaning of
the name is unknown. However, שֵׁת (Seth) sounds like the verb שִׁית (*sîth*;

---

3. The women rejoiced on Saul's and David's return from battle (1 Sam 18:7). A
form of ululation, a high pitched trilling sound, continues to be performed by women
during joyful celebrations in some traditional Jewish and Arab communities today.

appointed), and אֱנוֹשׁ (*'ĕnôsh*) is one of the four Hebrew words for "man."[4] Its general meaning of weak or limited man throws light on the character of the man named.

From Creation to Flood (Gen 5:1-32)

A new chapter in the family history of Eve and Adam begins with the first תּוֹלְדוֹת (*tôlēdôt*, generations) or list of male descendants. The Sethite genealogy bears resemblance to ancient Sumerian king lists, which also trace dynasties through ten generations, indicating that such listings were a common method for arranging information judged important enough to be remembered. Several features of this genealogy link it to the Genesis 1 creation account. They both state that humankind was made in the likeness of God and that they were made male and female. Made in the image of God, Adam now fathers a son in his own image and likeness. Though this genealogy mentions the birth of daughters, it traces patrilineal kinship through the eldest son.

The account of Enoch, the seventh generation, is noteworthy. His life span is the shortest of the antediluvian ancestors, but it holds special meaning. It corresponds to the number of days in the solar year and thus signifies completion. Furthermore, Enoch "walked with God" (v. 22), a reference to an intimate relationship. This feature, along with the fact that there is no mention of his death (God simply took him), led people to believe that Enoch was taken into heaven and would return before the end of time. The legend of Enoch and his journeys through the heavens grew over the centuries (Sir 44:16; 49:14). Traces of it can even be found in New Testament writings (Heb 11:5; Jude 14-15).

Earlier Lamech is noted for his vengeance; here he is known as the father of a remarkable son, Noah. נֹחַ (*nôaḥ*; Noah) comes from the verb נוּחַ (*nûḥ*; rest, comfort, relief). At the end of the genealogy the standard pattern breaks down. It notes the life span of Noah and then branches out to identify his sons Shem, Ham, and Japheth, the three important descendants who will continue the line after the flood.

This genealogy offered a sense of rootedness to the Israelites who had been dislocated and scattered by the exile, suggesting that the genealogical tradition itself is postexilic. It enabled them to trace their lineage back to

---

4. The others are אָדָם (Gen 1:26), אִישׁ (Gen 2:23), and גֶּבֶר (Job 38:3).

definite tribes and clans, providing them with identity, even though they might not have been able to lay claim to definite tracts of land.

Sin Abounds (Gen 6:1-4)

The genealogies featured the sons of the ancestors. The story now shifts the focus to their daughters. The passage raises several questions. Who are the sons of god? Who are the Nephilim? Which heroes of old were born of the union of divine fathers and human mothers?[5] The story itself suggests that it is an etiological tale explaining the existence of giants. But who are these giants?

The Hebrew expression בְּנֵי־הָאֱלֹהִים ($b^e n\hat{e}\ h\bar{a}$'$\check{e}l\bar{o}h\hat{i}m$) translated "sons of god" is really "sons of gods." Since הָאֱלֹהִים ($h\bar{a}$'$\check{e}l\bar{o}h\hat{i}m$) has often been translated "angels," some commentators translate it "sons of the angels." They claim that this translation is an example of a common ancient theme of angel marriage. Since ancient kings were often considered descendants of gods, some commentators believe that "sons of god" refers to dynastic rulers. The most obvious explanation maintains that the sons of god are some kind of divine beings.[6] They appear as such again in the book of Job (Job 1:6; 2:1), where they form the council of God, a remnant of Canaanite polytheistic religion. In that tradition as well as the traditions of other ancient Mesopotamian cultures, stories about the mating of gods and humans are quite common. Here again, Israel appropriated a common story of the ancient world and shaped it for its own purposes.

The Nephilim (נְפִילִים) appear only in this passage and again in Numbers 13:33 where the Israelites acknowledge that they themselves seem like grasshoppers in comparison with the Nephilim. This assessment has led some to envision the Nephilim as formidable enemies of gigantic proportion. The word is, however, derived from נָפַל ($n\bar{e}pal$, to fall), and so נְפִילִים (Nephilim) are literally the fallen ones. Hence, it could suggest divine beings who have fallen from some exalted position.

---

5. Gilgamesh, a legendary Sumerian king, is an example of such a hero.

6. For an overview of the various interpretations, see David J.A. Clines, "The Significance of the 'sons of God' Episode (Genesis 6:1-4) in the context of the 'Primeval History' (Genesis 1-11)," *Journal for the Study of the Old Testament* 13 (1979): 33–46; Victor P. Hamilton, *The Book of Genesis: Chapters 1-17*, The New International Commentary on the Old Testament (Grand Rapids, MI: Eerdmans, 1990), 262–64.

The behavior of these sons of god is reprehensible. They violate the line that separates the divine from the human, behavior that Israel always found particularly offensive. Israel's Holiness Code demanded strict observance of boundaries, for they believed that all things have their proper place and belong to a proper order. According to their understanding of purity, mixing members of two categories pollutes both categories. Furthermore, the language that describes the actions of the sons of god— they "saw that [the women] were fair[7] and they took wives for themselves" (v. 2)—recalls the story of Eve who also saw what was good and took what was forbidden (3:6). That first sin also sprang from the blurring of the line between the divine and the human: "you will be like God" (3:5). Though the women in this story did not actively seduce the sons of god, the story implies that their beauty caused the men to violate appropriate boundaries. Once again, women are characterized as temptresses.

There is much in this passage that is reminiscent of the earlier account. Just as God passed judgment after the first sin (3:14-19), so God passes judgment here (v. 3). The spirit of God that will not remain in human beings forever (v. 3) recalls the breath of life that made the man a living being (2:7). If God removes that spirit/breath, as this verse states, the human being will not survive. Flesh is an allusion to mortality since, as the earlier passage declares, "you are dust, and to dust you shall return" (3:19). In both passages the threat of death is mitigated. In the earlier passage, the couple is allowed to continue life, but outside of the garden; here the life span of human beings is shortened.

The implication that this sin was instigated by the attractiveness of the women is frequently coupled with the gender-biased reading of the first woman's desire for knowledge. Traditionally, the women in these stories have been considered both lacking in character (unable to withstand temptation) and boding evil (leading men into their sin). Might such negative depictions really reflect, however, Israel's polemic against a society's crediting women with divine characteristics? The sins committed in these stories are not merely violations of Israel's social mores. They are breaches of the boundary that separates what is divine from what is

---

7. Carol M. Kaminski claims that טוב means "good" and then compares the desire of the "sons of god" with that of Eve who saw that the fruit was "good" (Gen 3:6); "Beautiful Women or False Judgment? Interpreting Genesis 6:2 in the Context of the Primeval History," *Journal for the Study of the Old Testament* 32, no. 4 (2008): 457–73.

human,[8] and in orthodox Israelite theology, the female has no place in the realm of the divine. That place is reserved for the male.

In the earlier garden account, both woman and man willingly disregard the divine prohibition. Here, the women appear to be innocent victims of both the sons of god and their own fathers. The text says that the sons of god "took wives for themselves" (v. 2). Since there is no indication that the women were abducted, one can conclude that their fathers agreed to the unions. Thus, through no fault of their own, the women participate in the violation of boundaries. Presumably the Nephilim are the fruit of those unions. Although it was the sons of god who initiated the transgression, the punishment is meted out to human beings.[9]

Contemporary Reading: Invisibility and Blame

The biased and limited viewpoint of the biblical patrilineal genealogies cannot be denied. It is only recently that society has become conscious of the bias whenever it assumes that the category "men" includes, but does not name, women. Contemporary society has broadened the parameters of social institutions and practices and now can readily recognize the essential roles played by women. Therefore, without denying the ancient social bias, contemporary readers can incorporate an inclusiveness in their perceptions and interpretations.

It is much easier to remedy the invisibility to which women in biblical stories have been relegated than it is to deal with the blame for transgressions that they have too often been forced to bear. A simple mention and naming of women will make them visible. A serious reshaping of perspective is needed, however, to reverse unjustified blaming. Many women and men today have already begun such reshaping; they recognize the bias of the biblical author and refrain from laying blame where it does not belong.

---

8. Ibid., 36.

9. Kenneth Mathews maintains that, as was the case in the garden, it was the humans who transgressed the divinely established boundaries (Kenneth A. Mathews, *Genesis 1–11:26*, The New American Commentary: An Exegetical and Theological Exposition of Holy Scripture, vol. 1A [Nashville, TN: Broadman & Holman Publishers, 1996], 321). This would erroneously accuse the women for the transgression, where the passage says that it was the sons of God who violated the boundaries (6:2). Once again, the blame is placed on the women.

Chapter 3

"How Great Was Their Wickedness"
(Gen 6:5–9:29)

The account of the flood is one of the best-known narratives of the ancient world. Behind the story is probably a genuine experience of a deluge, whether of limited or extensive proportion. The exclusive focus on Noah underscores both the patriarchal structure in which Noah represents the entire human race and its androcentric bias, in which women are mentioned in the account only when they appear to serve male concerns.

Most troublesome is the fact that the punishment meted out to the human sinners engulfs the rest of creation, animals and Earth alike. Though Earth retains its fertility, the fruits that graced its surface are wiped out. This raises the question of theodicy, or the justice of God; why is the rest of natural creation punished when it is not guilty?

Warning of a Flood (Gen 6:5-8)

Human depravity has run rampant on Earth. What God originally saw as very good (1:31) has now become wickedness that is great (6:5). Not only are human beings guilty of actual transgression, but their inclinations are evil to the core. The anthropomorphic characterization of God is striking. God is grieved to the heart,[1] so much so that God regrets

---

1. עִצָּבוֹן (*ʿiṣṣābôn*; grieved), the verb describing God's state of mind in v. 6, comes from the same root as do the words describing the woman's pain of childbirth and

having made humankind. God, who carefully and providently created everything, now resolves to put an end to it. God is not acting capriciously, annoyed by thoughtless human behavior, as were the gods in the ancient Mesopotamian flood myths. God is genuinely aggrieved because of intentional human wickedness. Nevertheless, a ray of hope does flicker in this bleak picture: "Noah found favor in the sight of YHWH" (v. 8). This is the one who earlier was identified as the one who would bring relief (5:29).

Building the Ark (Gen 6:9–7:5)

The entire story unfolds in a chiastic structure (see "Aesthetics of the Text" in the introduction):

A   Noah is described as righteous (6:9-13)
  B   God instructs Noah to build and enter the ark (6:14–7:10)
    C   The flood commences (7:11-16)
      D   The waters rise (7:17-24)
        E   God remembers Noah (8:1a)
      D¹   The waters recede (8:1b-5)
    C¹   The waters dry up (8:6-14)
  B¹   God instructs Noah to leave the ark (8:15-19)
A¹   Noah offers sacrifice (8:20-22)

A second chiastic pattern identifies and repeats the span of time between several of these important movements in the story:

A   7 days warning (7:4)
  B   7 days warning (7:10)
    C   40 days of rain (7:17)
      D   150 days of cresting water (7:24)
        E   God remembers Noah (8:1)
      D¹   150 days of receding water (8:3)
    C¹   40 days of waiting (8:6)
  B¹   7 days of waiting (8:10)
A¹   7 days of waiting (8:12)

---

the man's arduous toil in trying to cultivate the land (3:16-17). This word indicates that sin brings great suffering both for humans and for God.

In both patterns, the center or main point is the same: God remembers Noah.

Noah is cast in the guise of a second Adam, the future of humankind resting on his shoulders just as it had rested on the shoulders of the first man. Adam was evidence of God's decision to create the human race; Noah represents God's decision to preserve it. The section opens with the third תּוֹלְדוֹת (genealogy). It identifies the threefold branch of Noah's male descendants (Shem, Ham, Japheth), who will play significant roles in the future of the human race. Noah himself is described as righteous and blameless. Like Enoch (5:22, 24), he walks with God, a reference to an intimate relationship with the divine. The description of his righteousness is intentionally placed in stark contrast with the corruption and violence of the world within which he lives.

כָּל-בָּשָׂר (*kōl-bāśār*, all flesh) usually means "all human beings" and only human beings.[2] Here, however, it refers to all beings with life in them.[3] Though the land was polluted by the innocent blood of Abel (Gen 4:10; see Num 35:33), Earth itself is innocent of transgression. The statement about its sinfulness reflects a perception held by many traditional peoples and affirmed by contemporary science, namely, that the fate of Earth and the living creatures that proceed from it and live upon it are inherently connected with the actions of humankind. Having all come from the same Earth (Gen 1:24-25), creatures are actually interdependent. Because of this interdependent interconnection, Earth too is said to be corrupt (vv. 11, 12) and full of violence (vv. 11, 13).[4] This violence leads to divine acrimony, not as arbitrary punishment from God, but as the natural consequence of the violence produced by sin.[5]

The story states that the flood occurred because "all the fountains of the great deep burst forth, and the windows of the heavens were opened" (7:11). Since one of the first acts of creation was the separation and confinement of the chaotic cosmic waters both above the dome of the

---

2. See Claus Westermann, *Genesis 1–11: A Commentary* (Minneapolis, MN: Augsburg Publishing House, 1984), 416.

3. Gen 6:12, 13, 17, 19; 7:15, 16, 21; 8:17; 9:11, 15, 16, 17.

4. The word for "corrupt" (שׁחת; *šāḥat*) is the same verb used in the divine speech: "I am going to destroy" (v. 13). In other words, corruption begets corruption.

5. Terence Fretheim, *Creation Untamed: The Bible, God, and Natural Disaster* (Grand Rapids, MI: Baker Academic, 2010), 54.

sky and beneath it (Gen 1:6-7), the flood was actually the undoing of creation. This meant that chaos, both cosmic and social, was now victorious.

The ark is to be three hundred cubits long, fifty cubits wide, and thirty
cubits high (6:14-16).[6] The noun תֵּבָה (*tēbā*; ark) is found in only one other
place in the Bible, as the basket in which Moses was placed (Exod 2:3, 5).
In both instances, the word refers to the means by which one chosen by
God is saved from dangerous waters. The detailed directions for building
the ark also call to mind similar detailed specifications for the construction of the ark of the covenant (Exod 25:10). Thus, Noah's ark, Moses'
basket, and the ark of the covenant are all instruments of God's saving
presence, assuring the people who are facing difficult times that God is
with them and thus they have a future.

מַבּוּל (*mabbûl*; flood) is found only in this narrative (6:17; 7:10, 17;
9:11, 15), in reference to this particular catastrophe (9:28; 10:1, 32; 11:10),
and in a reference to the related, original primeval chaotic waters (Ps
29:10). It is never an allusion to another disaster, implying that this flood
is considered unique among the early events in the history of the human
race. Having stated again and again that an end will be put to all flesh,
indeed everything with the breath of life, God makes an exception. Destruction will not be total. This flood will be a purgation of the world,
not its annihilation.

This account introduces the concept of covenant (6:18).[7] The covenant
God made with Noah and the rest of the natural world is asymmetrical,
since the partners here are not equals. It is also unilateral, not bilateral,
since God promises to enter into covenant with the natural world but
requires nothing of the covenant partners.

---

6. A cubit is the length of an arm from the elbow to the outstretched thumb,
approximately a foot and a half in length. Hence, the ark was about 750 feet long,
seventy-five feet wide, and forty-five feet deep.

7. Covenants were social transactions made between people and a king or a
god. Many of them were mutual agreements in which the parties took on specific
obligations toward each other. Penalties to be imposed for violation of these obligations
were determined before the pact was sealed. Other covenants were asymmetrical,
the stronger party imposing responsibilities on the weaker. All covenants included
an element of promise. Sometimes this element appeared to be more prominent; at
other times the focus was on the obligation.

The Flood (Gen 7:6–8:22)

The midpoint of this chiastic-structured narrative is reached: God remembered Noah (8:1). Throughout the Bible, the phrase "God remembered" usually means more than simply "calling to mind." It includes the notion of intervening with appropriate action, usually with divine mercy.[8] Here, God remembers Noah, his family, and all the animals sealed up in the ark, and God causes a wind to blow that will dry the land. The second half of the chiasm describes how God undoes the devastation of the flood. The scene recalls the first account of creation (Gen 1:2). In both stories, Earth is covered by the waters of the deep, and a wind from God sweeps over that chaos. It is as if creation begins anew after the flood.

The first thing that Noah does upon disembarking from the ark is build an altar and offer holocausts or burnt offerings. Appeased by this, God is sorry for having cursed Earth and having destroyed all living beings on it and resolves: "I will never again curse the ground because of humankind" (8:21). Human culpability is clearly stated, and God promises to protect the rest of the natural world from the consequences of human sin.[9]

Covenant with Nature (Gen 9:1-29)

The account of the covenant made with nature contains elements of both continuity and discontinuity with the first creation account. Both contain the admonition to be fertile, to multiply, and to fill the Earth; the same animals are listed; in both accounts humankind is commissioned to rule. Nevertheless, there are also marked differences. After the flood, the animals will not only be under human rule but also live in fear and dread of them for they will be food for human consumption.[10] A restriction is,

8. After the destruction of Sodom and Gomorrah, God remembers Abraham and leads him to a new settlement (Gen 19:29); God remembers the childless Rachel and opens her womb (Gen 30:22); God remembers the covenant made with Abraham and brings the Israelites out of Egyptian bondage (Exod 2:24).

9. Arbitrary species extinction, as well as the pollution, deforestation, and desertification of the natural world brought on by human arrogance, greed, and ignorance of the interdependence of all natural creation, question the applicability of this promise.

10. For some, permission to eat the flesh of animals has raised the matter of vegetarian versus carnivorous diet. Resolving this conflict by rooting the value of

however, imposed here: humans are not to eat flesh if its lifeblood is still in it.[11] The ancients recognized the sacredness of blood and its relationship with life itself. This prohibition seeks to curb the wanton slaughter of animals. This sign of respect for blood was a way of acknowledging God's sovereignty.

A threefold warning of divine sanction underscores the seriousness of the murder of a human. The victim of homicide is not merely a fellow man, as most translations suggest. The literal translation of the Hebrew אִישׁ אָח (*'ish 'āḥ*) is man-brother, a subtle reference to Cain's murder of Abel, suggesting that homicide is really a form of fratricide.[12] The penalty for murder is stated in a very succinct chiastic form:

A   sheds
  B   blood
     C   human
     C   human
  B¹   blood
A¹   shed

This is an expression of *lex talionis* or law of the talion, a juridical concept that states that the severity of the punishment can only equal, not exceed, the seriousness of the offense. Popularly known as an eye for an eye, a tooth for a tooth, this legal principle, found in the ancient Babylonian *Code of Hammurabi*, was meant to diminish or even rescind excessive blood vengeance (4:15, 23). This passage states that human beings

---

vegetarianism in the creation account is not as uncomplicated as some might suggest. One must ask: Is the issue behind vegetarianism one of preferred diet or of respect for the life of the animal? If it is preferred diet, the biblical story cannot be used as a justification for the practice. If it is respect for the life of the animal, this reason must be reconciled with the practice of offering animals in sacrifice to God.

11. According to a much later Levitical dietary law, the blood of the animal had to be drained before the flesh could be eaten (see Lev 7:26-27; 17:10-11, 14). This law was long-lasting, for at the time of Paul, it was one of the requirements placed on Gentile converts by the leaders of the church in Jerusalem (Acts 15:20). It is still observed by many Jews today.

12. Since women were viewed as part of the belongings of the patriarchal household (see Exod 20:17; Deut 5:21), their possible murder was considered a violation of the rights of the patriarch.

should be held in high regard because they are made in the image of God (1:26-27).

The scope of this covenant is quite broad. It is intergenerational (between God and Noah and his descendants) and global (with all the animals that were saved in the ark; vv. 9-10, 11, 12, 15, 16, 17). Initiated by God, it is unilateral, for while God assumes obligations, no comparable obligations are placed on natural creation. God seals this covenant with a concrete sign, a bow in the sky. Since the covenant deals with God's relationship with natural creation, this sign reflects the cosmic nature of the relationship. Rooted in God's promise, the bow is a natural signal that the storm has passed.

The bow in the sky certainly heralds the end of a storm. It may originally have represented, however, an archer's bow. In the Babylonian creation myth *Enuma Elish*, after conquering chaotic waters, the victorious god Marduk assigns the celestial bodies their stations in the heavens.[13] Once the enemy had been conquered and the rebellion quelled, Marduk hangs his weapon, an archer's bow, in the heavens with the other stars, thus indicating that peace and order have been reestablished. The bow in the Genesis account is also a sign that the natural forces of the cosmos have been stabilized and there is no longer need for God to enter into battle.

The genealogical details that follow the flood narrative (9:18-19) link that event with the history of the entire human race: "from these the whole world was peopled" (9:19). Nevertheless, the conduct of the men recounted in the story throws light on traditions that follow. The biblical narrative is an etiological explanation of the social situation of various peoples. The ethnic biases are striking. Ham/Canaan,[14] the disrespectful son, unmistakably represents the hated Canaanites. Shem, who represents the Israelites, is not only blessed by God but also promised Ham/Canaan as his slave. Japhet, the third son, is awarded expansive territory, which enables him to live among the tents of Shem where Canaan serves as his slave as well.

---

13. Gen 1:14-18 recounts similar divine action.

14. Details of the narrative are confusing. Noah's son Ham is the one who observes his father's nakedness, but it is Ham's son Canaan who is cursed because of this offense. Some scholars argue that this disparity points to the conflation of two previously independent stories. They maintain that an editor inserted the phrase "Ham was the father of Canaan" to explain the confusion. While the phrase indicates the relationship between Ham and Canaan, it really does not correct the discrepancy.

Several explanations of the crime committed by Ham/Canaan have been proposed. Some commentators argue that it was a grievous sexual offense such as castration or paternal incest. Others believe that it was maternal incest, a political move that signified the overthrow of the leader.[15] The action of Shem and Japhet in covering their father's nakedness suggests that the offense had more to do with public shame than with sexual impropriety. In an honor-and-shame society, honor is perhaps the greatest treasure one could possess.[16] Ham not only saw his father's nakedness but also made this known to his brothers, thus adding to his father's shame. The seriousness of such an offense against one's father is seen in the punishment meted out for such crimes: "Whoever strikes . . . curses his father or mother will be put to death" (Exod 21:15, 17; Lev 20:9).

This transgression underscores the final step in the total breakdown of fundamental human relationships. The recriminations in the garden pointed to the conflict between husband and wife, the murder of Abel demonstrated the animosity between brothers, and the disrespect of Ham now reveals the discord between children and parents. In each case, God punishes. In each case, however, God also shows mercy.

Contemporary Reading: A New Creation?

In many ways, life after the flood has been considered a new creation. Since sin was not eliminated, the newness was not complete. The flood itself was more of purgation than destruction. Earth, however, was purged, not the human race. Sin went right into the ark along with at least one of the descendants of Noah (Ham). In the minds of some, the purgation of the innocent Earth raises the question of theodicy (the justice of God). Others maintain that the interdependence of all Earth's creatures implies that the actions of one aspect or order of creation are really the actions of Earth generally. The biblical account of the covenant that God made with all creation appears to endorse this second perspective.

The covenant with creation underscores the mandate conferred on human beings in both creation narratives. Commissioned to function as

---

15. See Absalom's attempt to seize the monarchy from his father David (2 Sam 16:21).

16. Even today, in some traditional societies, it is better to take one's life than to lose honor or "face."

images of God, they are responsible for the rest of creation and are accountable to God in that regard (Gen 1:28); they are to serve and guard the garden (Gen 2:15). These passages imply that ecological responsibility is a mandate given to all humanity, not a choice that some ecosensitive individuals might make.

The sinfulness that both entered and exited the ark is manifested in the account's gender and ethnic biases. How the contemporary reader is to deal with the invisibility of women, obvious in this account as in earlier stories, has already been discussed above. The ethnic bias appears here for the first time. The universal human tendency to characterize oneself quite positively and one's rivals negatively should be acknowledged and addressed. Such characterization frequently reveals more about the one characterizing than the one being so characterized.

Chapter 4

"These Are the Descendants"
(Gen 10:1–11:26)

This last section of the Primeval History (Genesis 1–11) traces the paths of the descendants of those who were saved in the ark (10:1-32) by means of genealogies. As already stated, ancient Israel's descent was patrilineal, and so women were not usually included in the listing.

The Table of Nations (Gen 10:1-32)

The Table of Nations begins with the fourth תּוֹלְדֹת (*tôlēdôt*; genealogy)[1] of the book of Genesis. The people who descended from Noah are divided into three major groups as determined by their descent from one of his three sons. Since the principle of organization is political rather than racial or ethnic, the listing is less a genealogy than it is a Table of Nations. While many of the names identify individuals such as Nimrod, others name tribal groups such as the Amorites or geographic sites such as Sidon. Still others identify occupation such as the seafaring descendants of Japhet. The result is a kind of verbal map of the ancient Near Eastern

---

1. The exclusively male character of the genealogies is curious because the Hebrew word תּוֹלְדֹת (genealogy, generations, or descendants) is a feminine plural construct. Though יָלַד, the verb (*yālad*), from which the word generation is derived, should be understood here as "to beget," it more frequently yields the feminine meaning "to bear" or "to bring forth."

world (ca. first millennium BCE.) that includes territory as far north as the Black Sea, as far east as the Iranian plateau, as far south as Nubia, and as far west as the outlying Mediterranean coastlands.

The listings themselves probably originated as local or tribal legends that were then gathered together as diverse peoples were joined through treaties or marriage. Unlike similar ancient Near Eastern king lists that identify rulers and their military conquests, this listing of nations simply shows how far the human race had progressed to realize God's directive to fill the Earth.

Two genealogical entries stand out among the others. The descendants of Ham (10:6-20) represent four great nations, one of which is Cush. Known as Ethiopia in Egyptian texts, people of this land were dark skinned (Jer 13:23). Certain ideologies common in seventeenth- and eighteenth-century Europe justified the practice of enslaving people of African heritage, since it was Ham who sinned against his father Noah and was cursed by God to live as the slave of his brothers. Israel itself is not mentioned in this genealogy. A line of descent can, however, be drawn through Shem to the descendants of Eber,[2] the probable ancestor of the Hebrews. The precise location of the area inhabited by these descendants is difficult to determine. Some commentators believe that the names found within this genealogy originated as a list of cities with which Jerusalem conducted trade.

The entire Table of Nations consists of about seventy members, a number that means "completeness." This listing of peoples is meant to show that all the nations of the world, as diverse and distinct as they might have been, had a common origin.

The Tower of Babel (Gen 11:1-9)

The story of the tower of Babel, like that of the flood, is well-known. Its uncomplicated narration has, however, often clouded the apparent discrepancy between the story itself and its literary setting, as well as the fundamental meaning of its message. The very first verse raises questions. It maintains that the whole world had one language and the same

---

2. Eber (עֵבֶר) shares the same consonantal roots as does עָבְרִי, which means across or beyond, suggesting that a Hebrew was someone from across a boundary.

words. The Table of Nations in Genesis 10 explicitly states three times, however, that the various descendants of Japhet, Ham, and Shem developed their own languages (10:5, 20, 31). Various attempts to remedy this incongruity have been advanced. Some scholars hold that Genesis 10 and 11 should be reversed, thus placing the Table of Nations after the story of the tower. This might seem more logical to contemporary readers, but the order we have is the order determined by the final editors of the biblical book. Besides, there are many examples in the Bible of what seems to be incongruent, even contradictory. Authors and redactors in ancient Israel did not seem to be as troubled with what modern readers consider incongruity.

Other interpreters say that the placement of the tower narrative after the Table of Nations conforms to a recurring pattern found in the Primeval History (Genesis 1–11) that traces divine benevolence, demonstrated in the increase of the human family, followed by human rebellion followed by divine benevolence, etc. In this pattern, the recurrence of human transgression builds a narrative tension that prepares for the call of Abram and the ultimate election of a particular people through whom God's plans will be accomplished.

Still other commentators argue that the single language spoken by the whole world was simply a reference to the *lingua franca* of the ancient world, the common language used by all for the sake of international communication. If this is the meaning, then the language would most likely have been Babylonian, since this was the major power of the world, and Babylon's capital Sinar is mentioned in the passage. Ancient Israel would have resented the forced use of a Babylonian language, as often happens when a nation is conquered and occupied by a stronger nation, even if it were only for purposes of trade. This story contains many other derogatory allusions to Babylon. Thus, this explanation seems to be plausible.

However the placement of this story is perceived, it is certainly another example of human transgression and divine punishment. The story is an etiological tale providing an explanation of the name Babel (v. 9). Some have argued that it also explains the scattering of people. This latter view cannot be endorsed, because migration from the east, as stated in the passage, indicates that people had already been moving from place to place. At issue here is not their movement but their decision to settle in one place.

The story follows a chiastic structure:

A   unity of speech (v. 1)
  B   human settlement (v. 2)
    C   consultation for building a city and a tower (vv. 3-4)
        D   YHWH came down (v. 5)
    C¹   consultation for confusing language (vv. 6-7)
  B¹   human scattering (v. 8)
A¹   confusion of speech (v. 9)

Though the passage states that Israel's ancestors migrated from the east, enough details in the story indicate that they are still somewhere in Mesopotamia. They planned to construct their tower out of dried bricks held together with bitumen, a manner of construction common in Mesopotamia. The proposed tower calls to mind the ancient Mesopotamian ziggurat, a stepped, pyramid-style temple. The idea of such a temple could be behind the biblical story of the tower.

To build a city and a tower does not seem to have been the offense. Rather, it was the motivation of the people in doing so. They sought to make a name for themselves,[3] to establish themselves so that they would not have to be scattered abroad. They did not want to fill the Earth as God had commanded them. The city and the tower were concrete signs of the arrogance of the builders, just as eating of the fruit of the tree of knowledge of good and evil was a manifestation of the hubris of the couple in the garden. These are examples of human beings overwhelmed by human ambition. They want to be like God (3:5) or they want the reputation of being able to build a city with a tower whose top is in the heavens (11:4).

An ancient form of argument is employed next (v. 6). It is an argument from *a minore* or *a fortiori*, from the light to the heavy or from the heavy to the light. It can be characterized as arguing: If it is like this now, what will it be like later? In other words, God says: If, as one people with one language, they build a city with a tower that reaches to heaven, what

---

3. The arrogance of the people who desire a name for themselves becomes even more evident when in the following narrative God promises Abram, "I will . . . make your name great" (12:2); see Kenneth A. Mathews, *Genesis 1–11:26*, The New American Commentary: An Exegetical and Theological Exposition of Holy Scripture, vol. 1A (Nashville, TN: Broadman & Holman Publishers, 1996), 482.

might they try to do in the future? Two themes are woven together here: the human desire to reach beyond human limitations and the ancient theme of the jealousy of the gods (see Gen 3:5).

The consultation in which God engages reflects the widespread ancient notion of a divine council: "Let us make humankind" (1:26). The concept of God coming down suggests a three-tiered universe (the heavens, Earth, and the underworld) with God ruling from heaven. This view of cosmology and divine governance from heaven can be found in ancient myths such as *Enuma Elish*, which recounts how, after the cosmic battle was won, a palace in the heavens was constructed from which the victorious deity ruled heaven and Earth. The uniformity of language,[4] which resulted from the people's settling together, led to their arrogant plan to build a city with a tower that could reach heaven. God thwarted their plan by confusing their language. This act resulted in their being scattered all over Earth. In the past, people assumed that the confusion of language and the dispersion over Earth was a misfortune brought on by sin. According to the Table of Nations that precedes this account, diversity of language and the spreading of people across the land was God's original plan to fill the Earth. Surely this original plan cannot be seen as a punishment.

Understanding this story rests on our ability to grasp its literary character. There is a play on the words that refers to the rebellious action of the human beings and the chastising action of God. The consonantal root of the Hebrew word נִלְבְּנָה (*nilᵉbbᵉnâ*) translated "let us make bricks" (v. 3) is *l-b-n*. The consonantal root of the word נָבְלָה (*nābᵉlâ*) translated "let us confuse" (v. 7) is *n-b-l*. In an oral telling of the story, this reversal of consonants would be heard and its correspondence with the reversal effected by God's penalty would be grasped.

In a second play on words, the city is called בָּבֶל (Babel), because God confuses בָּלַל (*bālal*) the speech (v. 9). The city's name means "gate of the god." When the Israelites heard the name, however, they would

---

4. Uniformity of language among diverse peoples is usually imposed by the dominant group. Today postcolonial interpreters insist that diversity of language need not be seen as a curse that separates the human family but rather as a blessing that enriches it. See José Miguez Bonino, "Genesis 11:1-9: A Latin American Perspective," in *Return to Babel: Global Perspectives on the Bible*, ed. John R. Levinson and Pricilla Pope-Levinson (Louisville, KY: Westminster/John Knox, 1999), 13–16.

think not of the name itself but of confusion. All this suggests that in this story arrogance is the real sin and being made to babble foolishly is its punishment. Having been stripped of their arrogance, people now speak various languages as they are scattered around the world just as God had originally intended.

Genealogy from the Flood to the Ancestors (Gen 11:10-26)

The genealogy of Shem marks this passage as a new unit. Though the lineage is traced through the firstborn son and is patrilineal, this genealogy also mentions daughters. Though it does not mention the names of all of the descendants, it draws a direct line from Shem to Terah, the father of Abram, thus linking Abram, the ancestor of the Israelites, to Noah from whose descendants originated all the peoples of Earth. In this way, the God of their ancestors is identified as the universal God, the God of all peoples. The primeval age is now linked with the age of history.

Contemporary Reading: One Voice

Insisting on only one voice or one point of view is an exercise of power. Those who do not wield power because of their gender, race, ethnic background, economic status, etc. are well aware of how often their voices or points of view have been considered unwelcome or simply rejected. The story of the tower of Babel suggests that a plurality of voices and points of view is not only acceptable but actually willed by God.

Part 2

"I Will Make of You a Great Nation"
(Gen 11:27–50:26)

The second part of the book of Genesis, often referred to as the Ancestral History, recounts the origins of the major forbears of Israel. It
consists of three cycles of narratives. Because of the patriarchal character
of these stories, each cycle is known by the name of the respective patriarch—Abraham, Jacob, and Joseph—and all are told from a male point of
view, underscoring the male interests, values, and accomplishments of the
tradition. The most important themes in these cycles are lineage, which
is traced through the father (patrilineal), land, and divine protection—all
promises made by God to the heads of the ancestral households. When
women are featured in the stories, they are often portrayed as passive or
weak or as tricksters. Such characterization corresponds to the profiles
of women in strict patriarchal societies in which women are not allowed
to be self-assertive agents. Nonetheless, though cast in such roles, the
women in these stories still continually influence the course of history
in meaningful ways.

These stories also reflect the importance of land, the character of
which notably impacts the lives of the people. Often the biblical stories
cannot be understood adequately without some knowledge of this topog-
raphy. Five natural ecological zones can be identified: (1) the mountains in
the north stand in the path of the cloud-bearing winds, thereby providing
an abundance of rain needed for the prosperous farming; (2) at the foot

of the mountains, semiarid lowlands make farming a risk, yet the land is ideal for pastoral herding; (3) water flowing in the river valleys is dependent on runoffs from the humid highlands and varies in strength from season to season, thus making agriculture an unreliable occupation; (4) the extended narrow coast along the Mediterranean Sea links aquatic and land plants and animals, allowing seafaring occupations to thrive in this region; and (5) the arid land in the south, always subject to the possibility of drought, threatens the nomadic people of the area with famine.[1]

1. Daniel Hillel, *The Natural History of the Bible: An Environmental Exploration of the Hebrew Scripture* (New York: Columbia University Press, 2006), 26–39.

Abraham and Sarah
(Gen 11:27–25:18)

The stories about Sarah, Abraham, and the household all somehow relate to the major theme of this ancestral cycle, namely, the desire for a male heir through whom God's promises will be fulfilled. Several of the stories in this cycle recount events that jeopardize the fulfillment of that promise. Such stories build up anticipation for the eventual birth of the heir. Other stories recount measures that attempt to bring the promise to fulfillment even in the face of seemingly impossible circumstances. Though women are often absent, silent, or apparently insignificant in so many of these stories, the importance of the women should not be underestimated. Frequently the decisions they make influence the unfolding of the story.

Chapter 5

"Go from Your Country"
(Gen 11:27–14:24)

The first chapter in the story of Sarai and Abram and the household depicts them as migrants, traveling from Haran, a city in the area of Ur of the Chaldeans (11:28, 31), down the fertile crescent of the Near East, to the land of Canaan. The nomadic character of this household is sketched in these stories and includes some of the customs of the time. Abram is described as a landless sheikh whose importance is on a par with landed kings and the Egyptian pharaoh. His status can be seen in the access to other rulers that he seems to enjoy and in the deference he is shown by them.

Origins in Haran (Gen 11:27-32)

The patrilineal genealogy of Terah signals a new period in the overall narrative. It traces the immediate ancestry of Abram and is thus part of the Ancestral History rather than the Primeval History. Abram is the first name listed, suggesting that he was the firstborn and, therefore, the line would be expected to unfold through him. Consequently, a male heir would be important for the entire family. Sarai's barrenness is referred to twice, an unusual addition to a genealogy. Her barrenness adds to the vulnerability of this lineage. A unique characteristic of this genealogy is the specific information given about the women in the kinship structure. They are named, and their being named is telling. Both Sarai and Sarah, the new name, mean "princess"; Milcah, the name of Abram's brother's wife, means "queen." These names are aristocratic titles, associated with the cult of the moon deity in ancient Mesopotamia. The religious background of these ancestors and the importance of women in that early cult may be suggested here.

Migration from Haran (Gen 12:1-20)

Abram is told to leave his country, his kindred, and his father's household (v. 1). In traditional societies such as ancient Israel, one's identity, livelihood, security, and future were all rooted in one's status in the household, which was the center of religious, social, and economic life. Such a household consisted of several generations of a family—grandparents, aunts and uncles, and cousins. Abram is told to leave all this, to sever the most intimate bonds imaginable, and to migrate to a foreign land. The sacrifices involved in this move would have been felt by all the members of his household, members who actually had no choice in the matter. This would be particularly true for Sarai. By marrying Abram, she would have already left her family of origin and now, moving away from them, she would not be able to rely on protection from them should she be victimized in Abram's household.

The promise that God made to Abram includes a sevenfold blessing (vv. 2-3). Each blessing in its own way is astonishing. First, married to a barren woman, Abram is told that he will become a great nation. How will this happen? Will the line continue through Lot, who appears to be the only possible heir? Will Abram take another wife who might bear him a son? The fact that Abram has no heir and, because of Sarai's barrenness, probably will have no heir in the future is the first and the most decisive obstacle that must be overcome if God's intention that humankind "be fruitful and multiply, and fill the earth" is to be accomplished.

Second, directed to leave everything that made life meaningful, Abram is told that he will nonetheless be blessed. How will this happen? He may be the head of a new household with ample possessions, but he is not among his own people nor can he lay claim to any land, a fundamental requirement for greatness in the ancient world. Third, unlike the people of Babel who sought to make a name for themselves (11:4), God promises to make a name for Abram. How will a landless foreigner gain a reputation as a great leader among the neighboring nations?

Fourth, Abram will be the source of blessing for others. The blessing that he will receive will redound positively on those with whom he interacts; the manner in which other people treat Abram will determine the way God will treat them. Fifth, those who bless Abram will be blessed by God; sixth, those who curse him (the Hebrew has קָלַל [*qālal*], which means "disdain" or "treat with little account"), God will curse. This is an example of *lex talionis*—an eye for an eye, a tooth for a tooth, punishment that is equal to the crime. The final blessing also builds on the idea of being blessed through Abram. This blessing is extended to all the people of Earth. The universality of divine largesse is noteworthy for a people as ethnocentric as was ancient Israel. Still, this verse says more about Israel's concept of God than their sense of themselves as God's people. They may not always be open to others, but God is.

Verses 4-9 are a kind of itinerary that traces the movements of Abram and his retinue. They first stop near Shechem, which was not only a major Canaanite city but also a shrine to Canaanite gods. There they pitch their tents in the outskirts of the city, near a tree known as the terebinth or oak of Moreh.[1] Affording reverence to trees or rivers is quite common in traditional societies. It both recognizes the life-giving qualities of such natural phenomena and pays homage to the divine power behind them. It is near this tree that God appears to Abram and promises to give him the land into which he has migrated.

The altar that Abram builds was probably a simple pile of stones. Though the passage does not explicitly mention the offer of sacrifice, such an act of worship was the specific reason for building an altar. Though he is not a priest, like Noah before him, Abram is the leader of his household and as such is also their cultic leader. The point of the story is Abram's act of devotion in response to God's promise.

The people move from the vicinity of one shrine, Shechem, to that of another, Bethel. Here too an altar is built before the people leave and make their way to the Negeb, the southern border of Canaan. Though Abram and his household do not establish permanent settlements in Canaan, the altars that are built there physically mark the land as belonging to the God who promised this land to this people.

---

1. מוֹרֶה (Moreh) means teacher, suggesting that this was a place where oracles were received.

The account of the peril in Egypt (vv. 10-20) is the first of three similar ancestral stories (the other two follow in Gen 20 and 26). It can be examined from the perspective of each of the three major characters, Abram, Sarai, and Pharaoh. ("Pharaoh" really means "large house," but it came to refer to the one who lived in it.) The story opens with the report of a severe famine in the land of Canaan that compels Abram and Sarai to go down to Egypt and live there as resident aliens. Abram realizes that he personally is very vulnerable, for Sarai's beauty could place his life in jeopardy. Seeing her, Egyptian men might kill him so that she could be taken as one of their wives.

Such an action on the part of the Egyptians would violate the practice of hospitality that was held in such high esteem in traditional societies. These practices were, however, frequently violated. Should it happen to Abram, the promises made by God (11:2-3) would be thwarted. What is Abram to do? On the one hand, he and his household are confronted with starvation; on the other, both he and God's promise appear to be in jeopardy. He decides on deception. If Sarai agrees to act as his sister, he might be able to avoid this threat to his life. As a presumed brother in a patriarchal household, he would have some control over the bargaining that normally precedes marriage. He could bargain with the men over Sarai's future. Sarai apparently agrees to this ploy, for Abram is spared.

Sarai's point of view is quite different. The biblical text says that Abram asks her rather than simply commands her to agree with the ruse (v. 13: the Hebrew includes the word נָא [*nā'*], a particle that expresses request [please]). Sarai too realizes that she has very few options. She can refuse Abram's request and place his life in jeopardy. Or, she can agree to the deception and provide him a degree of safety. In either case, her own life probably will be spared, but she will surely be taken by the Egyptians. There is no indication in the text that Sarai knows of God's promise of descendants to Abram. From her perspective, Abram is asking that she sacrifice herself for him alone. She agrees and is taken into the harem of Pharaoh. Sarai forfeits her honor in exchange for Abram's life. This story exemplifies the androcentric perspective of the characters in biblical narratives as well as the storytellers and editors who transmitted the tradition. It shows that women were expected to serve the plans of men, even at their own peril if that was deemed necessary.

Pharaoh is really an unsuspecting victim of Abram's deception. The presents that he sends Abram are probably the bride-wealth that a groom normally gives to the family of the bride. Such presents are intended to compensate for the unborn children that the family relinquishes when the woman is incorporated into the household of the groom. Pharaoh is not only the victim of Abram and Sarai's deception, but he and his household become victims of divine justice as well. Pharaoh has violated the sanctity of marriage, even if unwittingly, and so reckoning must be exacted. This passage suggests that retribution is somehow built into the very act of impropriety rather than determined and executed by God. Becoming aware of what has really happened, Pharaoh immediately rids himself and his empire of the cause of the afflictions they are suffering. He sends Sarai and Abram away under heavy guard lest they try to return.

Abram's behavior not only is self-serving and disregards the welfare of Sarai as well as Pharaoh and his household but also demonstrates his lack of faith in the promises of God. His faith wavers when he is in personal danger. Though Sarai is asked to participate in the deception, she is treated like a pawn by everyone in the story. Abram trades her for his safety; the Egyptians take advantage of her social vulnerability in order to pursue sexual pleasure; and Pharaoh treats her like a piece of property as he first takes her and then returns her to Abram. It is Pharaoh, not Abram or Sarai, who finally recognizes the special divine protection under which this couple lives. The affliction he and his household have been made to endure because of the couple's deception prompts him to release her and send the entire retinue away. The guard guarantees their departure, for Pharaoh does not want to risk offending their God again, even unwittingly.

This story contains many of the features of the account of a much later sojourn in Egypt undertaken by the sons of Jacob. In both cases, the people go to Egypt because of famine (Gen 42:5). They are oppressed while living there (Exod 1:11) and are only released by Pharaoh when unbearable plagues strike the Egyptians (Exod 9:14). They leave the land loaded with gifts from the Egyptians (Exod 12:35-36). The present story, like the later one, demonstrates that once God makes promises, no obstacle is able to prevent their fulfillment.

Travels through Canaan (13:1–14:24)

Having been expelled from Egypt, Abram and his retinue return to Canaan. They pitch their tents near Bethel, the place where earlier they had built an altar to YHWH (13:1-18). Many commentators assume that the herds of animals received from Pharaoh account for the wealth Abram brought back with him. The increase in flocks and herds, originally a boon for the group, became a point of contention among them. The quarrels mentioned in the story were not between Abram and Lot but between their respective herders. This point offers a glimpse into the social conditions within an ancient nomadic clan. Though Abram was the head of the clan, the sons—or in this case the nephew—of the leader, led relatively independent lives, overseeing their own families, possessing their own flocks and herds, and employing their own herders. The head of the clan was, however, responsible for protection from outside threats, decisions about moving, and internal harmony.

The herders are quarreling over grazing land. Such disagreement implies that Abram and his clan are neither camel-riding Bedouins nor aimless wanderers. They are nomadic herders who live a kind of dimorphic existence, that is, semi-settled in places as they follow their herds in search of new pasturage. Though Canaanite tribes still occupy this land, God has promised it to Abram (12:7). Goodwill among kinfolk, however, is more important to him than control over a large expanse of territory, and, therefore, he is willing to relinquish some of the latter in order to secure the former. Abram had the right to apportion to another any part of this land he might choose. For some reason, he does not exercise this right. Instead, he allows Lot to decide where he would like to settle.

Lot's choice of land is telling in at least three ways. Rather than defer to his uncle, as one would expect from a junior member of a patriarchal household, he makes the first choice, choosing the lush land of the Jordan Valley. Unbeknownst to him, that choice will also be his undoing (v. 10). His choice of the land in the east takes him not only out of the jurisdiction of his uncle's control but also out of the land of promise. The cities of the Plain (also known as the Valley of Siddim) among which he settles, Sodom, Gomorrah, Admah, Zeboiim, and Zoar, are located a short distance from the southeastern tip of the Dead Sea in what is today a marshy salt land.

Lot chose the fertile Jordan Valley, but Abram is once again promised the rest of the land of Canaan. Added to this is the promise of descendants too many to count. This last point is important because Lot's departure left Abram with no close relative to be Abram's heir. No hint is given as to how the promise of descendants will be fulfilled. Once again Abram must rely on the trustworthiness of God's word.

Abram becomes entangled in international conflict (14:1-24). The cities in the Valley of Siddim rebelled against the much larger empires in the east. Such insubordination could not be tolerated, and so four kings from various sites in Mesopotamia mounted a military attack meant to punish the rebels. Two routes led from the Euphrates River to Egypt. The more direct route crossed the Philistine Plain and followed the Mediterranean Sea west to the major cities of Egypt. The inland route was longer. It passed on the eastern side of the Sea of Galilee, the Jordan River, and the Dead Sea as far south as what is today the Gulf of Aqaba where it turned west, crossing the Sinai Peninsula into Egypt. Since the defiant cities were located in the vicinity of the southeastern tip of the Dead Sea, the avenging kings took the longer route.

The report of the battle that took place in the Valley of Siddim resembles the royal inscriptions left behind on stone steles that testify to the royal military exploits (vv. 8-12). From the perspective of the biblical story, the important point of this account is the capture of Lot and his possessions. The reason given earlier for Lot's separation from Abram was the lack of adequate land for grazing their respective flocks (13:5-6). This story states that Lot settled in Sodom (14:12). He not only decided to make his home in a Canaanite city but also chose one known for its sinfulness (13:13). Mention of his possessions alerts us to the biased thinking of a patriarchal worldview that considers everyone and everything in a household to be possessions of the head of that household.

While all of this conflict is happening east of the Jordan River, Abram and his clan are settled in the west. Whether Lot made the decision to associate with the people of Sodom in this way out of religious indifference or foolishness makes no difference to Abram. Lot and his household are kin. Consequently, when he is notified of their plight, he feels obliged to rescue them (vv. 13-16). He allies himself with three tribes and is able to muster forces from his own kindred, 318 men of military age and ability. This large number of eligible warriors only hints at the actual size of Abram's clan. Employing the strategy of night attacks, they are able to force the invading armies as far back as the land north of Damascus. The enemy armies are not only defeated but also forced to relinquish the spoils of war that they had appropriated to themselves. The king of Sodom comes out to meet the conquering heroes, a gesture that denotes honor and high praise (v. 17).

It is important to understand the military conflicts initiated by Abram without trying to justify war itself. They were not wars of aggression, nor were they meant to quell rebellion. They were launched in order to repair the harm that was done to others, to seize the people and possessions that had been captured by four kings from the east, in order to return them. Abram did not personally benefit from these encounters. The fact that he returned the spoils of war to the conquered Canaanite peoples is evidence of this.

A very unusual episode interrupts the account of Abram's encounter with the king of Sodom (vv. 18-20). A second king appears on the scene, Melchizedek,[2] the priest-king of Salem. The bread and wine he offers are tokens of goodwill toward those who have been on a strenuous military campaign. Besides being a king, Melchizedek is a priest, and it is in this capacity that he blesses Abram. This is a most unusual event, because God promised that all families of Earth would be blessed because of Abram (12:3). Here he is being blessed by a priest devotee of another god. Furthermore, Melchizedek declares that the blessing actually comes from his god, El Elyon,[3] God Most High, the Creator of heaven and Earth.

Melchizedek's blessing is twofold. First Abram is blessed, and then El Elyon is blessed (which in this instance means "praised"). Abram's victory is an example of the power behind one of the promises made to him by God: "I will bless those who bless you, and the one who curses you I will curse" (12:3). Abram then offers a tithe to Melchizedek. Tithing usually refers to a yearly responsibility that acknowledges some form of proprietary claim by another. Abram's surrender of a tenth of what he has does not seem to be this kind of a tithe. It is most likely a form of offering frequently made after one has received a blessing. The material goods that Abram relinquishes are probably part of the spoils of war that he confiscated.

Several details of this account suggest that it is an etiological tale. Righteousness was considered one of the major virtues of the model Davidic king (1 Kgs 19:9; Ps 72:1). The Davidic king is also characterized as a priest-king similar to Melchizedek (Ps 110:4). Salem is usually associated with Jerusalem. While the story certainly enhances the portrait of Abram, it might really be a reinterpretation of an early ancestral story, which in this final form reinforces the importance of paying tithes at the sanctuary in Jerusalem.

---

2. The name Melchizedek comes from two Hebrew words, מַלְכִּי (*malkî*; my king) and צַדִּיק (*saddiq*; righteous), thus meaning "my king is righteous."

3. אֵל עֶלְיוֹן, El Elyon, which means God Most High, points to a Canaanite pantheon of gods hierarchically ordered, with this god as its head.

The last verses of the chapter resume the story of the encounter of Abram and the king of Sodom. The latter requests only the return of the people who had been taken captive by the four eastern kings; Abram can keep his own spoils of war. The story suggests, however, that the only property he confiscated was what originally was plundered from the people living in the Valley of Siddim. Though he did not presume to speak for those who allied themselves with him, Abram does not appear to benefit from the loss of others.

Contemporary Reading: Limitations of the Household

Several aspects of these stories are troubling. They flow from the patriarchal character of the household portrayed in the stories: divine promises are made exclusively to men; childlessness is blamed on women; men make decisions without consulting others involved; women are evaluated by male standards; women are sacrificed to achieve men's goals; sons are valued over daughters. How is one to understand such stories? Despite the perspective of these accounts, God is not confined by the limitations of patriarchy or patrilineality, any more than God is confined by the limitations of biased contemporary social or political structures. On the contrary, God's blessings enrich all. Still such sinful structures cannot be justified, nor should they be replicated today. They should be acknowledged for what they are and rejected. Contemporary readers must read beneath these limitations to discover God's all-inclusive blessings in the midst of human failings.

The stories of migration and war show that only the men in charge made decisions that affected the lives of everyone else. The benefits of migration, though presumably enjoyed by all, were always determined by the patriarchs. The concerns and values of others were considered inconsequential. While men were usually the combatants in war, many women and children were raped or killed in order to prevent the next generation of the enemy from surviving or thriving. Though the weapons of war have changed, the sufferings inflicted on the most vulnerable of the population have not. Too often their plight is considered unavoidable collateral damage. Here again the contemporary reader should not be satisfied with a simple literal reading of the account but must recognize how God is concerned with all people, even, and perhaps especially, the most vulnerable.

Chapter 6

"This Is My Covenant with You"
(Gen 15:1–17:27)

The patriarchal, patrilineal character of these narratives is blaringly obvious. As patriarchal head of his household, Abram is the only one with whom God communicates. Though the covenant touches the lives of all those within the household, it is made solely through Abram. Furthermore, in this society, the lineage is traced through a son, not through a daughter. Despite this bias, these chapters contain two versions of the making of the covenant (15:1-21; 17:1-27), with a story about Sarai's slave Hagar and the birth of her son Ishmael placed discretely between them (16:1-16). While this latter story exposes the cruel treatment of the foreigner, it actually softens the Israelite bias by underscoring a unique blessing given to Hagar. The blessing is doubly unique because it is given to a woman who is an Egyptian.

Cutting a Covenant (Gen 15:1-21)

The first words of the passage ("After these things"; v. 1a) link it with the previous episode describing Abram's victory over the aggressive Mesopotamian forces. Several features underscore the otherworldly character of what follows. The phrase "the word of YHWH came to Abram" (v. 1b) is associated with prophetic pronouncements. Related to this is the notion of divine revelation through the medium of a vision. Unexpected and profound experiences of God often engender fear in vulnerable human beings.

59

Consequently, at the time of a theophany or divine manifestation, God frequently offers words of encouragement: "Do not be afraid" (see Gen 26:24; 46:3; Num 21:34). The divine self-disclosure in this passage is heartening. God is characterized as a shield. As distasteful as military metaphors might be to some, it is used here to show that Abram and his household, vulnerable people in a land not their own, enjoyed divine protection. If God is Abram's shield, then Sarai, Abram, and the household have nothing to fear from others. The reward promised does not result from conformity to some standard of moral conduct, for no such standard is mentioned. Rather, it refers to the compensation one receives for work or military service. God is Abram's shield, and it is expected that Abram will fight God's cause.

Abram laments that protection and recompense are empty, because he has no offspring, no heir. The point of Sarai's barrenness has already been made (11:30). An heir was important, not merely to ensure that the wealth of the family or clan will remain within that group, but also to care for aging parents in their need, to take responsibility for their burials, and to look after their graves.

The identity of Eliezer, the one Abram presumes will be his heir, is difficult to determine. Many commentators believe that he was a slave born into Abram's household, and his roots can be traced back to Damascus. Others maintain that he was Abram's chief steward and the logical one to continue management after the patriarch's death. According to an ancient Mesopotamian custom, a man with no heir often adopted a member of his household to serve in that capacity. Such an arrangement is not what God has in mind, as the next scene makes clear. Once again a prophetic declaration announces a message from God (v. 4). Eliezer will not be Abram's heir. Rather, that privilege and responsibility will go to Abram's own flesh and blood. After renewing this promise of descendants, God confirms it with a concrete sign, insisting that Abram's descendants will be as countless as the stars in the sky. The metaphor not only is striking in its poetic force but also will be a permanent witness to God's promise to Abram. Each night when Abram gazes at the stars in the heavens, he will be reminded of that promise.

Reference to Abram's righteousness is an editorial comment, a kind of theological reflection on his character (v. 6).[1] Righteousness is usually determined by one's conformity to a standard of moral behavior. That is

1. This passage is essential to Paul's theology of faith; see Rom 4:3-5.

not the case here. Abram is regarded as righteous because he believed[2] God's promises that he will have a son of his own, and Abram has confidence in the reliability of God's word, despite the physical implausibility of its fulfillment. For this reason, Abram is reckoned as righteous.

God speaks again to Abram (v. 7), assuring him that the God who speaks to him here in the land of Canaan is the same God who called him to leave Ur of the Chaldeans. The identification demonstrates that this God is not confined to geographic boundaries as are the gods worshiped by the other nations. Rather, this God exercises dominion over all the lands of Earth and, therefore, is able to grant some of that land to Abram. Abram asks for some sign that will help him recognize God's plan; he is directed to prepare for a solemn ritual.

The ritual described is part of a covenant-making ceremony. In the rite known as "cutting a covenant," animals are slaughtered but not sacrificed. There is no mention of burning or eating them. The carcasses are arranged in parallel lines with a pathway between them. In the form of a self-imposed, dramatized curse, the covenant partners walk between these carcasses, thereby submitting themselves to a fate similar to that of the slaughtered animals should they violate their covenant promises.

Abram keeps guard over these carcasses, lest carrion birds confiscate the meat. The deep sleep that falls upon Abram is the same as the deep sleep that fell upon Adam before God took a rib from his side to fashion a woman (2:21). This deep sleep is a creative device that implies the human being is in no way involved in the actions underway. Just as Adam had no knowledge of the subsequent creation of the woman, so Abram is in the dark about future events. While Abram is in such a state, God speaks to him again, this time with a prophecy concerning the future (vv. 13-16).

God's prophecy to Abram is twofold. It states that before Abram's descendants take control of this land, they will be resident aliens in another land, enslaved and oppressed there. Four hundred years (v. 13) and four generations (v. 16) probably refer to the same period of time. Abram's descendants will not take control of the land until the Amorites, a Canaanite tribe then occupying the land, lose it as punishment for their sinfulness. The second part of the prophecy assures Abram of a long life after which he will be buried, presumably somewhere in the land of promise.

2. אָמַן (*'āman*, to believe) means to have confidence in the reliability of another.

The ritual that seals the covenant (v. 17) takes place in the dark of night, perhaps so that the full drama of the fire can be appreciated. Ancient people considered fire one of the four basic elements of Earth. Its remarkable properties led them to designate it a primary metaphor of divine power and mystery. Under the guise of fire, God walks between the separated carcasses, thus taking on the solemn responsibility of covenant fidelity. The absence of a comparable action on the part of Abram is noteworthy. Only God participates in the ritual; Abram remains in a trancelike state. This is most unusual, because covenants either bind both partners equally or the partner with less status is bound to the one with more. Throughout this ancestral tradition, it is God who takes the initiative: God makes the promises, and God assumes responsibility. These are all examples of divine magnanimity.

The Son of Hagar (Gen 16:1-15)

The story of the struggle between Sarai and Hagar[3] provides us with a glimpse into some of the social practices that affected women in ancient patriarchal societies. This story can be told from any one of three points of view, that of Sarai, of Hagar, or of Abram.

Sarai's story opens with a reference to her own barrenness. Though women are usually blamed for childlessness, Sarai is not willing to accept responsibility for her barrenness; she actually blames God: "You see that YHWH has prevented me from bearing children" (v. 2). The inability to bear children was a grave hardship for any woman in a patriarchal society, since the survival of the clan or tribe depended on the expansion of individual families. It was a particular affliction for the wife of the patriarch, for it was her responsibility to provide the next leader of the group. Thus, Sarai's barrenness was both a personal affliction and a condition that jeopardized the entire group.

The extant law codes of several ancient Near Eastern cultures state that a barren wife could engage a surrogate to bear a child in her place.[4] This

---

3. Though they are derived from different Hebrew roots, הָגָר (Hagar) sounds very much like הַ גֵּר (*ha gēr*; the alien). Thus the sound of her name identifies her vulnerable social status, and its meaning points to her future action that will put both her son and herself at grave risk.

4. In some patriarchal societies, women are still responsible for providing a solution for barrenness; see Dora R. Mbuwayesango, "Childlessness and Woman-to-Woman Relationships in Genesis and in African Patriarchal Society: Sarah and

child would then be adopted by the barren woman and thus become the legal heir of the husband. A second social custom evident in this story is the possession of slaves. Household slaves were very common in the ancient world. They were usually prisoners of war or individuals purchased from other countries. Female slaves were often given as marriage gifts by the family of the bride. Such slaves belonged to the wives and could not automatically be taken as concubines by the husbands. These customs throw light on Sara's situation. Unable to provide Abram with a child, she offers her Egyptian slave Hagar to him, stating that the children born of Hagar will become her own children (Gen 30:3). The ethnic background of Hagar is given but not that of Abram and Sarai, suggesting that the ethnicity of the patriarch and his household is the norm, an ethnic bias that minority groups are always forced to face.[5]

After Hagar conceives, Sarai is doubly afflicted. She not only has to bear the ongoing shame of barrenness, but now the pregnant Hagar treats her with disdain[6] as well. A third social custom enters the story at this point. Hagar's status within the patriarchal family has been altered. As a concubine of Abram, she is no longer a simple slave and cannot be easily dismissed. Sarai is the primary wife, however, barren or not, and Hagar is required to respect her. As head of the household, Abram is obliged to see that she does. This explains why Sarai blames Abram for Hagar's continued disrespect. Sarai's power over Hagar is limited, but if Abram does not correct the situation, Sarai can call on the justice of God to intervene. A law in the *Code of Hammurabi* states that a concubine who claims equality with the primary wife can be reduced to the status of a slave.[7] If Hagar had been reduced to that status, it would explain why Abram returned the jurisdiction over Hagar to Sarai. Resuming her authority over her slave, Sarai punishes her. In response to this, Hagar runs away.

Hagar from a Zimbabwean Woman's Perspective (Gen 16:1-16; 21:8-21)," *Semeia* 78 (1997): 27–36.

5. Lai Ling Elizabeth Ngan, "Neither Here nor There: Boundary and Identity in the Hagar Story," in *Ways of Being, Ways of Reading: Asian American Biblical Interpretation*, ed. Mary F. Foskett and Jeffrey Kah-Jin Kuan (St. Louis, MO: Chalice Press, 2006), 70–83.

6. קלל (disdain) is also translated as "curse." The choice of this verb indicates the seriousness of Hagar's offense.

7. The book of Proverbs warns against the same situation (Prov 30:23).

The conflict should not be considered simple rivalry between women over a man. It is much more serious than that. It threatens the inner harmony of a patriarchal family and challenges the structures that ensure inheritance. The vocabulary chosen indicates this. The word that identifies the wrong done to Sarai is חָמָס (*ḥāmās*), the same word for "violence" in the story that explains God's punishment of the people at the time of Noah (6:11, 13). Their sin was great, as is Hagar's disrespect.

Hagar's story is quite different. As a slave, she has no power to make decisions about her own life. Without being asked, she is given to the patriarch in order to produce a child that will not even be considered hers. The child will be adopted without her consent. She is raised in status from slave to concubine, not because of any merit on her part, but because of the child whom she will bear. Since a woman's importance is determined by her ability to bear children, it is understandable that she might disdain a woman who is barren, even if that woman is her mistress. Such behavior is not acceptable, however, and it is reported to Abram, who reduces Hagar back to the status of a slave. Once again she is handed over without her consent, this time to an angry mistress.

Abram's story presents still another point of view. Contrary to what some have held, Abram is not depicted here as a weak, irresolute man. Rather, he is a man who lives according to the social customs of his day. As a man, and particularly as the head of a large patriarchal family, he is expected to produce an heir. Since this has not come about, a surrogate birth through Sarai's slave and Sarai's subsequent adoption of the child appears to be the only legal path to take. As primary wife, Sarai exercises some jurisdiction within the confines of the patriarchal family itself, but Abram has ultimate authority. Respecting Sarai's role as primary wife and the honor that this accords her, he returns Hagar to the status of slave and to the jurisdiction of Sarai.

The scene of Hagar's encounter with God (vv. 7-14) is extraordinary in many ways. The family of Abram is well-established in Hebron, which lies in the southern part of Canaan, east of the Dead Sea. Shur, the locale where the encounter takes place, is on the northeastern border of Egypt. In other words, Hagar, the Egyptian, is close to her home. In the Bible, mention of geographic borders often represents a change in the status of a character or a point of decision making. Such is the case here. Hagar is confronted by an angel of YHWH, who addresses her three times: first with a question, the second time with a directive, and the third time with a promise. The mysterious angel of YHWH frequently appears in biblical narratives as a manifestation of God in some form. It is often the case that the one to whom the angel appears does not recognize the true nature of this visitor until after the meeting.

Hagar is not frightened but enters immediately into a very candid conversation with this mysterious visitor. Previously, when God confronted Adam with the question, "Where are you?" (3:9), and Cain with the question: "What have you done?" (4:10), both men tried to avoid a direct answer. When Hagar is asked, "where have you come from and where are you going?" (16:8), she provides straightforward answers. The messenger addresses Hagar by both name and social class. Referring to Sarai as her mistress, Hagar acknowledges her social status and the obligations that accompany it. She does not object when the messenger directs her to return to Sarai and to submit to the harsh treatment that, according to the social customs of the day, she does deserve.

The most unusual aspect of this account is the promise that is made to Hagar (v. 10). Usually a promise of descendants too numerous to count is made to the patriarchs (15:5), not to a runaway slave who is a foreigner. She is, in fact, the only woman in the Bible to whom such a promise is made directly. Here, remarkably, the blessing is transmitted through the mother. What follows are elements of a traditional birth announcement, the literary form employed here:

- a greeting by a messenger of God (v. 8)
- an announcement of pregnancy and birth (v. 11)
- a declaration of the name of the son (v. 11)
- a prediction of what lies in his future (v. 12)[8]

Since יִשְׁמָעֵאל (Ishmael) means "God has heard," the child will be a constant reminder to Hagar that God was aware of her distress and came to her aid. What appears to be a prediction of the future lifestyle of the child is really an etiological legend. It explains the fierce and independent way of life of the Bedouins who trace their ancestry back to Ishmael. This feature of the birth announcement is also important because it makes Abram the father of a people distinct from the people of Israel.[9]

8. Other birth announcements are found in Isa 7:14 and Luke 1:30-32.
9. Today Muslims trace their ancestry through Ishmael back to Abraham.

In a final feature of the account, this Egyptian slave confers a name on God. Since naming another is an expression of power over that other, presuming to name God might appear to be blasphemous. The text says that Hagar did name God, however, and the name suggests she recognized something of God's character. Furthermore, it is a woman who names, and it is a foreign woman at that. These details add to the extraordinary character of this account: heavenly communication, a promise of a multitude of descendants, a woman as the beneficiary of the promise, the attribution by a woman of a divine epitaph. These details may all point to the high regard in which Hagar's son and the people who descended from him were ultimately held by the descendants of Isaac.

Many of the divine epitaphs found in the Bible are descriptive characterizations of God, such as אֵל עֶלְיוֹן (*El Elyon*), which means "God Most High" (14:18-19). Others grow out of an experience of God, as does אֵל רֳאִי (*El-rŏ'î*), the name given by Hagar, which means "God who sees." Ancient Israelites held the majesty and power of God in such high regard that they were convinced they would never see (experience) God and survive. This conviction is behind Hagar's amazement that she has indeed seen God and yet has survived. Her experience and the name that she gives God are memorialized in the name given to the well where all of this happened. It is known as בְּאֵר לַחַי רֹאִי (*Beer-lahai-roi*), which means "well of the living who sees." Most likely, a tradition of an experience of God was associated with the well, and this story offers an explanation of its unusual name.

This chapter opened with Abram as a childless chieftain, and it closes with the birth of a son. At last the promise of descendants is fulfilled. The fact that Abram called the child by the name given by the angel indicates that he accepted him as his own son. However, is this child the adopted son of the primary wife or that of a concubine?

Sign of the Covenant (Gen 17:1-27)

The second tradition that recounts the covenant God initiated with Abram consists of a series of divine speeches. The first speech opens with divine self-disclosure (vv. 1-2). Here God reveals the divine title אֵל שַׁדַּי (*El Shaddai*), which is usually translated "God Almighty." Most commentators today believe that this title really means "God of the Mountain," a reference to the ancient belief that gods lived on a high mountain in the north. Abram is told to walk before God, which means "to walk in

God's ways and be blameless," thus binding him to a particular way of life. This directive is followed by promises of relationship with God and of multiple descendants. In an expression of reverence, Abram prostrates himself before God (v. 3).

God elaborates on the nature and characteristics of this covenant in a second speech (vv. 4-8). Abram is told that he will be the father not only of many descendants, that is, the progenitor of a large clan, but also of many nations, peoples outside of his own clan, as well as the father of kings. In order to symbolize this broad sweep of descendants, his name will be changed from Abram to Abraham. This new name אַבְרָהָם (Abraham), which means "father of a multitude," is also a play on the Hebrew words אָב ('āb), which means "father," and הָמוֹן (hāmôn), which refers to the "thunder of many people." A change of name means "a new era has dawned": a new identity has been conferred, and new responsibilities must be fulfilled.

Like the covenant made after the flood, this pact with Abraham and his descendants will be everlasting (17:7; 9:16). God's words close with yet another promise of land. Here, however, the land is explicitly named. It is the land of Canaan, the land in which Abraham now lives as a resident alien. This land will belong to him and his descendants forever.[10]

Gods' third speech (vv. 9-14) is a directive regarding the practice of male circumcision.[11] This practice was observed by many ancient people, including the Egyptians, the Edomites, the Ammonites, and the Moabites. It was not found among the Assyrians, the Babylonians, or the Philistines who were reproached for not circumcising their men (Judg 14:3). Circumcision was performed for medical, social, or religious reasons. From a medical point of view, it was considered a way of preventing illness or of facilitating intercourse. It was probably most important for social reasons, in which case it functioned as a rite of passage at puberty and a precondition for marriage. It acquired religious significance, often as a form of blood sacrifice.

---

10. This passage is often cited as evidence of the validity of modern Israel's claim to the land.

11. For an extensive discussion of the cultural and theological significance of circumcision, see Robert B. Cotte and David Robert Ord, *In the Beginning: Creation and the Priestly History* (Minneapolis, MN: Fortress Press, 1991), 67–70.

As described in this passage, circumcision became the sign of the covenant between God and the family of Abraham. This mark on the male reproductive organ, the organ that provided the seed of the next generation, served as an external sign of this covenant. The words of the biblical passage are quite explicit: "So shall my covenant be in your flesh" (v. 13). The fact that the covenantal sign was carried solely on the bodies of men demonstrates the erroneous notion that only men play an active role in the conception of new life. This notion further implies that women are merely passive recipients of the seed of life.

In ancient Israel circumcision was performed when male infants were eight days old, evidence that the practice was no longer a rite of passage into adulthood. Rather, it became an initiation into membership within a religious family. With circumcision, the boy now belonged to the people of God. Women enjoyed the privileges of the covenant and were bound by its regulations through their membership in a patriarchal family. Since, in addition to blood relatives, a patriarchal household included slaves and servants of many kinds, it was the householder's responsibility to guarantee that all male members of those groups were circumcised as well. The gravity of the observance of this religious practice can be seen in the severity of the sanction exacted if it was disregarded. Those neglecting the procedure would be excluded from the community. In a society that was community-based, as was ancient Israel, such excommunication was comparable to death.

Sarai and the child she will bear are the subject of God's fourth speech (vv. 15-16). Just as Abram's name was changed, so now Sarai becomes Sarah. Sarai is thought to have been an archaic form of the new name. Both names mean "princess." As with Abraham, the new name implies a new era, a new identity, and new responsibilities. The promises made to Abram earlier (vv. 4, 6) are now extended to Sarah: "she shall give rise to nations; kings and peoples shall come from her" (v. 16). The promise of descendants will be fulfilled through both Abraham and Sarah. This means, of course, that Ishmael will not be the heir.

Lest Sarah's significance be misunderstood and the biblical author credited with a gender sensitivity that is not appropriate for the time, a closer look at the passage will prove to be enlightening. The text certainly says that God will bless Sarah. The mention of Ishmael and the question of his participation in the fulfillment of the promises made to Abraham indicate, however, that the intent here is to identify the legitimate line of descent. Will it proceed through Sarah's son or through Ishmael? At this point in the story, not even Abraham is certain about this (v. 18). While Sarah's newfound fertility will certainly remove any shame that her former barrenness caused, she is still important only because of the child she will bear.

God's promise of a son through Sarah is incredible to Abraham. Convinced that he is too old to father a child and Sarah is postmenopausal, Abraham laughs. He believes that the promise of descendants will be fulfilled through his son Ishmael. God's fifth speech (vv. 19-21) is an affirmation of Sarah's impending pregnancy and an announcement of the name of the child she will bear. יִצְחָק (Isaac) is a derivative of the verb צָחַק (ṣāḥaq; to laugh). Just as Ishmael is a reminder that God hears (16:11), so Isaac is a reminder of Abraham's incredulity. Initially Abraham thought the promise would be fulfilled through Ishmael. What he did not consider was God's ability to bring life out of the bodies of a man and a woman who were past the age of giving life. Here Abraham is assured that this will happen, and he is further assured that the covenant promises will continue through Isaac.

There is a notable difference between the accounts of the promise made to Hagar (16:7-16) and the corresponding one to Sarah (17:15-16). In the first instance, the heavenly being carries on a conversation with Hagar directly; in the second, God speaks about Sarah to Abraham. Is this because the future of Sarah's son follows the patrilineal customs of the time, while there are no norms to follow in Hagar's case? Whatever the reason, it shows that the people of the time were not slaves to social custom. Rather, adjustments were made when the need arose, even if this meant that social customs ceased to be binding.

God does not forget Ishmael. Though he and his descendants are not included in the everlasting covenant that God made with Abraham, he will still be blessed by God. The words of blessing are the same as those found in the first creation account and the story of blessing after the flood: "I will bless him and make him fruitful and exceedingly numerous" (v. 20; see 1:28; 9:7).

The final words of this chapter depict Abraham carrying out the prescription of universal circumcision. Some commentators wonder why Ishmael was circumcised, since he was not to be included in the covenanted people. It might be an etiological explanation of why the boys of many Arab nations were circumcised when they reached the age of puberty. That very day signals the beginning of a new era. The foundation of the people of God is being established.

Contemporary Reading: The Weak Are Strong

In this account, both Sarai and Abram act in accord with the social customs of their day. Nonetheless, the social biases of those customs are glaring and are not to be replicated in today's society. These biases touch matters of gender, class, and ethnic origin, and as is so often the case, even today, one such bias is accompanied by another. Here, the value of both Sarai and Hagar is determined by their ability to bear children. Despite her reproductive fruitfulness, Hagar, the foreigner, is moved about like a pawn from one social class (slave) to another (concubine), and back again (slave). As an Egyptian, she suffers the double bias of class and ethnic origin; she is treated badly because she is a haughty slave and also because she is a foreigner.

Hagar is being victimized by the societal customs of the day, but she is also chosen by God for a divine revelation and a promise of extensive progeny. This is an example of a theme that runs throughout the biblical tradition: the weak of the world are chosen to confound the strong. Furthermore, like many people today, she employs names for God that correspond more closely to her own experience—and that new and unfamiliar name is acceptable and enduring.

In her own way, Sarai is also victimized by the social customs of the day. The only way for her to have a child of her own is through a surrogate who now disdains her; the only way to eliminate the disdain is to dismiss the surrogate and relinquish the child. Like many people today, she is caught in social structures that do not provide her necessary support. Abram, on the other hand, does not even seem inconvenienced by the social hardships that the women must face and, therefore, does not recognize the need to change the oppressive structures.

Chapter 7

"By the Terebinth of Mamre"
(Gen 18:1–20:18)

While the biblical narrative continues to recount the exploits of men, the subject matter of these stories focuses on woman. The stories do not, however, present women in a favorable light. Sarah is portrayed as unconvinced by the announcement of her future pregnancy; the daughters of Lot are offered as compensation for the desires of the lecherous men of Sodom; and Sarah is passed off as Abraham's sister in order to save his life. Though these women come through their respective predicaments unscathed, the men are not censored for their outrageous behavior. This indicates that neither the characters in the story nor the narrator judged such treatment of woman as reprehensible.

The Promise of a Child (Gen 18:1-16)

The account of Abraham's visit by three strangers is rich in cultural detail and theological meaning. An important story in its own right, it also acts as a linchpin in the ongoing saga. It parallels the previous narrative in which God promises Abraham an heir through Sarah (17:16), and it focuses on hospitality, which is the primary theme of the narrative that follows (19:2, 5).

The first issue that becomes apparent to any careful reader is the confusion over the number of visitors. Was there one, or were there three? The passage opens with the statement, "YHWH appeared to Abraham" (v. 1).

71

It then states that there were three men (v. 2). When Abraham speaks, his deferential address is singular: "My lord" (v. 3). YHWH plays an important role in the story but usually as one of the three visitors (vv. 13). Most scholars explain this discrepancy as evidence of two stories woven together into one: an account of a visit of heavenly beings and the prediction of the birth of a child. A fragment of a tablet from Ugarit, an ancient Mediterranean port city in the north, contains a legend of a divine being who receives hospitality from a man and in return announces the birth of a child. Many commentators believe that that ancient story is behind these biblical stories. Whatever the origin of the story, the confusion regarding the number of visitors does not detract from the force of the story as it stands today.

The events described take place in the stifling heat of midday, when travelers would be looking for shelter from the sun. Abraham sits at the entrance of his tent, which is pitched at Mamre, an oasis noted for its oak or terebinth trees (see 13:18; 14:13). There he would be out of the sun yet able to benefit from any welcome breeze. He sees three men standing nearby. He has not seen them approach. Given the circumstances of his location, this seems strange. In ancient literature, however, heavenly beings often appear and disappear in surprising ways. Faithful to the practice of hospitality, Abraham refrains from asking his visitors who they are, what they want, where they come from, or where they are going. Though no words are spoken, the men are subtly asking for hospitality.

The ancient Near Eastern world was perilous. Strangers who approached a settlement were considered a potential threat. The reverse was also true. Since strangers were outside the confines of their home and the safety that it provided, they too were vulnerable. In order to counter such danger, people devised a very intricate ritual of hospitality. Normally, one went out to strangers and offered hospitality. If it was not offered, the stranger was in peril. If it was not accepted, the settlement might face danger. In the ancient Near Eastern world, people understood that the practice of hospitality guaranteed safety to all involved.

As the host, Abraham initiates the protocol that hospitality directs (vv. 2-5): he runs to greet the visitors; he shows extraordinary respect through his profound bow; he prevails upon them to accept his hospitality by allowing him to have the dust of their journey washed from their feet and to provide the shade of the tree for their comfort; he suggests that they eat something. If any of these gestures is declined, his hospitality is rejected and the visitors thereby reveal themselves as dangerous strangers. Their response is, however, straightforward and accepting: "Do as you have said" (v. 5).

The story then describes the lengths to which Abraham, the host, goes in order to extend hospitality to these unknown visitors (vv. 6-8). His initial offer of a little bread is simply a polite expression suggesting that he is really going to no trouble in caring for their needs. In reality, he is expected to prepare as sumptuous a meal as he is able. The measurement, the three seahs, is equivalent to about eight liters or two gallons of fine flour. It will make more round flat loaves than three men can eat. A second example of extravagance is the choice of meat. A lamb or a goat would certainly be more than enough. Nevertheless, Abraham selects a tender calf. He serves this feast with both fresh milk and rich curds. Finally, while Abraham supervises the preparation of the feast that Sarah and the servants prepare, according to custom neither he nor anyone from his household eats with his guests. Instead, he stands to the side, ready to serve them. For their part, the visitors accept everything that is done for them, thus placing themselves in Abraham's debt and eliminating any possibility of their being a threat to his safety.

The story shifts its focus from Abraham's attentive care for the strangers to their interest in Sarah (vv. 9-15). Uncharacteristically, they ask Abraham about her. Even today in Bedouin society, it is considered inappropriate to ask about another man's wife or possessions. Abraham informs them that she is in the tent where, according to custom, women belonged, away from prying eyes. She was, after all, involved in preparing the meal that they have just consumed (v. 6). It is strange that these visitors who appeared from out of nowhere know her name. More than this, they announce that Sarah will bear a son. Surely these are not ordinary human beings. Though the visitors are speaking to Abraham, their message is really meant for Sarah, who is in the tent, just behind the speaker, listening to what is being said about her. Once again, the difference between Sarah and Hagar becomes evident. The messenger of YHWH spoke directly to Hagar, telling her that she would bear a son (16:11). Here, Sarah is addressed only indirectly.

Sarah's response to hearing that she will give birth to a son is the same as Abraham's response when he first heard the news; she laughs (v. 12) as he had laughed (17:17). In both instances, the advanced age of the couple is mentioned. This passage also states that Sarah very demurely reveals that she is postmenopausal. If anyone knows that she is long past her childbearing years, Sarah certainly does. Her incredulity springs from her personal experience of the cycles of her body. She realizes that it is absurd to think that one her age should once again have the freshness of youth and enjoy the pleasures of sexual union. Though Sarah laughs to herself, the man speaking with Abraham knows that she has laughed. Who is this mysterious man?

The identity of one of the visitors is soon made known. It is YHWH who speaks to Abraham (v. 13) and questions Sarah's laughter. The incredulity of first Abraham and now Sarah springs not from a lack of faith but from a realization of the limits of human reproductive potential. Abraham and Sarah are correct, for according to the laws of nature, they are far too old to have children. With God, however, all things are possible, even the impossible. YHWH repeats the prediction of the birth of a son that will take place within the year. Since it is YHWH who, though in the disguise of a traveler, has made this prediction, the idea of bearing a child is no longer a laughing matter. It is not even a mere possibility; it is a fact.

The visit is concluded; Abraham's graciousness has been demonstrated; the prediction of a son has been made. The visitors set out for Sodom. Fulfilling his responsibilities of hospitality, Abraham walks a short distance with them. Little does he know the role that he or they will play in the future of his nephew Lot and the city in which Lot has taken up residence.

The Fate of the Cities (Gen 18:17–19:38)

The story of the destruction of Sodom and Gomorrah falls into two distinct parts: a discussion between Abraham and God regarding the fate of the cities (18:16-33) and the account of Lot's plight and the destruction of the cities (19:1-38). The story opens in an unusual way. YHWH engages in an internal reflection, wondering whether or not Abraham should be told about the impending fate of the cities (vv. 17-19). The initial promise made to Abraham, the promise that he will be a great nation and a blessing for others (see 12:2), is the reason YHWH considers disclosing the disaster. It is as if the blessing and its partial fulfillment have made Abraham God's confidant.

The identity of Abraham's mysterious visitors is now made clear to him. They are heavenly beings come to punish the sinful cities. God heard cries against the inhabitants of Sodom and Gomorrah but is unwilling to act on hearsay alone. The exchange between Abraham and God is really a theological probing of the issue of justifiable punishment. Abraham's questioning does not challenge the legitimacy of punishment itself, but it questions its scope. Punishment should fit the crime. The stories of Adam and Eve and of Cain illustrate how such punishment is exacted. Just punishment is not as easily determined, however, in cases where an entire group is being judged. The account of the flood is an example of this. There are many similarities between the story of the flood and the situation facing the cities of Sodom and Gomorrah, but there is one noteworthy difference. In this account, the fairness in the inevitable suffering of the innocent along with the guilty is being explicitly questioned (v. 23).

Besides being individuals in their own right, people are also members of corporate bodies. They share in and contribute to a corporate identity. In other words, they enjoy the common benefits of the group, and they carry common responsibilities. What is called a corporate personality is more prominent in traditional or tribal societies than in modern, individualistic ones. This perspective, which is widespread in the Bible, is the basis of the theological discussion between Abraham and God. Will the innocent suffer with the guilty? Or will the righteousness of fifty, forty-five, forty, thirty, twenty, even ten offset the wickedness of the majority? In either case, the entire corporate body will experience the same fate. They will either be punished, or they will be saved.

This theological discussion also raises the question of theodicy, or the justice of God. Abraham asks, "Will you indeed sweep away the righteous with the wicked?" (v. 23). The answer he gives to his own question pits the righteousness of God against the concept of collective punishment: "Far be it from you to do such a thing. . . . Should not the judge of the earth do what is just?" (v. 25). While Abraham's series of questions might be seen as a form of Near Eastern haggling, as some commentators have suggested, it is really a theological probing meant to discover the conditions requisite for reversing the frightful fate of the cities. Abraham seeks to discover the basis and scope of divine justice. The scene ends with Abraham realizing God's willingness to save but assured no certainty that the conditions for that salvation are present. Are there enough innocent people to save the cities?

After Abraham's discussion with God, there is an obvious shift in the story (19:1-38). Abraham steps into the wings and Lot takes center stage. As the broader story unfolds, the identity of the three visitors becomes clearer, as does the major reason for their visit. While YHWH stayed behind to speak with Abraham, the other two visitors proceeded toward

Sodom (18:22). The two are angels, messengers of God, who have come to destroy the sinful city (vv. 1-28). They enter the city in the evening, intending to spend the night in the open square, as those traveling through the vicinity apparently often did. Lot is sitting at the gate of the city, the place where commercial transactions take place, where public meetings are held, and where juridical matters are decided. His presence there suggests that to some degree the men of the city have accepted him as a legitimate resident. When Lot objects to their plan to exploit the visitors, however, they show that they have not really accepted him, for they sneer at him and call him an immigrant (19:9).

Seeing the two strangers, Lot immediately extends hospitality to them, just as Abraham had done earlier (18:2-5). The text gives no reason for their initial rejection of his offer. It may simply be part of the protocol of hospitality; strangers should not appear to be overly eager to accept it. After all, the open square did offer a suitable place for spending the night. Lot insists, and the angels accept, setting the stage for the drama that will unfold.

The townsmen's attempted sin against the visitors is twofold: a violation of the social duty of hospitality and an attempt at gang rape. While homosexual relations among men were accepted in many ancient societies, gang-raping of men was not. The story clearly states that all the men of the city, both young and old, demanded that Lot turn his guests over to them. Women and children were never included in such calculations, for they were considered merely part of the patriarchal household. The sinfulness of all of the men shows that God's willingness to spare the city will be thwarted, for ten righteous men cannot be found (see 18:32). Faithful to his responsibilities of hospitality, Lot refuses their demands and offers, instead, his two virgin daughters.

Mention of Lot's sons-in-law (19:14) suggests that his daughters have been betrothed. Betrothal or promise of marriage was considered the first phase of the marriage itself. Even though a woman continued to live in the household of her father, she was considered married. This period provided time to make arrangements for gathering both the dowry of the woman and arranging for the corresponding bridewealth of the man. Therefore, Lot offers daughters who are not only virgins but also committed to other men.[1]

---

1. A later law will consider the sexual assault of a betrothed virgin a capital crime (Deut 22:23-27). This proscription has little to do with deference for the young woman but is meant to protect the sexual "property" of the man to whom she is betrothed.

Traditionally, the sin of Sodom and Gomorrah has been identified with homosexuality. In fact, sodomy takes its name from the attempt of the men of the city to have sexual relations with Lot's heavenly visitors. The fact that Lot's daughters might be handed over in place of the men indicates, however, that the crime had less to do with homosexuality than with a serious violation of the precepts surrounding hospitality.

This explanation of the offense in no way mitigates the appalling nature of the crime. In fact, Lot's offer of his daughters in place of the two angels lays bare two aspects of the story that are not condemned by the author, suggesting that such behavior was probably common in the original community. The first aspect is the readiness to compromise the physical integrity of a woman in order to safeguard a man.[2] The second issue is the willingness to allow the gang rape of the women. Lot was not censored by the author for such behavior, for the women were, after all, considered his property.[3]

Though he was faithful to the practice of hospitality, even at his daughters' expense, Lot chose not to follow the instructions of the heavenly messengers. He actually hesitated leaving the city, and he objected to the directive to flee to the mountains. The man who chose the lush land of the Jordan valley rather than honor his uncle Abram by deferring to him in the selection of land (see 13:10-11) once again chooses what he thinks will be to his advantage. Rather than fleeing to the mountains, he prefers to find refuge in Zoar, one of the five cities located on the southeastern tip of the Dead Sea (14:2, 8). He tells the heavenly visitors that: "that city is near enough to flee to" (v. 20). For Lot's sake, that city is spared the destruction that consumed Sodom and Gomorrah.

2. This is the second time in the Abraham-Sarah cycle that such behavior is reported. The first time appeared in the story of Abram and Sarai in Egypt (12:10-20).

3. A similar story of the acceptability of such violation of a woman is recounted in Judges 19. In one of the most brutal stories in the Bible, a man of Gibeah is said to have offered his virgin daughter to a lecherous crowd in order to save his male guest. For his part, the guest, who was a Levite, forcibly volunteered his concubine, who was seized by the crowd and gang-raped. Upon his return home, the Levite further mutilated the body of the violated woman, dismembering it and sending the severed pieces throughout the territory of Israel. This final act of barbarity was meant to show how *he* had been affronted in Gibeah. At no time was the plight of the poor woman considered.

Just as the flood story might well be grounded in the memory of an actual water disaster, so it is possible that the report of the destruction of Sodom and Gomorrah contains details of a real catastrophe that enveloped cities once located at the southeastern tip of the Dead Sea. Some commentators believe that the destructive forces described here resulted from a shift in the tectonic plates under the Great Rift, a valley that runs from northern Syria south to Eastern Africa. Such a shift could have produced an earthquake that released sulfuric gases or petroleum that could ignite. Others maintain that the disaster was caused by a form of volcanic eruption. Whatever the case, the entire area, with the exception of Zoar, is destroyed. As with the account of the flood, this story reports that the natural world, though innocent of transgression, suffers the fate of sinful human beings, an issue that continues to be of great concern to many interpreters today.

The episode about Lot's wife is also etiological in origin. The area south of the Dead Sea is known for its well-weathered limestone formations. One of these formations may have precipitated this legend. The significance of the narrative is found less in the inquisitiveness of Lot's wife, than in the gravity of the taboo that was pronounced: "do not look back" (v. 17). The actions of God are not meant to be observed by the human eye.[4] Though the directive was addressed to Lot as head of his household,[5] the entire household was expected to comply with it. Lot's wife violated the injunction, and so she was punished. The story does not say why it was his wife who acted in this way and not Lot himself or one of his daughters or their husbands. Perhaps the salt formation that precipitated the legend lent itself to being seen as a woman rather than a man. Whatever the origin of the tradition might have been, a biased tradition claiming that the reason can be traced back to women's innate inquisitive nature has grown out of this story. Lot is now left with only his two daughters.

The story of Sodom itself ends where it began, with YHWH and Abraham on a rise overlooking the city (v. 27; see 18:16). The story of Lot continues in the next chapter, a chapter that parallels an account of events that transpired after the flood. Noah, who was saved from the

---

4. God cast Adam in a deep sleep when the woman was fashioned from one of his ribs (Gen 2:21), and Abram fell into a trance while God walked through the separated carcasses at the time of the establishment of the covenant (15:12, 17).

5. The words are all second-person masculine singular.

disaster, became intoxicated and was taken advantage of in his vulnerability (19:30-38; see 9:18-23). Though Lot had asked to escape to Zoar rather than flee to the mountains, he was afraid to stay in that city, and so he eventually settled in the hill country after all.

Lot's sons-in-law do not take his warning seriously and refuse to leave the city with Lot, his wife, and his daughters. With the deaths of their prospective husbands, Lot's daughters realize that their father provides their only chance of bearing children who would continue his line and guarantee their own security. Thus, they set aside social restrictions against incest in order to forge a future. Unlike Ham who earlier is cursed for having taken advantage of Noah's nakedness (11:22-27), the women are judged negatively neither by Noah nor by God. It is biased interpreters who claim that their behavior is shameful.

The story is an etiological legend, explaining the origin of two peoples who are distant from yet somehow related to the Israelites. The sons of Lot's daughters become the ancestors of the Moabites[6] and the Ammonites, people who eventually settled on the east side of the Jordan River and who often play significant roles in the history of Israel.

In many ways the account of the destruction of Sodom and Gomorrah parallels the earlier story of the flood (Gen 6–8). Both narratives describe total destruction resulting from widespread and unrepentant sinfulness. In both cases, one man is singled out for deliverance and the members of his household are saved along with him. Once the catastrophe has ended, the favored man in each story is overcome by the intoxicating power of wine and taken advantage of by one or more of his children. Finally, the offspring of the perpetrators of this shameful act become nations that have troublesome relations with Israel (Canaanite tribes [10:15-19], Moab and Ammon [19:36-38]).

The Promise Preserved (Gen 20:1-18)

The story of Abraham and Sarah settling in the territory of a foreign ruler is similar to an earlier account (12:10-20). The structure of these two stories is basically the same: the patriarchal family migrates to a foreign land; the ruler of that land takes an interest in the wife, thus endangering

---

6. מוֹאָב (Moab) means "from father," and בֶּן־עַמִּי (Ben-ammi) means "son of my people."

the patriarch's life; the patriarch tells her to say that she is his sister, thus safeguarding himself; the wife is taken into the harem of the foreign ruler, thus placing her and the promise of an heir through her in jeopardy; the actions of the foreign ruler bring down divine punishment, thus revealing the true identities of the patriarchal couple; the wife is returned along with gifts from the foreign ruler; divine punishment ends.

In the past, scholars explained this apparent repetition as evidence of parallel versions. Many scholars today maintain, however, that the second account is not a genuine literary story but rather a reworking of the first one in order to address some of the questions that that account left unanswered, particularly the question of guilt. This second story raises another obvious question: Why did Abraham place himself and his family in jeopardy a second time? Some commentators hold that the movements of the group reflect the occasional change of pasture that is part of nomadic life. Though God promised the land of Canaan to Abraham and his descendants, they were still resident aliens in the land and, therefore, vulnerable to the people already settled there. Furthermore, the play on words between גְּרָר (Gerar), an area south of Beersheba near Gaza, and גֵּר (*gēr*; sojourner) reinforces the people's status in the land.

This account explicitly states that Sarah was indeed Abraham's half-sister. Although later Israelite law will forbid such unions (Deut 27:22), in this case a marriage between siblings does not appear to be censured. As head of the patriarchal household, Abraham would be the one who arranged the marriages of the women of the group. This means that he handed Sarah over to the king of Gerar, since there is no indication that she was taken by force. While Abraham acted in this way in both stories, his behavior here is more troubling, since it seems to have occurred shortly after the heavenly visitors assured him that Sarah would bear a child within the year. Because he feared for his own safety, he placed in jeopardy both the integrity of Sarah and the promise of an heir. Sarah's advanced age here, a detail that does not seem to be a problem for the author, strengthens the argument that this story is really a reinterpretation of an earlier one.

The revelation of God to the king is unusual, not because the medium is a dream, but because the recipient is a foreigner. Furthermore, he is the one who had just taken the wife of another man into his harem. Such an act was regarded as a serious violation of the integrity of that other man (see 2 Sam 12:8, 11). In fact, to seize a man's harem could be considered an act of war (see 2 Sam 16:20-22). Thus God pronounces the sentence on the king: "You are about to die" (v. 3). God reaffirms the king's claim that he is innocent of the grievous sin. Besides, he has not yet been intimate with Sarah. Guilty of a mistake, he is innocent of a crime. This is the only way to explain the affliction he does experience (vv. 17-18). A wrong has been committed and so balance must be restored. God intervenes to save a foreign king who had been duped, lest he suffer the consequences of a more serious transgression.

The comparison between the integrity of the king of Gerar and the cowardice of Abraham is clearly sketched. The two questions posed by the king are telling: "What have you done to us? How have I sinned against you?" (v. 9). In order to save himself, Abraham has not only placed Sarah and the promise of an heir in jeopardy but also put the entire kingdom of Gerar at risk of divine retribution. The king is concerned for others; Abraham thinks only of himself. He offers a threefold defense: he was afraid that the people of Gerar did not fear God but would kill him in order to take Sarah; he insists that he did not really lie, for Sarah was his half-sister; ultimately Sarah did agree to present herself as such.[7] With this threefold excuse, Abraham takes no responsibility for his actions.

In the earlier account, after returning Sarai, Pharaoh sent Abram and Sarai out of his country with the flocks and slaves that might have served as legitimate bridewealth. The king of Gerar also provides flocks and slaves, but he does not expel Abraham and his retinue. He allows them to settle where Abraham chooses. Then, contrary to custom, the king turns to Sarah, addressing her as Abraham's sister, not his wife. The huge amount of money that he gives may appear to be the monetary compensation paid to the nearest male relative of a woman who has been violated. The king says, however, that it is really for her exoneration or vindication (v. 16). People knew that she had been taken into his harem. Therefore, her reputation was damaged. The Hebrew expression כְּסוּת עֵינַיִם (*kesût 'ênayim*) means "covering of the eyes." In other words, the critical eyes of others will be covered, and Sarah will be seen in a favorable light.

The need for vindication and reinstatement in the good graces of a traditional society prompted various practices. One such practice was the

---

7. The patriarchal customs of the day would have prevented Sarah from refusing to accept Abraham's plan.

bestowal of excessive wealth on someone unjustly accused of wrongdoing. This obvious good fortune which was seen by all was considered an external acknowledgment of innocence (see Job 42:10). Though the money was given to Abraham as the head of the patriarchal household, the king clearly stated that it was intended for Sarah's vindication.

Despite his glaring shortcomings, Abraham is still identified by God as a prophet. He functions as a prophet, not in bringing the word of God to others, but in praying for them. God tells the king that Abraham will intercede for him (v. 7), and at the end of the story, Abraham does (v. 17). Thus, the initial promise made to Abram is fulfilled: "In you all the families of the earth shall be blessed" (12:3).

Once again, though the major actors in this drama are the men, their use and abuse of the woman is the reason for their struggle. Sarah is a pawn, used by Abraham to safeguard his own life and intended to be used by the king for his pleasure. Though the story says that she is exonerated, it is really the king who is exonerated. If she was not violated, it is because of his actions, not hers. He may not have planned to have relations with another man's wife, but he was ready to do so with someone's sister. In either instance, Sarah had little or nothing to say about it. The king showed more concern for Sarah than Abraham did, however, for he realized that because of his actions she would be criticized. In order to remedy this, he did what he could to confirm her innocence.

Contemporary Reading: Women at Risk

The vulnerability of women in a patriarchal society becomes blatantly evident in the stories in this section. Even the value of their reproductive potential, so cherished in many stories, is set aside when the safety of men is in jeopardy. Not only is there total disregard for the inherent dignity of the women here, but the cowardice of the men is laid bare. Moreover, neither the characters in the stories nor those who compiled the stories register disapproval of such behavior. This is evidence that bias against women has been handed down generation after generation. Most, though not all, societies today recognize the heinousness of such unashamed disregard of the human dignity of women. Nonetheless, the road to total mutual gender respect is still long and hard.

Chapter 8

"YHWH Took Note of Sarah"
(Gen 21:1–23:20)

The stories in this section deal with issues of life and death. Sarah's barrenness is seen as the primary obstacle to the fulfillment of the promise to Abraham of an heir. Rather than understand Sarah's physical condition as an obstacle, however, one could well see it as a ploy used by God to demonstrate divine power, for the promise of descendants is eventually fulfilled through Sarah. It is only in God's good time that she conceives, and the child of promise is finally born. A kind of reverse parallelism exists between Sarah's inability to bring a child to life and Abraham's charge to take the life from that child. At the end of the section, Sarah's burial marks the fulfillment of the dual promise, an heir and possession of the land.

Sarah's Child (Gen 21:1-34)

The extraordinary character of Isaac's birth (21:1-7) is underscored by the way Sarah's pregnancy is reported: "YHWH dealt with Sarah as he had said, and YHWH did for Sarah as he had promised" (v. 1). The progression of her pregnancy and of the child's birth may have been natural, but the fact that she became pregnant at all was God's doing. From the very beginning, Sarah's child is marked as exceptional.

Abraham performs prescribed cultic duties (vv. 3-5). He names the child Isaac and circumcises him when he is eight days old, thus fulfilling the requirement set down when God entered into covenant with him (see 17:10-12). The laughter that originally prompted the name of the child (see 17:17; 18:12) appears here as well (v. 4). While Abraham's and Sarah's previous laughter was engendered by incredulity, however, this laughter springs from joy. Isaac not only reminds his parents of their lack of faith in the face of the ridiculousness of a possible pregnancy at such an advanced age but also is the source of their joy. The advanced age of the couple is a constant reminder of the marvels that God can and does work to accomplish the divine promise.

In many ancient Near Eastern societies, children were nursed until they approached three years of age (see Macc 7:27). It was common practice to celebrate the time of weaning by a rite of passage. Weaned, the child was no longer an infant but had moved safely into childhood, the next phase of life. In a society where infant mortality was quite high, weaning was considered a milestone. Isaac had survived infancy and, hence, Abraham celebrated the event with a great feast. The joy and celebration found in the previous verses are turned into resentment and hardship (vv. 8-21). The tension between Sarah and Hagar described in an earlier account (chap. 16) now encompasses their respective sons as well. The rivalry exists on at least three further levels. On the level of the story, it is a rivalry between two women. Since one woman is a legitimate wife and the other is a slave woman who has become a concubine, it is a rivalry between social classes as well. Finally, as the story unfolds, it becomes clear that it is also a rivalry between two peoples, the Israelites and the Ishmaelites.

The fury of this rivalry is ignited when Sarah sees Hagar's son playing with her son. Some commentators claim that he was not playing with Isaac but laughing at him. This latter translation provides an explanation for Sarah's anger and what appear to be the drastic steps she takes to correct an unacceptable situation. Various social customs of the day offer sufficient reason for Sarah's reaction. The *Code of Hammurabi* stated that the child of a concubine could inherit along with children of free wives. Sarah does not want this to happen, not only for Isaac's sake, but for her own as well. Since she may have to face dependency on her son for care and protection in her old age, she does not want to risk losing any of the inheritance.

Hagar had been Sarah's slave and, thus, Sarah had exercised control over her (16:2). She lost that control, however, when she gave Hagar to Abraham as a concubine. Now the only way she can influence Hagar's life is through Abraham. A second ancient Near Eastern custom ensured that a concubine who bore a child could not arbitrarily be cast out. If she were dismissed, she was to be awarded her freedom and the freedom of her child, along with some financial support in exchange for relinquishment of any part of the inheritance the child might have been awarded. Sarah demands that Abraham act in conformity with this custom. This story provides a glimpse into the influence exercised by a major wife over matters internal to the patriarchal household.

Abraham's distress over this matter lays bare his attachment to Ishmael, who is, after all, his son. He acquiesces, but with regret. He acquiesces to God's directive, however, not merely to Sarah's demand. God states once more that the promise made to Abraham will be fulfilled through Isaac. Lest there be conflict over this, it seems important to separate the sons. Still, God promises Abraham what was earlier promised to Hagar, that a great nation will spring from Ishmael (v. 13; see 16:10). In both accounts, God appears to work through social customs that discriminate against the foreign slave and her child. Nevertheless, God promises them a blessing of their own while acting in this manner.

The story of the dismissal of Hagar and her son is heartrending (vv. 14-21). Abraham himself, not one of his servants, sees them off. They depart at daybreak, enabling them to travel a distance before they must face the heat of the day. Abraham furnishes them with bread and water, the bare necessities.[1] If Abraham is camped near Gerar (20:1) and Hagar wanders in the wilderness of Beersheba, she has been traveling southeast. Her water is gone, a great peril in desert land. She cannot bring herself to watch her son die of thirst, yet she cannot abandon him.

Twice in one verse, the text says that "God heard the voice of the boy" (21:17). God speaks to Hagar through a messenger: "Do not be afraid"— the typical words of reassurance at the time of a divine manifestation (see 1 Sam 4:20; Luke 1:30) because God hears the cries of the oppressed (see Exod 3:7). The promise made to Abraham that this son will be a great

---

1. In the earlier tradition (16:1-16) the child is much older. If Abraham was eighty-six when Ishmael was born and one hundred when Isaac was born, Ishmael would have been sixteen at the time of Isaac's birth and eighteen or nineteen when Isaac was weaned. The discrepancy indicates that the present story originated in a different tradition. Here, the depiction of a small child underscores the vulnerability of Hagar and Ishmael, a major focus of this story.

nation is repeated to Hagar. She then sees the well, fills the water skin, and gives the boy a drink. They have both been saved.[2]

Eventually, this freed Egyptian slave arranges for the marriage of her son to another Egyptian woman. This is very unusual since, in patriarchal society, the father usually made such arrangements, and if not the father, then the eldest brother. In Ishmael's case, however, his father has abandoned him and he has no elder brother. Here is a case in which the woman steps forward and fulfills a social responsibility normally assigned to a man. Such a situation demonstrates that strict role assignment often stems from gender bias rather than presumed female incompetence.

This story is sometimes seen as an etiological legend that explains certain characteristics of the Ishmaelites. They are Bedouins who are skilled with bow and arrow. They live in the wilderness of Paran, a stretch of land south of Canaan in the Sinai Peninsula. Finally, they have an uncommon relationship with the Israelites: both peoples trace their origins to Abraham; they are not allies, but they are not always enemies either.

The final segment of this chapter (vv. 22-34) resumes the account of Abraham's dealings with Abimelech, the king of Gerar (see Gen 20). Discrepancy of details suggests that two traditions have been woven together, one reflecting political circumstances present at the time of the monarchy, when these narratives were likely composed or edited, and a much older tradition reflecting ancient customs attached to the digging of wells and the planting of trees. The king of Gerar is accompanied by Phicol, the commander of his army—a definite show of force. The king has reason to fear Abraham, for the king and his people suffered greatly when he unwittingly took Sarah into his harem. He acknowledges his vulnerability, stating that God protects Abraham despite his underhanded behavior. The king now seeks a nonaggression agreement with him that will guarantee straightforward dealings in the future. Abraham's response is short and to the point: "I swear it" (v. 24). A solemn oath has been declared, and the commander of the king's army is witness to it.

It is then Abraham's turn to raise the issue of a well that Abimelech's servants had seized. Wells were indispensable for nomadic herders like Abraham and his household. Furthermore, caravan routes through the wilderness were established near such wells. Those in charge of the wells

---

2. Just as there is a play on words with the name Isaac, so there is a comparable play with יִשְׁמָעֵאל (Ishmael), which means God has heard affliction (16:11).

benefited from the exchange of goods that took place there. Abraham is very concerned that his well has been confiscated by the people of Gerar. The king claims lack of knowledge of the matter. Somewhat wary, Abraham seeks a form of guarantee. Offering Abimelech sheep and cattle, he initiates a covenant.

The number seven is an important etiological detail, for בְּאֵר שֶׁבַע (*Beer-Sheba*), the place where this transaction occurred, means "well of seven." A gift of ewe lambs is most unusual. Female animals are much more valuable than are the males of the species, because of their potential for breeding as well as for the milk that they produce. The fact that these sheep were lambs points to a long future of productivity. Abraham is presenting Abimelech a gift that he cannot refuse without being guilty of insult. The value of this gift highlights the importance Abraham places on control of this well. The two men swear an oath that seals the covenant. This detail of the story prompted another etiological tradition regarding the name of the well, Beer-sheba, which means "well of the oath." The complexity of the passage is seen in the fact that two oaths are sworn and two meanings for the name of the place are remembered.[3] This discrepancy probably resulted from the conflation of two traditions.

The story ends with Abraham performing two cultic acts. First, planting a tree was considered a sacred act comparable to building an altar. Because of the extraordinary fertility of trees and the shade that they provide in the wilderness, they were thought by some to be sacred and the home of a god. Second, calling on God was considered a cultic act. The name that Abraham used to call on God is אֵל עוֹלָם (*El Olam*), which means "God Everlasting." This could have been the name of the deity worshiped at a pre-Israelite shrine that was already set up in the area. These actions signal that the second part of God's original promise to Abraham has finally been fulfilled. Though it is a very small plot, Abraham now possesses a parcel of the land that God promised him.

A Test of Trust (Gen 22:1-24)

The account of Abraham's willingness to sacrifice Isaac is one of the best known and most disturbing stories of the Bible. The Jewish

---

3. Mention of the Philistines poses an anachronistic problem because the Philistines do not appear on the scene until the twelfth century BCE.

community refers to it as the binding of Isaac, rather than the sacrifice of Isaac. The former designation indicates that Isaac was bound but not sacrificed. The text itself identifies its message when it states, "God tested Abraham" (v. 1). While Abraham thinks that he will offer his precious son as a sacrifice, and Isaac experiences his own binding, the reader knows that it is all a test. When God calls out to Abraham, his response is immediate and telling: "Here I am." It is the appropriate response of a man who enjoys a covenantal relationship with his God, a man who finally sees that the promises this God has made to him over the years are at last being fulfilled.

God asks for a burnt offering or holocaust, the most solemn of Israelite sacrifices. Abraham offers no objection. His only response to God's directive is immediate obedience. Behind this narrative is probably the ancient practice of child sacrifice.[4] This practice had a very complicated history in ancient Israel. There is no doubt that it was practiced at an earlier time.[5] Those texts that retain traces of the practice, however, also include its abrogation in favor of animal sacrifice (Exod 13:12; 34:19-20). Though some child sacrifice did continue in Israel as late as the monarchy (1 Kgs 16:34; 2 Kgs 21:6), it was forbidden under penalty of death (Lev 20:2-5). Here, the author probably employed details of a very old cultic practice that was no longer observed in order to highlight the total devotion of one of Israel's earliest ancestors.

The description of the journey to the place of sacrifice is poignant. Abraham and his company leave early in the morning before the heat of the day will make travel unbearable. The three days' journey reflects the typical period of time set aside as preparation for an extraordinary event.[6] Some commentators believe that Abraham carried the fire and the knife because they were too dangerous for Isaac to carry. The fact that Isaac carried the wood for the sacrifice indicates, however, that he was not a small child. The conversation on the way between Isaac and

---

4. As horrendous as this practice was, it should not be equated with child abuse, as some contemporary interpretations have suggested. Child abuse is a sadistic violation of the dignity of the child; child sacrifice is an abhorrent form of appeasing the deity.

5. There is evidence that the original people of Jericho practiced foundation sacrifice. This was the practice of sacrificing the firstborn son and then burying him in the foundation of the city, thereby ensuring the prosperity of the city (Josh 6:26).

6. Three days in the tomb (Matt 27:63).

Abraham serves to heighten the emotional impact of the story, as do the obvious naïveté of the son and the grim determination of the father. Abraham's response to Isaac's query about the absence of an animal for the sacrifice ("God will provide") might explain the name of the mountain, Moriah.[7]

Isaac's naïveté turns into acquiescence as he seems to allow himself to be bound. His passive behavior throughout the narrative shows that he is not the major figure in the story. He simply responds to Abraham's instructions. It is Abraham who is called by God and directed to offer a sacrifice; it is Abraham's devotion to God that is being tested. Once this devotion becomes clear, Abraham is told to lower the knife. If this mountain had not been a cultic site before this event, it certainly became one as a result of it. Having offered a ram in place of his son, Abraham names the site יְהוָה יִרְאֶה (*YHWH yir'eh*) "YHWH will provide [will see to it]".

Once Abraham has demonstrated his unquestioning devotion to God, the angel of YHWH calls to him again. As earlier in this story, the content of the message delivered shows that it is really YHWH who is speaking to Abraham. God renews the promise of a multitude of descendants too numerous to count (see 12:3; 15:5). This promise is then reinforced with an oath that is meant to assure Abraham of God's dependability. The trial is over; the test has successfully demonstrated Abraham's devotion.

Sarah plays no role at all in this story. Still, some contemporary commentators insist that this mother, who acted aggressively to ensure that her son alone would be Abraham's heir (21:10), would never have allowed Abraham to attempt this sacrifice. Though the story is certainly rooted in patriarchal customs, mother-love would not in any way ameliorate the drama. In fact, it could possibly blur the focus on its principal theme. Just what is that theme?

It is not child sacrifice; the horrendous practice is merely the occasion for the test that Abraham must endure. Nor is it simply a test of obedience; Abraham's obedience is the external manifestation of his profound religious disposition of trust. At issue is whether or not Abraham trusts God. Furthermore, it is a trust not that God will intervene in Abraham's

---

7. יִרְאֶה (*yir'eh*), translated here as "provide," really means "he will see," referring to the lamb that God will see. Some scholars maintain that מֹרִיָּה (Moriah) is a play on the sound of the verb. The Samaritans claim that Mount Gerizim in Samaria was the place of this test.

problematical situation but that God will fulfill the promise of an heir. This is a test to discover whether or not God chose the right man for that promise. Just as Abraham had been told to leave the past behind and to trust in God (12:1), here he is told to relinquish the future and, once again, to trust in God.[8] God might be depicted in a negative light in this situation, but it seems that the only way that ancient Israel could demonstrate the depth of Abraham's character is to have God test it to its limits.

Abraham's obedience, though difficult to understand at times, is active, not passive. He accepts and he responds. He does not initiate because it is God's plan that is unfolding, not his. If that plan is to be brought to completion, and if Abraham is to play any part in it, he will have to accept the role into which he has been cast and trust the one whose story is being told—and that one is God. Though there is no evidence of this in the story, some explain Isaac's silence as a feature of a rite of passage in which young men are made to face and accept mortal danger before assuming all of the rights and privileges of an adult male. What remains clear, however, is his importance in the story, despite his passive behavior. All the hopes for the future rest on Isaac. While it appears that his well-being is set in opposition to Abraham's obedience, at issue is not Isaac himself but the promise of the future that he represents. Consequently, the dilemma is really about clinging either to Isaac as the hope of the future or to God in whose hands the future is held.

The chapter ends with genealogical information about the family of Abraham's brother Nahor, which provides the genealogical background for the story of the courtship of Rebekah, which appears in the next chapter. Since biblical genealogies trace descent through the sons, the names of women were included only as markers of male descent. This explains the mention of Milcah, who bore Bethuel, the father of Rebekah. This inclusion reinforces the opinion that, though patrilineal in character, this short genealogy supports the importance of Rebekah.

8. The idea that God tests individuals or groups in order to discover the authenticity of their virtue is not an unfamiliar theme in the Bible. It is found in several other places. For example, God tested the Israelites when they were in the wilderness (Exod 15:25; 16:4) and when they attempted to take possession of the land that had been promised to them (Judg 2:22). Job's loss of family and possessions and ultimately his physical affliction were also meant to test his virtue (Job 1:11; 2:5).

Sarah's Death and the Purchase of Land (Gen 23:1-20)

The purpose of Abraham's purchase of land is stated six times in this chapter: he needs a place to bury the dead members of his household (vv. 4, 6, 8, 11, 13, 15). While the bulk of the chapter describes the intricate transaction of the sale of the land, it opens with the report of Sarah's death and closes with mention of her burial. In this way, ensuring final respect for Sarah becomes the presenting reason for the events that transpire. The text does not explain why Sarah died in Hebron and not further south in Beer-sheba where they had pitched their tents. Nor does it explain the origin of the name Kiriath-arba (קִרְיַת אַרְבַּע), which means "city of four." The point here is that Sarah has died and Abraham has nowhere to bury her body.

The customary mourning rites that Abraham most likely performed included weeping loudly, tearing his garments, putting on sackcloth, disheveling his hair, cutting his beard, scattering dust on his head, fasting, and sitting in silence for a prescribed period of time. Once he had completed these rites, Abraham sets out to secure land for the tomb of his dead wife.

In the ancient Near Eastern world, the exchange of land was a very complicated venture. A people's identity was often tied to the land on which they lived. Moreover, ownership of the land was usually communal and, therefore, kept within the tribe itself. These customs render Abraham's purchase of land quite significant. This account reflects several characteristics of ancient financial negotiations. The transaction itself takes place in three distinct stages, each of which is marked by typical Near Eastern exaggeration. Abraham approaches the Hittites (vv. 3-6), most likely at the city gate where the men gathered to conduct the business of the city. He identifies himself as a stranger and an alien, thus acknowledging his vulnerability and his total dependence on their graciousness. His self-effacing demeanor is appropriate because he is indeed an outsider but also because he has come to the people as one wanting to purchase some of their land. His request might be considered quite presumptuous. Lest the people of the city think that he has ulterior motives, he immediately presents them with his plight. He is a landless alien who needs a burial site for his recently deceased wife. He is not a threat; nor is he asking for charity. He intends to pay for the land. Near Eastern courtesy requires that the people of the city attend to this valid and universal need.

The Hittites respond to Abraham's request with great respect. They address him as lord and refer to him as prince. They acknowledge that he is no ordinary prince or tribal chief, but a prince of God. In Near Eastern custom, Abraham exaggerates his humble state, and the Hittites overstate his importance. True to custom, they will not be outdone in graciousness, and so they allow him to choose from their choicest burial sites.

The second round of negotiations (vv. 7-11) begins with Abraham bowing low before the people of the city in a sign of respect. They have offered any site he wishes; he asks only for a cave belonging to a man named Ephron. Abraham does not expect to be given this cave freely; he is prepared to pay full price for it. The extraordinary generosity of the men of the city makes it difficult for Ephron to refuse Abraham's request, for he is asking less land than the people originally offered him. The cave in question is at the far end of a field, so relinquishing it would be a relatively easy matter. Abraham asks that this transaction be made in public, at the gate of the city where all major business is enacted, thus formalizing it. Addressing Abraham as lord, Ephron agrees to sell the cave but insists that Abraham take the entire field in which the cave is found. Once again Abraham is offered much more than what he requested.

The third stage in the negotiations (vv. 12-18) begins with Abraham bowing to the citizenry yet again. Turning to Ephron, Abraham declines the more extensive offer, restating his intention to pay for what he receives. His disadvantage, however, now becomes evident. Ephron is in total charge of the transaction. His seeming generosity ("I give you the field"; v. 11) was not meant to be taken seriously. It is an example of Near Eastern exaggeration. He is willing to sell, but on his terms. He decides both the extent of the land that is purchased and the price that is exacted. Four hundred shekels of silver is an exorbitant price to pay for a field.[9] Ephron makes light of this, claiming that this is an insignificant amount of money for men as wealthy as they are. There are several reasons why Abraham can hardly quarrel with this. Most importantly, he needs the burial site as soon as possible. Furthermore, he is a foreigner and, as such, he has little or no legal recourse. Finally, Near Eastern decorum prevents him from backing out of a transaction that takes place in public, particularly

9. In the future, Jeremiah will buy a field for seventeen shekels (Jer 32:9).

at this point in the negotiations. And so Abraham agrees and weighs out the stipulated amount of silver.

While it appears that the promise of land is being fulfilled, purchase of the field in Machpelah is really important for another reason. Having left their land of origin at God's command, it seems only right that the ancestors be laid to rest in land that had been promised them. Besides, purchase of one field would not have given the ancestors the right to claim the entire land. With the purchase of this land, Abraham now has a burial place for his wife Sarah, himself, and any descendants who might decide to be buried there.

Contemporary Reading: Hardship Overcome

This section contains several stories of hardship, even brutality. The story of Hagar and Sarah has been repeated again and again whenever social customs pit one woman against another over job security, various ways of parenting, even different ways of expressing themselves. The feminist movement is intent on fostering genuine self-identification and self-determination of women. It manifests its authenticity when it legitimately champions such diversity.

The ancient writer may well have considered Hagar a minor character in the Abraham/Sarah saga. Nevertheless, many contemporary women see her otherwise. Strengthened by a revelation from God, she assumes total responsibility for her son. In the absence of male family members who normally negotiate marriages, she makes the necessary arrangements. This is a woman who is not afraid to step forward when the needs of others are not being met, regardless of whether the task is traditionally considered woman's work.

Abraham's dealings with Abimelech and Ephron uncover the bias and vulnerability often experienced by immigrants. Despite the fact that he is powerful and wealthy, Abraham must defer to the people of the land, cautious that he not appear devious or demanding. Despite his diffidence and straightforward manner, Ephron still takes advantage of him. Abraham is not naïve; he knows how such transactions are carried out. He bides his time and accepts the unfair treatment, because he really wants the field. Very often, those in a society who are economically or politically powerless know how to get what they need or want despite their powerlessness.

Perhaps the most troubling feature of this section is Abraham's willingness to sacrifice Isaac. This is not simply a gender issue, for in Israel, mothers sacrificed their children just as fathers did (see Lam 4:10), and the ancient Near Eastern people revered female deities who were just as brutal as were the male deities (Tiamat in ancient Babylon). This is deeper than a gender issue. Without exonerating Abraham, the real culprit in the story is God. How could God ask a father to sacrifice his son? The reader knows that it is only a test (22:1), but Abraham did not. If it is only a test, how could God require such a ghastly act? This is a terrible depiction of God. It is a characterization that continues to hold sway, however, in the minds and hearts of many people today who ask: Why did God cause an innocent child to suffer the ravages of cancer?

It is easy to say that this was the only way the righteousness of Abraham could be revealed. In this, the story of Abraham is similar to that of Job. Nevertheless, the cruelty of God in both stories still stands forth. In the face of such tragedy, some might conclude that God is indeed cruel; others may admit that much of the terrible suffering in the world is simply beyond human understanding.

Chapter 9

"The Woman Whom the LORD Has Decided Upon"

(Gen 24:1–25:18)

Rebekah plays the major role in most of the stories in this section. She is the one who meets the requirements for a suitable wife set by Abraham; she is the one who, like Abraham, agrees to leave her home and journey to a strange land; she is the one who is given a blessing that promises her a multitude of descendants.

The Choice of Rebekah (Gen 24:1-66)

In a patriarchal society, the importance of finding the right wife for the son who will be heir of the household cannot be overemphasized. This is one of the patriarch's most serious responsibilities, for the future of the household depends on it. Marriages are arranged by the chief men in the respective families. Depending on the customs of the specific group, the bridal couple may or may not be included in the choice of a partner. In such societies, marriage is understood primarily as a legal agreement between families and only secondarily as an emotional attachment between individuals.

Groups practice one of two forms of marriage, exogamous or endogamous. Exogamous marriages are unions between members of different tribes or clans. When such groups enter into treaties with each other, they often exchange daughters in marriage. Despite the fact that this practice often requires great sacrifice on the part of the women, it is meant to strengthen the ties that are established between various groups as well as foster the cultural exchange that results from these unions. Such exogamous marriages are a frequent practice of groups enjoying a strong sense of identity, one that is not threatened by diversity and change. Endogamous marriages are unions between persons who are members of the same tribe or clan. Groups that practice this form of marriage determine the degree of blood relationship that is allowed. True siblings are seldom permitted to marry. Marriages between cousins, however, are quite common. Endogamous marriages ensure the purity of the male bloodline.[1]

Several social customs are operative as Abraham plans to secure a wife for his son. First, the seriousness of this venture is seen in the form of the oath that Abraham requires of his servant. It is not unusual that those taking an oath hold some sacred object in their hand.[2] Here, Abraham directs his servant to place his hand under Abraham's thigh, near his genitals. This action suggests some aspect of generativity and is found in passages in which an elder is acting out his last will before death.[3] This meaning is certainly implied here. The servant is directed to swear that he will not procure a wife for Isaac from among the people of Canaan, clear evidence that Abraham's group practiced endogamy.

The seriousness of a move away from one's land of origin allowed the woman the right to decline a marriage offer. Nevertheless, Abraham believed that the God who called him from his land of origin and brought him to this land would guarantee success in the search for a wife for his son. The servant took ten camels and a treasure trove of choice gifts, an indication of Abraham's wealth. He made his way to the common well that was just outside the city of Nahor. While the city gate was the place where men gathered to conduct the business of the city, the well was the place where the women congregated to converse and exchange news as they drew water. It was there that the servant hoped to find a wife for Isaac.

In most patriarchal societies, procuring water for household use as well as for the care of animals was assigned to the women and/or children

---

1. Purity of the bloodline concerns lineage and inheritance, not racial prejudice, as might be the case today.

2. Swearing on the Bible is a modern example of such a practice.

3. Jacob's request of Joseph; see 47:29.

of the family. It is also customary for young women to come to the well to get water for the evening meal and for the night. Such is the case here. It is near evening; the day's journey is over; the camels are tied and thirsty; the stage is set for the encounter with Rebekah (vv. 11-27). As the servant waits, he prays for success in his search for a fitting wife for Isaac; he asks for a sign. In fact, he is very specific in his description of the scenario that will reveal to him God's choice.[4] Almost immediately Rebekah appears with her jug, and the ritual of hospitality unfolds.

Though normally men do not speak to women in public, not even to their wives, an exception is made at the well, for the need of water supersedes all other considerations. Still, even in this circumstance, gender propriety dictates that the man initiates the exchange.[5] The servant approaches Rebekah and asks for only a little water. It would be impolite to ask for more. For her part, the young woman shows great respect when she addresses the servant as "Sir." She then outdoes herself in generosity. She lets him drink his fill of water, much more than he requested. She then immediately attends to the needs of his animals, even without his asking her to do so. Since a camel normally needs about twenty gallons of water, Rebekah takes on a significant task in watering ten camels. The servant notes her generosity in spirit, her alacrity in service, and her familiarity with the needs of animals—all admirable traits of a suitable wife in this culture. She seems to be acting out the scenario he had outlined in his prayer. Add to this the fact that she is a young woman, beautiful, and a virgin (v.16).[6] He would have known she was a virgin by the way she was dressed, for married women were customarily extensively covered.

The gifts offered by the servant are lavish. A shekel of gold is about twelve grams or four tenths of an ounce. Bracelets weighing ten shekels alone would be equivalent to about four ounces of gold. Since Rebekah is the daughter of Abraham's nephew, the requirement of an endogamous marriage can be met. While Rebekah states that her father's house has ample room and provisions for the servant and his animals, as a woman she does not have the authority to extend such hospitality, and so she

---

4. The search for God's will in this way is not uncommon; see Judg 6:17; Isa 7:11.

5. Jesus initiated conversation with a Samaritan woman; see John 4:7.

6. Both בְּתוּלָה (*bᵉtûlâ*) and עַלְמָה (*'almâ*) are translated "virgin" (vv. 16, 43). The first word refers to a young woman with childbearing potential; the second refers to one who is still under the care of her father's household.

runs back home to inform those in charge. God has heard the servant's prayer and so he bows down in grateful worship.

The fact that Rebekah runs to the household of her mother, not that of her father, suggests that there is a major change in the nature of that particular household. Though her father Bethuel is mentioned later in the story (v. 50), Rebekah's brother Laban is the one involved in arranging the marriage, implying that he is the head of the household and is assuming the responsibilities of that role.

Some interpreters maintain that Laban's interest in this encounter is not totally out of hospitality. He sees the gifts his sister has received and he recognizes their value. He can only benefit if he entertains such wealthy visitors. So, as head of the household, he goes out to the well where Abraham's servant waits with his retinue and camels. Laban extends hospitality to the visitor and assures him that the servants will also be cared for. He does not yet know the identity of this man and so his greeting, "Blessed of YHWH" (v. 31), is probably simply a polite recognition of the man's obvious wealth. According to custom, the feet of the travelers are washed, and then food, most likely prepared by the women of the household, is provided for them.

Before he partakes of any food, the servant recounts in great detail the events that have brought him to the city of Nahor, to the household of Laban (vv. 34-49). He suggests that these events unfolded according to the plan of God. Laban too recognizes the hand of God in all that has transpired, and so he and his household comply with the marriage proposal. Contrary to some misunderstanding, bridewealth or bride-price is not a purchase of the woman. Rather, it is a form of compensation to her family for their loss of her reproductive potential and the labor that she ordinarily contributes to the family, for in patrilocal (father-locale) arrangements, the woman's reproductive potential and labor enhance the household of the husband's father. Only after offering such gifts do the servant and those who were with him accept the full hospitality that Laban offers.

The next morning the visitor announces his intention to return to Abraham immediately. Laban's family argues for a prolonged visit, perhaps for time to prepare for Rebekah's departure. The servant insists. Because the family is not ready to concede, the decision is left up to Rebekah. It is unusual that the prospective bride is consulted on this very important matter. Perhaps it is because this marriage, though endogamous, will take her far away from her family of origin and, presumably, she will never see them again. Rebekah expresses her willingness to go, and so arrangements are made for the departure.

While the man offers bridewealth to the family of the woman, the woman generally brings a dowry with her to the marriage. This usually consists of personal items such as clothing, jewelry, and cosmetics. Though no dowry is explicitly referred to here, a nurse and other maids are mentioned. The number of Rebekah's attendants could explain why Abraham's servant brought more camels then he and his companions required. Rebekah has what she needs in order to enter into a marriage with self-respect. She resembles Abraham, for she too is expected to leave her family of origin and go to a foreign land. Like Abraham, she does not question the expectation but responds willingly and trustingly. As was the case with Abraham's household, Rebekah's servants have no say in the matter of their departure. Decisions about their lives are made by those in charge.

Blessings for descendants are usually associated with the patriarchs or their sons. Unfortunately, comparable blessings bestowed on women are frequently overlooked. Though God promised Abraham, "I will bless her [Sarah] and she shall give rise to nations; kings of peoples shall come from her" (Gen 17:16), Hagar was granted a blessing directly from the angel of YHWH: "I will so greatly multiply your offspring that they cannot be counted for multitude" (16:10). Here it is Rebekah's mother and brother who bless her: "May you, our sister, become thousands of myriads" (24:60). This blessing is a typical farewell blessing, a wish for many children and for protection from enemies. It is also a play on the sound of her name רִבְקָה (*ribᵉqāh*; Rebekah) and the basis of the blessing: יְבָרְכוּ (*yᵉbārăku*; they blessed) and רְבָבָה (*rᵉbābāh*; myriad).

While this story depicts what were most likely typical events in the lives of ancient Near Eastern people, it is unusual as a biblical account. Most of the earlier stories portray God as actively involved in the lives of the people. God created the first man and woman and conversed with them (Gen 1–3). God spoke directly to Noah, explicitly guiding him every step of the way (Gen 6–9). God called Abraham and intervened in his life again and again (Gen 12–24). In this story, God seems to have receded into the background. True, Abraham's servant prayed for a clear sign, but God does not step in and direct events in an unambiguous manner. Rather, this story demonstrates how God works through the very ordinary experiences of daily living, through the specific customs and cultural mores of a particular people, limited as they might be. It was through the observance of the rituals of hospitality and the fidelity to marriage practices that God provided a way to hand down to the next generation the promises made to Abraham.

Commissioned by Abraham, the servant returns to Isaac. This point and the fact that Abraham is no longer mentioned at all in the story suggest that he has died and Isaac has now taken his place as head of the clan. Furthermore, when Rebekah questions the servant about the identity of the man she sees in the distance, Abraham's servant identifies Isaac as "my master" (v. 65). Loyalty would be transferred in this way only if Abraham was dead. Furthermore, Isaac is living somewhere in the Negeb, in Beer-lahai-roi (the well of the living who sees), not at Mamre or Beer-sheba where Abraham usually pitched his tents.

When Rebekah discovers that the man she sees walking in the field is Isaac, her behavior conforms to traditional practice. She quickly dismounts, lest her prospective husband be forced to look up at her as she sits on a camel. She also covers her face, for it is customary that a man not see his future wife's face until they are married. She moves into Sarah's tent, since it would be inappropriate for her to live with Isaac before they are married. Once they are married, however, Rebekah takes Sarah's place as the chief woman in the clan. The love that Isaac had for Rebekah (v. 76) was more than emotional attachment. The word אהב (*'āhēb*; to love) has covenantal connotations implying an enduring legal commitment.

The End of an Era (Gen 25:1-18)

Most scholars maintain that the end of the Abraham and Sarah cycle of stories serves at least two principal purposes. First, it explains the relationships that existed between Israel and several of the Bedouin tribes with which Israel had frequent contacts, relationships that were sometimes friendly and at other times quite contentious. Second, it demonstrates the fulfillment of the promise that God made to Abraham, a promise that he will be the father of nations, not merely a multitude of descendants: "I will make nations of you" (17:4, 5, 6).

This text does not explicitly say that Abraham's second wife Keturah is a concubine. The way Abraham disposes of his wealth, however, suggests that she is, for his other descendants are referred to as "sons of his concubines" (v. 6), and only Isaac receives an inheritance (v.5). קְטוּרָה (Keturah) means "incense," suggesting that the people who trace themselves back to Abraham through her specialized in the trading of spices.

The scene that follows this genealogy (vv. 7-10) has a deathbed character to it. In it, Abraham makes provision to bequeath his wealth to his descendants. Though Isaac is Abraham's primary heir (v. 5), Abraham gives gifts to his other sons and then sends them away so that they cannot constitute any kind of challenge to the inheritance of Isaac. The verses follow the structure of an ancient death notice: the age at death is given (175 years old; v. 7); the statement of death is published (v. 8); the place is burial is announced (v. 9). Abraham was "full of years, and was gathered to his people" (v. 8), a typical ancient Near Eastern way of saying that he lived a full life and then died in peace. The report of Abraham's burial states, "His sons Isaac and Ishmael buried him" (v. 9). They laid him in the cave that Abraham had purchased as a tomb for Sarah. There is no earlier mention of the reunion of the estranged brothers, no description of Ishmael's journey from the wilderness of Paran (see 21:21). This detail, at the conclusion of the Abraham-Sarah cycle, may be an example of the editor's desire to resolve all questions about Abraham's descendants that might still exist in the Abraham-Sarah cycle.

The final תּוֹלְדוֹת (genealogy) of the Abraham-Sarah cycle sketches the descendants of Ishmael (vv. 12-16). The listing shows that the promise made to Abraham regarding Ishmael was eventually fulfilled: "He shall be the father of twelve princes" (17:20), the number twelve suggesting a formal federation of tribes. Princes were major political dignitaries who wielded significant power over their subjects. The employment of this term here indicates that Ishmael's descendants were very powerful men. Finally, as always, these genealogies trace lineage through male descendants, only mentioning women when it is important to know which wife or concubine gave birth to the particular son.

The report of Ishmael's death follows the customary format: the age at death is given (137 years old; v. 17a); the statement of death is published (v. 17b). The place of burial is not, however, mentioned here. Instead, the geographic area in which Ishmael's descendants pitched their tents is cited. This area is quite extensive, as would be expected for nomadic Bedouin people.

With this genealogical information, the first cycle in the Ancestral History is brought to a close. After a long and frustrating period of time, the promises made to Abraham have been fulfilled. Though Sarah's son is marked as the legitimate heir, Abraham's fame and importance are spread through the world through his other sons. Furthermore, though he lived as a nomad throughout his lifetime, and the same will be true of his descendants for a generation or more, Abraham can lay claim to at least two parcels of land: the place of the well near Beer-sheba (21:25-30) and the field at Machpelah purchased as a burial place for Sarah (23:11-20). Leadership of the people of God now passes to a new patriarch. The promises will now be fulfilled in and through Isaac and Rebekah.

Contemporary Reading: The Importance of a Woman

Though these biblical stories are fundamentally accounts about men and their exploits, the women in the stories play very significant roles. First, it is their reproductive potential that moves both the lineage and the story itself forward. The description of Rebekah is an example of this. Though she acts in accord with the patriarchal customs of her day, it is her extraordinary demonstration of hospitality that convinced Abraham's servant that she would be the right wife for Isaac. Furthermore, though within her rights to refuse to leave her kin and her country, she agreed to the proposal with the result that the lineage would be continued through her.

Isaac and Rebekah:
Jacob, Leah, Rachel, Zilpah, and Bilhah
(Gen 25:19–36:43)

There are very few stories that feature Isaac and Rebekah. Many scholars question whether the narratives about Isaac and Rebekah constitute a genuine cycle of stories. They contend that these accounts probably originated in individual tribal circles, and they have been handed down as a literary bridge between the other two collections. Nonetheless, it is Rebekah, not Isaac, who plays the major role in most of the stories. It is to her that God reveals the choice of the younger son over the elder, a theme that runs throughout this section (25:23); she is a focus in the sister/wife drama (chap. 26); and she is instrumental in seeing that Jacob grasps the blessing of Isaac.

Chapter 10

"Rebekah Became Pregnant"
(Gen 25:19–27:46)

The Children in Her Womb Struggled (Gen 25:19-34)

The unit opens with תּוֹלְדֹת (*tôlêdôt*), the genealogy of Isaac, situating him squarely within the family of Abraham and then introducing Isaac's own family history. It also identifies the lineage of his wife Rebekah. As daughter of Bethuel, the son of Nahor (22:20-23), she too is kin of Abraham. Mention of her brother Laban will prove to be important in a future episode (27:43). The birth of the firstborn son was a memorable event in the life of a man, particularly the head of a patriarchal family. It was a sign that the man would live on into the future through his descendants.

Like Sarah before her, Rebekah is barren (25:21; see 11:30). As was the case in the earlier tradition, the inability to conceive children was always considered a limitation of the woman. Despite the male bias, this unfortunate situation was probably intended by the author to underscore the unique character of the child that will ultimately be born. That child will be a child of promise, the circumstances of its conception demonstrating that it is God's design that is being fulfilled, not simply the very human longing for offspring. Isaac entreats YHWH for a child, a sign that he recognizes that any conception will be effected through the power of God.

Rebekah eventually conceives, but the pregnancy is very difficult. The biblical author's interpretation of both the pregnancy and the birth of twins foreshadows the troubling future of the descendants of Isaac and

Rebekah. The hardship of the pregnancy is due to the wrestling of the twins that Rebekah is carrying. ץ צ ר (*r-s-s*) translated here as "struggle" really means "smash" or "crash against," implying a violent encounter. In great distress Rebekah consults YHWH. This prayer is different from the earlier one offered by Isaac. Rebekah probably has turned to some kind of religious practitioner or she may have traveled to a shrine in order to receive a word from God. Her search for an explanation is successful and she is blessed with an oracle or divine response. She is told that the struggle within her is not simply the kicking of the unborn. Rather, it represents the rivalry of siblings, the strife between two opposing nations, and the conflict between two competing ways of life. She is also told that the outcome of this struggle will result in the reversal of the prominent social custom of primogeniture, the dominance of the elder over the younger. The struggle is expressed in a parallel fashion (v. 23) in which the principal idea is simply repeated:

two nations	are in your womb	
two peoples	born of you	(shall be divided)

The reversal of the social custom is expressed in an X form of parallelism that contrasts ideas. The younger one will be dominant, not the older:

In traditional societies, multiple births are considered an anomaly. Since human births are normally single and animal births are multiple, the character of the infants is often questioned. Are these infants really human? Are they some kind of animals? Or might they be somehow divine? In this story the twins are definitely considered human, but they are also symbolic of something else. Since the firstborn of a family or clan was considered the firstfruit of the womb and was awarded unique rights and privileges, the birth of twins often brought confusion. How can there be two firstborn? This matter does not seem to be a problem here.

Creative imagery is used to describe the twins at their birth (vv. 24-26). Their names are determined by appearance in the case of the first one born and by behavior in the case of the second. The details of Esau's appearance suggest Edom, the land that his descendants eventually will inhabit.[7] The second infant is born gripping the heel of the first. The contrast between the brothers is also found in their manner of living and, like Abel and Cain before them, in their choices of occupation. Esau prefers the open field, a place of uncultivated land; Jacob is less adventurous, choosing to live in tents. Esau is a skilled hunter; though it is not explicitly stated, Jacob is probably a shepherd. Isaac prefers Esau because of the game he provides his father; no reason is given for Rebekah's preference of Jacob. Most likely, the distinct profiles of the brothers are meant to characterize the two future nations that they represent, namely, Edom and Israel.

The preeminence of the younger brother over the elder is illustrated in the story of Esau's relinquishing his birthright (vv. 29-34). Several details of this story reinforce the characterizations of the brothers. Jacob is described as cooking a stew, a household task usually relegated to women. Such a trait might explain his mother's preference of him. Esau's hunger hints at his failure to ensnare game. The tenor of his appeal to Jacob indicates that he is a rough man with coarse speech. He refers to the stew as אָדֹם (*'ādôm*; red stuff), another play on the sound of the word "Edom." The author seems to suggest that the temperaments of these two men represent those of the nations they symbolize. Thus, the Edomites are characterized as irresponsible and boorish while the Israelites are shrewd and highly civilized. The ethnic bias in such characterization is undeniable. One is reminded of the contrasting profiles of Cain and Abel (4:1-16).

Jacob is willing to accommodate his brother's desire for food but not without being granted something in return. What he asks for is totally out of proportion to Esau's request. Esau asks for some of Jacob's food; Jacob asks for Esau's birthright, the honor of primogeniture that attends being the firstborn. Esau's behavior appears to be a spur-of-the-moment reaction to hunger, while Jacob's seems quite calculating. The audacity displayed in Jacob's demand is matched by the foolishness of Esau's acquiescence, for he places the immediate satisfaction of his hunger over the lifelong

---

7. The Hebrew word that denotes Esau's red coloring sounds very much like אֲדוֹם (Edom). Similarly, שֵׂעָר (*śē'ār*; hair) sounds like שֵׂעִיר (Seir), another name for Edom (32:3). The second child, is named יַעֲקֹב (Jacob), which comes from עָקֵב (*'āqēb*; heel).

responsibilities and privileges of having been the firstborn. Lest at a later date Esau attempt to renege on his decision, Jacob insists that he swear an oath to ratify this agreement. Esau does so. The author of the story is quite critical of Esau, saying that he despised his birthright. This is a grievous offense in a society in which birthright and lineage are paramount.

A Trip to Gerar (Gen 26:1-35)

The stories in which Isaac plays a major role are found in Genesis 26. These stories seem to be independent units that were simply randomly collected in an attempt to devise some kind of Isaac–Rebekah cycle. Internal connections among the stories can be detected, however, that suggest a well-structured literary composition. It appears that the stories about Rebekah and Isaac were intended to show that in many ways Isaac's life was comparable to Abraham's. This similarity made Isaac the legitimate heir to the promises God made to his father.

Genesis 26 opens with a report of a famine in the land of Canaan. This was a very common experience, especially in the southern part of the land, in the Negeb where Isaac dwells (24:62). Like his father Abraham before him (12:10) and his descendants after him (42:1), Isaac probably turned to Egypt for relief. God appears to him, however, and directs him to remain in Gerar (vv. 1-6). Though the promises made by God to Abraham can be found in several places, the reference here recalls the episode of Abraham's willingness to sacrifice his beloved son. At that time, God renewed those promises:

> I will indeed bless you, and I will make your offspring as numer-
> ous as the stars of heaven and as the sand that is on the seashore.
> And your offspring shall possess the gate of their enemies, and by
> your offspring shall all the nations of the earth gain blessing for
> themselves, because you have obeyed my voice. (Gen 22:17-19)

Isaac himself is the fulfillment of the promise of descendants; the promise of land is being fulfilled little by little as the ancestors acquire sections of the land of Canaan. Finally, the episodes in this chapter present Isaac as a source of blessings for others.

Parallels exist between Isaac's placing Rebekah in jeopardy and Abraham's comparable behavior. The characters in this drama play the same roles as did those in an earlier episode (Gen 20:1-18): Isaac is willing to risk the safety of Rebekah as well as the promise of descendants through her; the unsuspecting foreign ruler is first duped by the ruse and then frightened of the impending consequences; Rebekah is treated like a pawn, handed from one man to another without having any say in the matter. Despite these similarities, this episode does possess some unique details (vv. 7-11), specifically, reference to brother-sister marriages.

The distinctions between brother or sister and cousin are not made in many traditional societies. Those belonging to the same clan are considered brother and sister. This kin designation does not exonerate Abraham or Isaac of the guilt of their deception. The women may indeed have been related to them as clan-sisters, but here they were primarily their wives, and it was the husband-wife relationship that threatened the safety of the men and about which they deceived the foreign rulers into whose land they had entered.

In this instance, Rebekah does not seem to have been brought into the harem of the king (12:15; 20:2). It is almost by accident that Abimelech discovers the truth of the relationship between Isaac and Rebekah. In fact, there is a bit of humor in the story. Abimelech looks out the window and sees Isaac fondling Rebekah. It is most unusual that there would be any public display of intimate behavior in a society with the kind of moral constraints to which ancient Israel was committed. The scene itself strikes one as being implausible. Furthermore, the Hebrew word צָחַק (ṣāḥaq; fondle) means "laugh" or "play with" and comes from the same root as does the name Isaac. The humor in the play on the sound of the name Isaac and the word for laughter is also present in this episode.

The next small unit (vv. 12-14) sets the stage for the conflict that follows. Nevertheless, it also ties what follows with what preceded in the first verses of this chapter. Isaac settled in Gerar because there was a famine in the land where he had been living (v. 1). The abundant harvest that is reported in these verses points to the wisdom in obeying the directive given by God: "Settle in the land that I shall show you. . . . I will be with you and will bless you" (vv. 2, 3). In addition to the hundredfold harvest that he was able to produce, Isaac also acquired flocks and herds of animals. His good fortune became a threat to the people among whom he lived. Reference to them as Philistines presents a problem in dating. The people known as the Philistines do not appear on the scene until about 1200 BCE. Mention of them here could be an anachronistic error on the part of the biblical author, or it might simply be a reference to the people then living in the region that would eventually be known as Philistia.

The envy of the Philistines is such that the king orders Isaac to leave the area. Therefore, he and his retinue return to the place where they had originally been encamped (v. 1). The rest of the chapter traces the itinerary of the people as they move from place to place in search of water. Previously, Abraham had wells dug in that area, wells that the Philistines stopped up with Earth (vv. 15, 18). Isaac now reopens these wells so that he has access to the precious water he will need, and he gives the wells the names originally given by Abraham.

Though naming is a way of claiming proprietorship, Isaac and his people are faced with conflict here. The dispute over water rights results in naming the well עֵשֶׂק (*Esek*), which means "contend" or "challenge" (v. 20). A second well is dug, the opposing sides argue over these water rights, and this well is שִׂטְנָה (*siṭnâ*; quarrel or enmity). These are not frivolous disagreements. Water is essential for the survival of people, animals, and any crops that might be coaxed out of the ground. It is particularly valued in a land such as ancient Canaan where drought often threatened and famine resulted. Water rights or privileges are essential here. Isaac's people dig a third well. There is no quarrelling over the right to this water, however, and thus the well is called Rehoboth (רְחֹבוֹת), which means "open space."

What follows is a second theophany or manifestation of God (vv. 22-25). This revelation reiterates the promises made at the beginning of the chapter (vv. 2-5). Together they bracket the struggles that Isaac has with the people of the region of Gerar. This literary structure, which includes a promise ("I am with you"), suggests that Isaac and his people are protected by God even when they face the opposition of others. This revelation also includes a divine self-disclosure: I am the God of your father Abraham, a remarkable characterization of God. It implies an intimate relationship between God and an individual and, correspondingly, with all of the people of that individual's family. God promised, "I will be with you" (v. 3) and has demonstrated that "I am with you" (v. 24). The designation "God of Abraham" affirms this. Though only the patriarch's name is part of this divine designation, by implication the name indicates that this is the patron God of the entire household.

Isaac's ostensibly amicable relationship with the people of Gerar seen in the account of the well at Rehoboth is unmistakable in the events that follow (vv. 23-33). Abimelech, his advisor, and the commander of his army arrive at Isaac's encampment. When a suspicious Isaac questions them about their change in attitude toward him, they confess that they now realize that God is with Isaac and to be at odds with Isaac is to risk the wrath of God. Without realizing it, their present way of thinking illustrates the force of God's initial promise to Abraham: "I will bless those who bless you, and the one who curses you I will curse; and in you all the families of the earth shall be blessed" (Gen 12:3). Isaac makes a covenant of peace with the people of Gerar (v. 28). By providing both food and lodging for his visitors, Isaac graciously fulfills the obligations of Near Eastern hospitality. The next morning the covenant is ratified with an oath, a promise of nonaggression, and the partners separate in peace. This collection of stories about Isaac closes with the report of the digging of yet another well. Called Shibah or "oath," it is located in the place is known as בְּאֵר שֶׁבַע, Beer-sheba or "well of the oath."

The report of Esau's marriage (vv. 34-35) reintroduces the Jacob-Esau drama that began in Genesis 25 and that will continue in Genesis 27. This brief notation points to another parallel between Isaac and Abraham. Both men fathered two sons. In each case, the lineage of the father passed through the second son, not the firstborn: Isaac in the case of Abraham, and Jacob in the case of Isaac. In each case, the elder son who was passed over entered into an exogamous marriage, that is, marriage with a woman outside of his clan or tribe. Abraham's son Ishmael married an Egyptian woman (21:21), while Isaac's son Esau married women who were Hittite and Hivite, respectively (v. 34). No reason is given for Esau's choice of wives, but Isaac and Rebekah were embittered toward him because of this decision.

A Resourceful Mother (Gen 27:1-46)

The description of the conflict between Jacob and Esau begun in the previous chapter is resumed. What is clearly an internal family story actually contains very important social practices. These include the rights of the firstborn, the power of a deathbed blessing, and endogamous marriage. Themes of parental favoritism, deception, and sibling rivalry are woven throughout. The bulk of the story consists of interactions between two major characters: Isaac and Esau (vv. 1-4), Rebekah and Jacob (vv. 5-17), Jacob and Isaac (vv. 18-29), Esau and Isaac (vv. 30-40). This is followed by a report of Rebekah's intervention in order to secure Jacob's safety (vv. 41-46).

The very first verses of the chapter set the stage for the drama. Conscious of impending death, Isaac calls his favorite son Esau to himself in order to bestow the prized blessing (vv. 1-4). Such death blessings determined the destiny of the son by transferring the father's own vitality and by promising the son good fortune (Gen 49). It was customary to call all of the heirs together at this time, not just one. The fact that Isaac summons only Esau, and does so privately, flags the first instance of deception in the story. This not only shows favoritism on the part of Isaac but also demonstrates his attempt to thwart the plan of God that was revealed to Rebekah at the time of her pregnancy: "the elder shall serve the younger" (25:23). Once again, the reason for Isaac's preference of Esau is stated, namely, he was fond of the game that Esau provided (25:28).

Rebekah's overhearing the conversation between Isaac and Esau has often been interpreted negatively. Such a view overlooks the social customs of the time. In ancient Near Eastern patriarchal societies, the women of the household were normally neither consulted nor informed about the plans made by the men. Confined to the inner sanctum of the tents, they frequently discovered these plans by overhearing discussion of them.[8] Rebekah's eavesdropping and the measures she takes to secure Isaac's blessing for Jacob (vv. 5-17) have been seen by many as evidence of devious manipulation on her part. This gender-biased view fails, however, to recall God's words to her: "the elder shall serve the younger" (25:23). Isaac might attempt to undermine God's plan, but she will not. While it is true that she engages in deception and trickery, these are the ploys that powerless people are often forced to utilize in order to achieve their ends. Here, Rebekah uses them in order to achieve God's ends.

This story is framed by passages that highlight yet another reason Rebekah might have resorted to deception. The previous chapter ended with a report of Isaac and Rebekah's embitterment at Esau's marriages outside of Abraham's clan (26:34-35). This chapter ends on a similar note of displeasure with such unions. In this way, the story of deception is bracketed by concern for marriages within the kinship structure. Some commentators fault Isaac for not arranging an endogamous marriage for Esau, a marriage with women from his own people. If Esau now receives Isaac's blessing, his marriages with foreign women might in some

---

8. When the visitors told Abraham that Sarah would bear a son, "Sarah was listening at the tent entrance" (18:10).

way challenge the legitimacy of the heir of the promises made by God. Rebekah's intervention prevents this from happening.

Rebekah's instructions to Jacob begin and end with unyielding insistence: "Obey my word" (vv. 8, 13). It is not that Jacob is weak and can be easily swayed, as some have claimed, but that Rebekah is resolute. Taking advantage of her husband's weakened condition, she also takes advantage of the situation. Esau has been sent out to procure wild game. Rebekah sends Jacob to select two kids from the nearby flock.[9] By the time Esau is able successfully to track down game, kill it, and prepare a meal for his father, Isaac will have been served the kind of tasty dish Rebekah knows he will enjoy, and he will have bestowed his blessing on Jacob.

The objection that Jacob poses has little to do with the deceptive character of his mother's plan. Rather, he questions the possibility of its success. He argues that Isaac's loss of sight will not prevent him from recognizing the true identity of the one offering him a meal. His voice differs from Esau's; his clothes do not carry the aroma of the open fields; and most importantly, his skin is not hairy. Jacob is afraid that he will be discovered, and, rather than receive his father's blessing, he will be cursed. Rebekah's response, "Let your curse be upon me" (v. 13), is curious. Her willingness to assume any curse that Isaac might pronounce seems somewhat disingenuous. She would certainly know that, just as the father's blessings cannot be revoked, neither can a spoken curse. Therefore, if Isaac does curse Jacob, she will not be able to take its consequences upon herself. Her insistence in this matter is less an example of maternal devotion than a way of reassuring the dubious Jacob that this plan will accomplish God's plan as revealed to Rebekah earlier.

Jacob does as Rebekah directs. Then, in order to assuage Jacob's concerns that this deception will be discovered, she provides Jacob with some of Esau's clothing, which still retains traces of his scent. She next takes the skins of the kids she prepared as the meal and covers Jacob's arms, thus simulating Esau's hairiness. The scheme is now ready to be set in motion.

The scene of the interaction between Jacob and Isaac (vv. 18-29) is fraught with tension. At any moment, Jacob's true identity could be revealed. Throughout the episode, Isaac is not fully convinced that the man before him is his son Esau. When Jacob addresses him, Isaac first seeks

---

9. Kids, young males of the flock, were killed for meat because they were expendable. The more valuable female lambs were needed for breeding.

verbal verification of his identity (v. 18). He then asks how the wild game could have been caught so quickly and the meal prepared is such short a time. Jacob's response—"Because YHWH your God granted me success" (v. 20)—can be understood on two different levels. While it answers Isaac's question about the shortness of time, Jacob knows that it also suggests that the success of the ruse is part of the divine plan. Isaac asks to touch Jacob's hands in order to make sure that they are hairy. Recognizing the voice as that of Jacob, Isaac notes that the hands are like those of Esau (v. 21). Finally, he leans close to Jacob in order to kiss him, thus enabling him to detect and recognize any scent that might be on his clothing (v. 27). In each case, Jacob very carefully plays his part in the ruse, and Isaac is duped.

The blessing that Isaac speaks over Jacob has a dual focus. It includes fertility of the land (v. 28) and authority over other nations as well as within his own family. Without realizing it, Isaac is actually declaring that, indeed, "the elder shall serve the younger" (25:23). The conclusion of the blessing is reminiscent of God's original blessing to Abraham (12:3): "Cursed be everyone who curses you, and blessed be everyone who blesses you!" (v. 29).

When Esau arrives on the scene, he discovers that his father has been taken in by the deception and he himself has once again been supplanted by Jacob (v. 36). This brother has tricked him out of both his בְּכֹרָה (*bᵉkōrā*; birthright) and the בְּרָכָה (*bᵉrākā*; blessing) that accompanies it. Jacob has certainly lived up to the name "supplanter" or "heel-gripper." Isaac and Esau are shaken when they realize what has happened. Isaac trembles violently with fear and alarm (v. 33), and Esau cries out in extreme distress. They both realize that the die has been cast; the blessing has been given away and it cannot be recalled. The promising future for which Esau hoped has been snatched from his grasp.

In desperation, Esau begs his father for a blessing for himself but to no avail. Isaac bestowed the entire primogeniture blessing onto Jacob, who can now claim the blessings of abundance and the privilege of dominance. For his part, Esau's future will be the reverse of Jacob's. While Jacob is promised "the dew of heaven, and of the fatness of Earth, and plenty of grain and wine" (27:28), Esau is told that "away from the fatness of the earth shall your home be, and away from the dew of heaven on high" (v. 39). Jacob's future is promising: "Let peoples serve you, and nations bow down to you. Be lord over your brothers, and may your mother's sons bow down to you" (v. 29); but Esau's is dismal. His life will be one of servitude and violence: "By your sword you shall live, and you shall serve your brother" (v. 40).

Esau's resentment toward Jacob (vv. 41-45) resembles that of Cain toward Abel (4:5), and he plans to resolve this problem in the same way Cain resolved his, by means of fratricide. Once again Rebekah is apprised of a plot against her favorite son, and she steps in to save him.[10] She instructs Jacob to flee to Haran, to the house of her brother Laban. The reason she gives to Isaac for Jacob's departure is the need to find a wife for him in her family rather than from among the Canaanites, as Esau did. Thus, Rebekah conceals the underlying reason for Jacob's departure by appealing to Isaac's duty to arrange an endogamous marriage. This plan will both remove Jacob from the threat of Esau's wrath and guarantee an endogamous marriage in which the family's cultural and religious values will be guaranteed. Rebekah assures Jacob that the separation will only last a short time. Little does either of them know that it will be twenty years before Jacob returns to the land of promise. By that time, Rebekah will have died. The mother and favored son will never meet again.

Contemporary Reading: Protector of the Promise

Rebekah is truly a remarkable woman. Having shown that in leaving her country and her kin her trust was equal to that of Abraham, she now spurns social mores in order to ensure that God's plan will be accomplished, and she does this more than once. In violation of hierarchical standing in the family, she maneuvers her second-born son into the position of privilege, thus demonstrating that social custom can sometimes be a hindrance to the working of God in the lives of women and men. Although ordinarily the primary man in the household arranges marriages, it is Rebekah who steps forward to do so on behalf of her now blessed son. She also saves the lineage determined by God by preventing the violent death of this son.

10. In the later Jewish tradition, Rebekah is perceived as a prophet and comes to know about the danger facing Jacob through some kind of divine revelation; see Gen. Rab. 67.9.

Chapter 11

"The Daughters of Laban"
(Gen 28:1–30:24)

The stories in this chapter focus on the women who enter into and change the direction of Jacob's life. The women are Leah and Rachel, his wives, and Bilhah and Zilpah, his concubines. Many of the dynamics found in these stories reflect the prevailing kinship structure and the cultural practices of the day.

Wives for Jacob and Esau (Gen 28:1-9)

Jacob plays a major role in the first part of this passage (vv. 1-5), while Esau is dominant in the second (vv. 6-9). The entire passage addresses the marriage practices of Isaac's family. In the earlier narrative, Esau had made up his mind to kill his underhanded brother once their father died (27:41). There is no mention of such a treacherous plan here. Previously, Esau made marriage choices independent of the family preference for endogamous unions. Here, he is aware both of Jacob's compliance to their parents' desire that he marry within the family and of the displeasure he himself caused them by marrying Canaanite women.

In the earlier narrative, it is Rebekah who urges Jacob to flee to Haran to elude Esau's wrath. Here, it is Isaac who instructs him to go to Paddan-aram in northern Mesopotamia, and the reason given is to acquire a wife (v. 1). This is evidence of two versions of the story.

The blessing that Isaac bestows on Jacob is very different from the one he was earlier tricked into giving. It is a composite of the commission given to the first man and woman at the time of creation (1:28), the promise made to Abraham at the time of his initial call (12:2-3), and the renewal of that promise to Isaac (26:3-4). It attests that Jacob is the legitimate recipient of the ancestral promises.

The focus shifts to Esau (vv. 6-9). This elder son of Isaac and Rebekah did not conform to family custom when he married Canaanite women, and he is now aware of how this behavior displeased his father. In an attempt to remedy this, he marries Mahalath, Ishmael's daughter. It is difficult to understand how he might think that this marriage would return him to his father's favor, for Ishmael himself was the son of an Egyptian woman (25:12), and Esau later married another Egyptian woman (21:21). With this family background, Ishmael's daughter would not have Mesopotamian roots and would not meet the criterion for an endogamous marriage for Esau.

The Dream at Bethel (Gen 28:10-22)

The report of the episode that took place on the way to Haran is a dream narrative, of which there are several in the Bible (20:3; 31:24; etc.). Such experiences are considered portents of future events, glimpses into a different and mysterious world. Scholars agree that this account contains elements from various sources. The oldest version was probably a local sanctuary narrative that provided an explanation for the sacred character of the place. Most likely, this sacredness resulted from a theophany or manifestation of God. Cultic practices and rituals grew up as people came regularly to the shrine in order to pay homage to God or to experience divine favor. Finally, all of these elements were woven into an episode in the story of Jacob's escape to Haran.

No explanation is given for Jacob's spending the night in the open rather than enjoying the comforts of ancient Near Eastern hospitality in someone's dwelling. Perhaps as a man escaping the murderous plans of his brother, he chooses privacy outside of a town rather than expose himself to possible disclosure. Or it might be required by the character of the story that describes an experience of God, which marked the site as a sacred place. The sun has set, and so under the cover of darkness Jacob finds a place to sleep. Nothing leads him to believe that this site is in any way extraordinary. His experience during the night will radically alter this assumption.

Jacob's dream contains both visual and auditory revelatory details. He sees a ladder and angels, and he hears God speak. Mention of a ladder calls to mind the stepped ramps that were part of the ancient Mesopotamian ziggurats or temples as well as the stepped pyramids of Egypt. These religious structures enabled worshipers to ascend toward heaven in order to meet the deity who, they believed, would descend to Earth. The ladder that Jacob sees is a way of passage joining heaven and Earth. The point of connection between heaven and Earth, an image that is found across many traditional cultures, is called the *axis mundi* or axis of the world. It is considered the navel of the world, or the point of the world's beginning. It is no ordinary place.

God's words to Jacob are significant. They begin with divine self-disclosure. This is YHWH, the God of Jacob's ancestors. This momentous experience shows that now the God of his ancestors is also his God. God is here identified with a particular people, not merely with this specific place. Furthermore, this God is not confined to one location but is associated with a people who move from place to place. The ladder might mark this spot as the place where heaven and Earth meet, but God will be with this people wherever they might go.

The divine self-disclosure is followed by a renewal of the ancestral promises of land and descendants (see 12:2-3). God here makes a fourfold promise to Jacob: "I am with you. . . . [I] will keep you wherever you go. . . . [I] will bring you back to this land. . . . I will not leave you until I have done what I have promised you" (v. 15). The importance of the presence of God as protector cannot be overestimated, particularly for a man whose life is in peril and who has been forced to flee from his country. Though Jacob is traveling to his ancestral home, that place is unfamiliar to him. Still, he has nothing to fear, for God will keep him safe wherever he might be. The third promise must have been very comforting. God promises Jacob that he will not be a sojourner in a foreign land for the rest of his life. Rather, he will return to his home. God's promises end with the assurance that eventually the promises will all be fulfilled.

When Jacob awakes from his dream he becomes aware of the momentous significance of his night-dream experience. What he might have once considered a random site, he now sees as an awesome place. He calls it "house of God" and "gateway to heaven." He sets up the stone upon which he had rested the night before, making it a pillar, a memorial stone that will stand as a witness to the sacred event. He then pours oil

over the stone, a ritual act that consecrates it as a sacred object. He names
the site בֵּית־אֵל (Bethel), which means "house of God."

The second title he gives the place, "gateway to heaven," simply describes what he witnessed in his dream. The phrase might be a polemic
against the Mesopotamian boast that Babylon is really the *axis mundi*.
The reason for this boast is the fact that the name of the city (*bab-il*)
means "gate of god." This story provides an explanation of the origin
of the shrine, the origin of its name, and the origin and meaning of the
memorial pillar that was part of the shrine.

Jacob then makes a vow to God. A biblical vow is different from an
oath. An oath is a straightforward promise, while such a vow has a con-
ditional quality to it. It is a promise to perform a particular act, if God
will grant a specific favor. If God will provide divine presence and protection, provisions needed for his journey to Haran, and safe return to
his father's house, Jacob will choose this deity as his own God. Jacob
then reaffirms the importance of the memorial pillar, and he promises to
tithe. Offering God one-tenth of one's property and goods was a way of
acknowledging that all of one's goods rightly belong to God. This practice
was considered cultic because it was usually offered at a shrine. There is
no suspense in this offer; there is no wondering whether or not God will
accept the terms of Jacob's vow, for God already promised everything
that Jacob here requests.

Arrival at Haran (Gen 29:1-14a)

Jacob comes upon a well in the open country, frequented by nomadic
herders. Droves of sheep are simply gathered around the well but are not
yet being watered. The well seems to be the common property of several
herders who water their flocks at the same time, probably to ensure that
no one will take unfair advantage of the precious water. His warm greeting
is probably meant to assure them that he is not a threat. He poses three
questions, to which he receives three direct and succinct answers. Courtesy
requires that the shepherds respond to him, but caution demands that they
provide a stranger no more information than is necessary. The fact that
they are from Haran indicates that the city is close by and Jacob's journey is
almost at its end. They acknowledge knowing Laban, but they are reluctant
to offer any personal information about him to this stranger. Since Laban's
daughter Rachel appears on the scene, they direct all other questions to her.

Rachel, not Laban's servants, brings her father's flock to the well. In this culture at this time, young unattended girls had more freedom of movement than did married women. The former were often given charge of the animals, especially if there were no sons in the family, while the latter were usually confined to the household. Jacob's response to Rachel's arrival is both spontaneous and curious. He immediately rolls back the stone so that she can water the flock, disregarding any protocol that might have been in effect. He then kisses her and bursts into tears as he identifies himself as being related to her father. The kiss would hardly be a passionate kiss, since he has never met her before, but rather the customary Near Eastern greeting of relatives. Rachel's response is to run and tell her father, who immediately comes out to meet his kin. Upon arrival at Laban's home, Jacob provides enough information about their mutual family for Laban to be assured of Jacob's genuine kinship.

This scene is reminiscent of another scene depicting a young woman at a well (24:10-33). In both stories, the patriarch (first Abraham and here Isaac) is seeking a wife for his son in the city of Nahor. In each case, as evening approaches someone comes upon a well and there meets a young girl who eventually will become the bride. When she discovers this man's relationship to her family, she runs home to deliver the news. Despite the similarities, there are also several important differences. Here, no expensive gifts are given the girl's family. In fact, the unfolding story will show that Jacob has no source of income and is forced to work for his uncle. Furthermore, what might appear to be a chance meeting is in all probability an example of the fulfillment of one of the promises made by God: "Know that I am with you and will keep you wherever you go" (28:15). Bone and flesh is a formula of kinship equivalent to our contemporary expression "flesh and blood": "You are my kin, you are my bone and my flesh" (2 Sam 19:12).

Jacob has successfully escaped his brother's wrath by fleeing to his ancestral home. The next narrative will treat the accomplishment of his second goal, finding a wife for himself in his uncle's family.

The Struggle between Rachel and Leah (Gen 29:14b-30)

After Jacob stays in Laban's household for a month, the question of wages for work surfaces. He is neither a servant nor a slave and so is deserving of a different kind of compensation, the kind due a relative who provides service to the household. It is Laban who raises this matter, in an apparent show of concern. Jacob does not ask for wages; he asks for a wife. He has chosen Rachel, the girl he met at the well. Unlike the servant of Abraham who "brought jewelry of silver and of gold, and garments" as bridewealth (24:53), however, Jacob apparently left the land of Canaan without goods or property. In lieu of material goods, he offers to work for seven years in order to earn what would be more than equivalent to generous bridewealth. Though Jacob is a free and willing laborer, the agreement he strikes with Laban makes him beholden to his uncle.

Laban agrees to the proposal, stating, "It is better that I give her to you than that I should give her to any other man" (v. 19). This agreement reflects a form of endogamous union known as cross-cousin marriage, a situation in which a man marries a cousin from his mother's side. It should be noted that the women have nothing to say about the choice of a husband. As father in a patriarchal structure, Laban decides for Rachel, as earlier he did for his sister Rebekah (24:51).

But Laban has two daughters, Leah and Rachel. The author's description of Rachel is quite straightforward: she was beautiful in form and appearance (v. 17b). The description of Leah, however, is not as easy to determine. Although רַךְ (*rōk*) describes her eyes as tender, soft, or delicate, some commentators translate the word as weak, erroneously suggesting that Leah was ugly and giving this as a reason why Jacob did not love her. This kind of interpretation cannot be rooted in the biblical text itself but emerges from a bias of the interpreter.[1]

After working for seven years for bridewealth, Jacob asks for Rachel in marriage. Laban agrees and makes arrangements for the wedding. A Near Eastern wedding was an elaborate event, for it marked the beginning of a new branch of the family. It began with a procession to the bride's home in order to bring her to the place where the ceremony was to be conducted. There, the marriage contract was read out loud. This was followed by a large celebratory meal. The bridegroom would then take his new wife, who throughout this entire celebration had been heavily veiled, into the nuptial chamber where the union would be consummated. They would rejoin the festivities the next day and continue the weeklong celebration.

---

1. All cultures have standards by which they judge the beauty of both women and men. Any suggestion that one who does not measure up to these standards will not be loved is without foundation.

Laban takes advantage of the custom of heavily veiling the bride and tricks Jacob into marrying Leah, a deception of which Jacob becomes aware only the next morning after having consummated the marriage the night before. In great distress he cries out, "What is this you have done to me?" (v. 25), the very words used by Pharaoh when Abram tricked him (12:18) and by Abimelech when Isaac acted in the same way (26:10). The family so skilled in deception has now been deceived itself. Laban not only tricks Jacob but also turns Jacob's own ruse upside down in order to justify his action, appealing to the custom of marrying the elder daughter before the younger. Jacob can hardly protest this action, since he had reversed the primogeniture order of preference by putting the younger (himself) above the older (his brother). Demonstrating once again that he has the upper hand, Laban directs Jacob to complete the week of marriage celebration. At the end of the festivities, Laban will give him Rachel to be his wife. There will, however, be a price to be paid. Jacob will be required to work for Laban for seven more years.

There is very little that Jacob can do in protest. Though unknowingly, he accepted Leah as his wife and consummated their union, so he can hardly repudiate her in the midst of the wedding celebration. He loves Rachel and wants to marry her, yet he has no bridewealth to offer in her case. He probably should be grateful that Laban gave him Rachel before rather than after the second seven-year period of labor was completed. So, at the end of the celebration that marks Jacob's marriage to Leah, Laban gives him his daughter Rachel as his wife. As part of their dowries, each daughter is also given a slave girl: Zilpah belonging to Leah and Bilhah to Rachel.

This entire narrative demonstrates the powerlessness of women in patriarchal societies when it comes to marriage. Their role is to produce heirs who will continue the bloodline of the patriarch. The personal preferences of the women are irrelevant. Leah was certainly aware of the ruse, but she was a pawn in her father's plan and had no option but to remain silent. The narrative also underscores strict class lines. Zilpah and Bilhah are slaves who become the maidservants of Leah and Rachel. They are given to the brides as if they were property, which, in that culture, they were. The patriarchs may have male servants (see 24:2), but these male servants do not seem to have been handed from one master to another as were the female slaves. It is clear that women universally suffered because of gender bias, and women in social classes that were themselves marginal suffered doubly.

The Children of Wives and Maidservants (Gen 29:31–30:24)

Commentators agree that the passage that describes the birth of twelve of Jacob's children is a composite of earlier traditions. This final form, however, marks the end of linear genealogies that trace lineage through a single line of descendants. While earlier birth narratives confirmed the fulfillment of the promise of a descendant (17:16), this passage attests to the fulfillment of the promise of a multitude of descendants (15:5; 26:4). This is a family story, however, not a political one. The focus is not on the children themselves but on the rivalry that exists between the primary mothers. This rivalry is based on two interrelated themes, namely, Leah's being unloved by Jacob and Rachel's inability to conceive. Some commentators consider this a petty rivalry, one in which two women are fighting over the same man. Such an incorrect judgment overlooks certain cultural values that determine the status of women in a patriarchal society.

Because of the importance of progeny and the constant threat of extinction in the ancient world, childbearing was considered a woman's primary contribution to the family and, by extension, to the clan. Her position in the family was determined by her ability to produce children, particularly sons, when lineage was traced through male offspring. The status for which women competed was not only accompanied by present benefits but also a guarantee of future advantages. The son's good fortune guaranteed his care of his mother as she aged. Thus, with such vital matters at stake, tension between Leah and Rachel is hardly an example of petty rivalry.

The explanations given for the names of the children show that the sentiments of the mother at each birth have more to do with her relationship with the child's father than with the joy in having brought a child into the world. The present narrative reveals how the respective situations of the sisters (unloved in Leah's case; barren in Rachel's) are the forces that moves the story forward. It opens on a very poignant note: "When YHWH saw that Leah was unloved, he opened her womb" (29:31). Besides showing that God is mindful of those who suffer through no fault of their own, this statement shows that fertility is really a gift from God.

Leah names her firstborn Reuben, a name that really means "behold a son." Leah herself says, however, that the name means "YHWH has looked on my affliction" (29:32), and she believes that since she has borne Jacob a son, he will now love her. She conceives again and proclaims that the name of her second son, Simeon, means "YHWH has heard" (v. 33). She further maintains that the third son, Levi, will ensure that "my husband will be joined to me" (v. 34). Finally, at the birth of the fourth son, Judah, she cries out, "I will praise YHWH" (v. 35). After the birth of the fourth son, she stops conceiving.

Throughout Leah's pregnancies, Rachel remains barren. She is now desperate to have a child (30:1-8). She becomes both envious of Leah and resentful toward Jacob. Her demand that he give her children suggests that she does not take responsibility for her barrenness. The four sons born of Leah are evidence, however, that Jacob is able to father a child. Rachel reverts to the custom employed by Sarah before her (16:1-2). She gives Jacob Bilhah, her maid, to bear a child in her name. The phrase "She may bear upon my knees" implies adoption. It probably originated from the custom of placing the child on the knees of the one adopting, a practice that would call to mind the bringing forth a child from between one's legs. Bilhah gives birth to a son whom Rachel names Dan, claiming that "God has judged [vindicated] me" (v. 6), and a second son whom she names Naphtali, crying out, "I have wrestled with my sister and prevailed" (v. 8).

The competition does not end; it only increases. Since she is no longer conceiving, Leah also turns to her maidservant Zilpah who bears sons who are then taken by Leah as her own. She names them Gad, which means "good fortune" (v. 11), and Asher, which means "happy" (v. 13). For a time both Rachel and Leah were unable to conceive, and so they sought remedy in a fertility drug. The mandrake is a Mediterranean plant whose roots were considered both an aphrodisiac and an aid in conception. Rachel asks her sister to share them with her. Leah's response reveals the antagonism she feels toward Rachel: "Is it a small matter that you have taken away my husband? Would you take away my son's mandrakes also?" (v. 15). Leah is correct in calling Jacob her husband, because she is the first wife. The arrangement that Rachel proposes for Leah (a night with Jacob in return for some of the mandrakes) suggests that, though Leah has marital rights, Jacob has been avoiding her bed in favor of Rachel's.

The tables have been turned. Now it is the wives who take charge of the sexual behavior of the husband (vv. 16-21). Leah has hired (rented) Jacob for the night. Once again it is God who enables Leah to conceive. She bears a fifth son and calls him Issachar, which means "my hire" (v. 18). She bears a sixth son, Zebulun, which means "good dowry" (v. 20). Finally, she gives birth to a daughter, Dinah. No meaning is given for the name, but it probably means "vindication." The addition of the name of a daughter in the list that will eventually identify the twelve tribes has raised some questions. Some commentators contend that since Benjamin, the twelfth son, will not be born for some time, the name of this daughter completes the listing of twelve names. Others believe that its inclusion sets the stage for an upcoming story in which Dinah plays a major role. Either or both reasons can provide an adequate explanation.

Rachel recognizes that it is God who enables her finally to conceive, not the mandrakes, when she acknowledges that God has taken away her reproach. The name she chooses for her son is Joseph, a name that is also a prayer: "May YHWH add to me another son" (v. 24).

Although Leah and Rachel play the major roles in the drama that unfolds in these stories, the tension between them results from their respective relationships with Jacob. Yet Jacob does nothing to alleviate the tension. In fact, he exacerbates it by blatantly favoring Rachel over Leah. He actually becomes a pawn in the hands of his wives, first by being given their maidservants as his concubines and then by being hired out for a night by one wife for the other. The man who is heir to the ancestral promises is portrayed here as having less than stellar character.

Contemporary Reading: Is Biology Destiny?

The struggle between Rachel and Leah centers on fertility and the status that it provides within the household. This is not an issue of lineage, as was the struggle between Jacob and Esau. The final promise of a multitude of descendants is made to Jacob. It is from his offspring generally, not from a specific individual, that this promised multitude will spring. Here again are cultural mores that pit one woman against another. Furthermore, the contraposition sketched is much more serious than simply the behavior of the women. It strikes at the very core of their sexuality. Their value is determined by their ability to conceive and bear children. The fact that this ability is essential to the survival of the people does not lessen the burden placed on the individual woman. In fact, it probably added to the burden. In a culture that stigmatized infertility, there is no indication that the tension between the women was ever really resolved. In many cases, this stigma still exists today, and women are often left to resolve it in their own lives.

A second appalling aspect of this account is Jacob's apparent lack of concern. It was his responsibility to ensure harmony in his family, and he failed in this regard. He does not even appear to be concerned about Rachel's sense of inferiority and Leah's haughty attitude, the rift between the two sisters, or the surrender of Bilhah and Zilpah for the sole purpose of procreation. In fact, he benefits from this exploitation of the women, for the initial rivalry results in his sexual relations with all four of them.

Chapter 12

"Let Us Make a Covenant"
(Gen 30:25–32:2)

The relationship between Laban and his son-in-law Jacob, which began so amicably with typical Near Eastern hospitality, quickly deteriorated because of deception and mistrust. Laban tricked Jacob. Now Jacob, a trickster himself, will dupe Laban. Jacob's wiliness appears to have been contagious, for Rachel devises her own ruse against Laban. Ultimately, the discord is resolved by entering into a covenant of nonaggression.

Laban Is Tricked (Gen 30:25-43)

Jacob decides to return to his own country and, if possible, resolve the tension surrounding one of the reasons for his initial departure, namely, the wrath of his brother. Returning home is, however, more difficult than leaving it. Laban did not treat Jacob with the openness his original hospitality suggested, nor is he eager for him to leave now. After all, for the last fourteen years, Jacob has proven himself to be a valuable worker. Jacob's labor for fourteen years earned him bridewealth, not savings. Furthermore, though a relative, he is indebted to Laban and thus does not enjoy the benefits due a full member of his uncle's household. Though Jacob followed patrilocal customs, as an indebted laborer, he lived in the household of his wives' father. Now that he has fulfilled his responsibilities to Laban, it is understandable that he would want to return to his family of origin.

According to an ancient custom, a slave could be freed after six years of labor. If, however, that slave had been given a wife by the master, the wife and any children born to them were required to remain with the master, as if they were his property. The slave had to choose, either his freedom or his family (Exod 21:3-6). This custom might stand behind Laban's insistence that his daughters and grandchildren belong to him, not Jacob (31:43).

On the surface, the exchange between Jacob and Laban appears to be quite cordial. A close reading of the text shows, however, that these men do not trust each other. Laban acknowledges that Jacob is the reason he has prospered, and he seems willing to pay Jacob whatever wage he suggests. Ancient Mesopotamian records indicate that those who tended the flocks of others were normally given a wage of 20 percent of the lambs born that year. Jacob has another plan in mind. In what appears to be a show of deference to Laban, whose name (לָבָן; *lābān*) means "white," Jacob agrees to claim only the colored animals.

Jacob's trick stems from the belief that whatever the female animal saw at the time of mating affected the offspring born. Animals in heat usually breed where they drink. Jacob strips the bark of fresh shoots of some nearby trees and stands these shoots upright in the watering trough. Thus, Laban's white goats bring forth kids that are striped, speckled, and spotted. Jacob perpetrates a comparable ruse with the white sheep, placing them in front of dark or speckled sheep, ensuring that they will give birth to speckled or spotted lambs. Jacob is particularly attentive to the stronger animals, knowing that such animals breed strong offspring. Since he does not apply this method to the weak white animals of Laban's flock, they produce more weak white offspring. What today would probably be considered magical manipulation as well as selective breeding was practiced by many herders in the ancient world.

The Tricksters Escape (Gen 31:1-24)

Jacob's plan to leave Laban's household is then endorsed by a revelation in which God both directs Jacob to return to the land of his birth and promises to be with him (v. 3). He presents his plans to Rachel and Leah (vv. 5-13). Trusting neither Laban nor anyone from his household, Jacob takes his wives out into the countryside where there is less opportunity for eavesdropping. There, he points to how their father took advantage of him in order to defraud him. Jacob assures his wives that God, who at Bethel promised to be with him (28:15), appeared to him here, instructing him how to breed the animals so that his own flocks prospered while Laban's are weakened. This very God now directs him to return to the land of his birth.

Rachel and Leah are willing to leave. The secrecy and deception surrounding this departure provide a glimpse into some of the family customs practiced at the time. Though Leah and Rachel were married, they lived in their father's household and, thus, were under his jurisdiction. They could not leave without their father's permission or without renouncing his rights over them. This was also true of their children. Second, normally the brides shared in some of the bridewealth. There was no bridewealth in Jacob's case, however; his labor was substituted for property. Still, the daughters should have enjoyed some of the prosperity that Jacob's labor earned for their father. This did not happen. Instead, Laban kept it all for himself, treating his daughters and their children like foreigners instead of family. Thus their decision to leave their father's household was justified.

Rachel and Leah need no convincing. They direct Jacob to heed the words of God. Though in biblical narratives women are often depicted as subservient to the plans of men, they were not devoid of all rights. It is clear that Jacob needed the approval of the women to act on his plan, even though the plan was revealed to him by God. Like Rebekah before them, Rachel and Leah would be leaving their family of origin and their homeland far behind them. Such a drastic move required their consent.

Some form of deceit seems to mark every major episode in Jacob's life story: he deceived his own father (27:1-29), on the night of his wedding he was deceived by Laban (29:23), deception and trickery ruled the labor agreements between Jacob and Laban (30:25-43). Now, the actions of Rachel correspond to this pattern (v. 19). The household gods that Rachel steals might have been representations of ancestors, meant to guarantee protection and blessing for the family. Her motive for the theft is not given. She might have considered them part of the inheritance of which she was deprived by her father's greed. Or, she could have taken them for protection on the long journey into a land that was foreign to her. Whatever the case, Rachel deceives her father and flees her homeland.

Preparations for departure must have been quite complicated, for Jacob had a large family with servants, extensive flocks, and shepherds.

Furthermore, though he placed his wives and children on camels, movement of such a vast entourage would have been very challenging. The timing was right, however, for Laban and his men were out shearing sheep. The time of shearing was also a time of feasting, so Laban would have been too occupied to know what Jacob was doing. Jacob and his company traveled for three days before Laban was told of their departure. It then took him seven days to overtake Jacob. The place where this occurred is Gilead, a mountainous region in central Transjordan.

This part of the story ends with an example of God's provident care of Jacob. Both at Bethel and in Paddan-aram, God promised to be with him to protect him (28:15; 31:3). The night before Laban confronts Jacob, God appears to Laban in a dream and warns him not to do any harm to Jacob, another example of how God sides with those in the right, even if they are weak, as opposed to those who are stronger. Laban should not have been surprised at this revelation. In the face of his own earlier prosperity, he had acknowledged that it was through Jacob that God had blessed him (30:29). It was clear to Laban that Jacob was indeed the chosen one of God.

The Covenant at Mizpah (Gen 31:25–32:2)

Laban's anger toward Jacob is not masked. He presents himself as the one who has been aggrieved, a devoted father whose daughters and grandchildren have been kidnapped and whose property has been stolen. He characterizes Jacob as a marauding enemy who has treated Laban's offspring as prisoners of war. Laban claims that by his deceptive actions, Jacob has deprived him of providing the traditional farewell ceremony required when individuals leave the household of the *pater familias*. He further claims that such behavior on Jacob's part has not only insulted Laban but also shamed his daughters. By always referring to them as his daughters and not as Jacob's wives, Laban is laying claim to his authority over them.

Three times Laban accuses Jacob of deception: "flee secretly and deceive me and not tell me" (v. 27). The characterization of Jacob's actions as foolish (v. 28) is more sinister than might appear at first glance, for foolish behavior carries dire consequences. In an implied show of force, Laban reminds Jacob that he has the power to do him harm. He assures him that it is only the protection of God that preserves Jacob from swift and deserved punishment. Finally, Laban accuses Jacob of the theft of the household gods. Such gods were often handed down within the family as part of the inheritance. Since Jacob is only a relative through marriage, he does not have a right to Laban's gods. That theft is a very serious offense.

Jacob responds to each of Laban's accusations, offering an explanation for his surreptitious departure and denying even knowing of the theft of the household gods. He insists that he was afraid that Laban would reclaim his daughters by force. Both men refer to the forceful seizure of the women, as if they are property under male control. Ignorant of the part Rachel played in the theft of the household gods, Jacob asserts his own innocence as well as the innocence of those in his company. In fact, he pronounces a solemn curse on anyone who might be culpable. The penalty of this curse is death. Little does he know that the guilty one is his own beloved wife.

The scene of Laban's frenetic search is both suspenseful and humorous (vv. 33-35). He rummages through all the tents, ending with Rachel's. This passage provides a glimpse into the living arrangements of a polygamous household that enjoys a degree of economic means. Each woman has her own tent or living quarters, which the husband visits at night. It is within these accommodations that the children of the respective women are raised.

Rachel's pretense matches her husband's propensity to deceive. When her father enters her tent he finds her sitting on a camel saddle in which she has hidden the household gods. She does not stand to greet him, claiming that she is indisposed because of her menstrual period. The scene of Laban feeling all about in the tent calls to mind Isaac feeling the disguised arms of Jacob (27:21-22). The success of Rachel's ruse stems from Israel's laws regarding ritual purity. Since it was believed that "the life of the flesh is in the blood" (Lev 17:11; see Gen 9:4), people were forbidden to touch blood unnecessarily. If they did so, they were considered ritually unclean, forbidden to participate in cultic ceremonies. Furthermore, they were required to avoid anyone or anything that was ritually unclean, lest they too be affected by such uncleanness. This ritual custom carried no moral implications. One was restored to ritual purity after a period of time (Lev 15:25-27). This explains why both menstrual and birth blood rendered women ritually unclean for long periods of time.

Claiming that "the way of women is upon me" (Gen 31:35), Rachel knows that Laban will touch neither her nor the saddle on which she sits and in which she has hidden the household gods, lest he be rendered ritually impure. Moreover, she is relying on Laban's presumption that if she is menstruating, her condition of ritual impurity would be a blasphemous act, for she would be rendering a household god unclean by polluting it with her blood. As it is, she is in fact ridiculing the household god by merely sitting on it.

Laban's search of the camp lays bare his distrust of Jacob. Not only has Laban treated him unfairly and without respect and now wrongly accuses him of theft, but his actions show that he considers him a liar. This is highly insulting in a society where a man's word is held in honor. Jacob's countercharge is scathing (vv. 36-42). He first demands that Laban produce evidence of theft if he can and let their respective kinsfolk decide on guilt or innocence. He then recapitulates his years of faithful service to Laban in the face of Laban's abuse of power. What he describes reflects some of the legal protection the Mesopotamian *Code of Hammurabi* afforded shepherds. Often left to their own devices for months, they were allowed to eat from the flock without having to reimburse the owner. It also states that they were not accountable for the loss of any animals that might have been eaten by wild beasts. Jacob claims that while he was working for Laban he never took advantage of these rights, but he bore any loss himself.

Jacob then asserts that his present prosperity was acquired despite the obstacles Laban placed in his path over the last twenty years. It was only because God was with him, protecting and blessing him, that he was able to prosper. He insists that Laban's treatment of him went far beyond that of a strict employer, for Laban did what he could to keep Jacob from earning enough to facilitate his departure. Furthermore, Laban was obliged to ensure that Jacob would not leave empty-handed (Deut 15:12-14). Jacob identifies the God who provided for him as his ancestral deity—the God of Abraham and the Fear of Isaac. This divine epitaph, which appears only in this chapter, probably means "the God of whom Isaac stands in awe." Perhaps Jacob identifies God in this way to impress Laban with the awesomeness of the God who is protecting him.

Without relinquishing his claim of authority over his daughters and their children, Laban turns this claim to his own benefit. In a posture of magnanimity of heart, he suggests that he and Jacob establish a covenant, an agreement of nonaggression that will allow both men to save face and will guarantee peace for all involved. The report of the establishment of this covenant contains several duplications. There seem to be two different agreements, two sacred symbols that memorialize the covenant, two names given for the site, two deities called upon. Most commentators maintain that two sources have been woven into one report. There is no agreement, however, over which details belong to which source.

It was common practice to set up a pillar as a memorial stone, as Jacob did after the mystical experience he had had at Bethel (28:18). On some occasions, stones were piled into a heap or mound rather than set up as pillars. These mounds often served as landmarks or as burial monuments. In this instance, the mound is meant to serve as a witness to the covenant. Sharing a meal was also a part of covenant making. A meal establishes, on a very personal level, a bond between the covenant partners. What appear to be different names for the site stem from the use of different languages. גַּלְעֵד (Galeed) is Hebrew for "heap of stones"; יְגַר שָׂהֲדוּתָא (Jegarsahadutha) is the same expression in Aramaic. Finally, מִצְפָּה (Mizpah), which means "watch post," is a play on צָפָה (sāpâ; watch).

Once again Laban turns to the topic of his daughters, expressing concern for them. Since he prevails upon Jacob not to marry any other women, the ill-treatment to which he alludes is probably somehow connected with the conjugal relationship. In a patriarchal society, the primary way a woman might be humiliated was by denying her conjugal rights. Since an earlier narrative suggests that Jacob acted in just such a way toward Leah (30:15-16), Laban's concern is well-grounded. He might also be concerned that his daughters and grandchildren not be required to share any of Jacob's wealth with other possible wives and children. Finally, Laban reminds Jacob that, though others might not be aware of any mistreatment of his daughters, God will know; God will know if the covenant between the two men is violated in this way.

The agreement that is made between the two men has an international character. The pillar and mound of stones now mark land boundaries, boundaries that will later separate the lands of Israel and of Aram. Laban calls on the patronal deities of Jacob and of his own ancestors to act as guardians of the covenant between the two men. Should the covenant be violated, the god of the wronged party will exact justice on the offender. The possibility of the involvement of two gods suggests that monotheism has not yet been accepted by Israel's ancestors. They do practice monolatry, however, the worship of only one God. Jacob accepts the terms of the agreement and, calling on God by the title Fear of Isaac, takes the oath that binds him to the covenant. The episode ends with a sacrificial meal.

After the two companies go their separate ways (32:1), Jacob is met by angels, messengers of God. This meeting calls to mind a similar encounter of heavenly beings (28:12). The earlier experience occurred at night during a dream just before Jacob left the land of his birth and entered Haran, the homeland of Laban. The present event takes place as he is about to leave. These two experiences mark Jacob's going out of his land of origin and his coming into it, as if they are signs of God's protection of Jacob as he crosses borders. Recognizing the presence of God in this encounter, Jacob names the place מַחֲנָיִם (Mahanaim), which means "God's camp." This experience reassures him as he prepares to meet his estranged brother Esau.

Contemporary Reading: Family Wisdom

The stories in this section are replete with deception. Laban tricks and cheats Jacob, Jacob tricks Laban, and Rachel deceives her father. The motivations of these deceptions are, however, very different. Laban takes advantage of his privileged position and tricks Jacob out of the woman he desires for a wife and then cheats him out of some of his rightful earnings. In this way, Laban seeks to exercise unfair control over the vulnerable Jacob. For his part, Jacob takes advantage of his role as herder of Laban's flock and tricks Laban by using magical powers. Thus he guarantees financial security for himself and his family. Rachel believes that she has been unjustly deprived of her share of an inheritance. Therefore, she takes what she believes is her right, and she deceives her father lest he discover what she has done.

Jacob and Rachel demonstrate how those who do not enjoy power and privilege often resort to trickery in order to achieve what they believe is their right. Social mores of the day might accuse Jacob and Rachel of wrongdoing. The biblical author, however, does not. In fact, their actions are seen as necessary means to bring to fulfillment the promise of God revealed long ago in a dream at Bethel.

Chapter 13

"You Have Contended with [the] Divine"

(Gen 32:3–33:20)

The Jacob who returns to Canaan is a very different man from the one who much earlier fled for his life with his wronged brother in hot pursuit. This man has been chastened by disappointment, victimization, and hardship. Responding to God's command to return to his home in Canaan, he knows that he will have to face Esau along with his previous treachery. He has no idea how his brother will receive him. He can only trust in God's promise to be with him.

Appeasement (Gen 32:3-22)

Jacob no sooner resolves the conflict between himself and Laban than he turns to face what may well be the hostile intent of his brother Esau. Jacob does not presume familiarity. When he left Canaan, Esau was breathing threats of violence against him, so Jacob has no idea how his brother will receive him now. Therefore, following customary ancient Near Eastern protocol, he sends an official delegation to Esau, announcing his arrival. The words he uses signal the formal approach his delegation is to take: "Thus you shall say to my lord Esau . . . 'Thus says your servant Jacob.'"

While Near Eastern courtesy requires obsequious speech (my lord . . . your servant), this custom serves Jacob quite well. It is because of Jacob that Esau is not prosperous in Canaan but has been relegated to the land of Edom. Now, on his way back to his own homeland, Jacob must pass through Edom. Like any traveler, he is bound to show deference to the chiefs of that land. In doing so, he also humbles himself before the brother he so grievously wronged. Mention of Jacob's wealth is not meant to impress Esau but to assure him that Jacob can provide the customary gift of honor offered the inhabitants of the land. It also shows that Jacob is ready to turn over some of his possessions to Esau as reparation for the harm he did in the past and to gain Esau's favor.

The messengers return with the report that Esau, along with a retinue of four hundred men, is coming to meet Jacob. One cannot help wondering whether this reflects the words spoken to Esau by Isaac years ago when he begged him for a blessing: "By your sword you shall live" (27:40). Jacob has reason to be afraid. He cannot escape Esau this time. If he turns back, he will have to face Laban again. Furthermore, his caravan, which includes women and children along with extensive herds and flocks, will never be able to outdistance a troop of four hundred men. All Jacob can do is prepare for attack. He divides the animals into two camps—a play on the word Mahanaim, the name he gave to the site (v. 3), the name that means "two camps."

In prayer, Jacob addresses God with titles identifying God as the patron of his ancestors, the patron who promised protection and favor. Using covenant language, חֶסֶד (*ḥesed*; steadfast love) and אֱמֶת (*'ĕmet*; faithfulness), Jacob reminds God of God's commitment to him. Only after this appeal to divine magnanimity does he entreat God's protection. In the past Jacob might have been concerned solely for himself, but now he must also consider women and children. Furthermore, these very children are the fulfillment of God's promise. Surely God will not renege on this promise and allow these children to be destroyed.

Jacob proceeds with the conventional practice of gift giving. The reiteration of obsequious language, identifying Esau as lord and Jacob as servant, is meant to allay any bitterness Esau might still be harboring toward Jacob. Here occurs a play on פָּנֶה (*pāneh*; face) that is lost in translation. The word appears four times in verse 20, the literal translation of which might read, "I will cover his face (atone to him) in gifts, the [gift] going before my face (ahead of me) . . . so that I will see his face (appease him), perhaps he will lift up my face (forgive me)." The importance of this word is seen later in the story in the name Jacob gives the site (v. 31).

Wrestling during the Night (Gen 32:23-33)

The account of Jacob's wrestling during the night raises several questions: Why is Jacob attacked? With whom does he wrestle? Is it a man, as the text states? Or an angel, as the story has been traditionally understood? Or is it God, as the name of the site suggests? Why is Jacob left with a limp? What does the change of name signify? Several of these questions remain unanswered.

The Jabbok, an eastern tributary of the Jordan, is a turbulent river that flows through a deep ravine about twenty-five miles north of the Dead Sea. Fording this river with a large assemblage of people and animals would have been a challenge for even the most experienced herders. In order to avoid the heat of the day, caravans frequently traveled by night. This explains the timing of Jacob's movement. No reason is given for Jacob's remaining alone once the caravan has crossed the river. Some commentators maintain that the master's place was at the rear of the company, ensuring that there were no stragglers but that all were safely accounted for. If this is the case, then Jacob's separation from the group might be explained.

Most likely, the story originated as an ancient animistic folktale associated with the spot where frequently the river was crossed. Like many tales of this kind, it told of a river spirit or demon that guarded the place of fording and that had to be appeased in order to ensure a safe passage. Demons of this kind threatened only at night and retreated with the light of day. Such a folktale has been reshaped into a story about Jacob and now provides an explanation of the name of the site, Jabbok.[1]

The text identifies Jacob's assailant as a man; however, this man has more than human ability—but then, so does Jacob. The struggle may have been simply a feature of the folktale, but it is described in the Bible as an actual event. Jacob's subsequent limping is evidence of this. Both the struggle and Jacob's resulting disability correspond to some of the standard elements of a saga. In this type of narrative, a hero makes valiant efforts to overcome a seemingly insurmountable obstacle and is eventually successful. In some sagas, the hero does not escape without having to bear some form of injury that witnesses both to his physical weakness and to his ultimate strength.

---

1. Note the play on words: יַבֹּק (Jabbok), אָבֵק (*'ābaq*; struggle), and יַעֲקֹב (Jacob).

As the day begins to dawn, Jacob demands a blessing. No blessing is given, but his name is changed to Israel. The biblical text provides an explanation of the name: one who has "striven with God and with humans, and [has] prevailed" (v. 28). A change of name always signifies a change in destiny. Jacob's new name links him with a future nation. Though Jacob himself will not always be called Israel, his descendants will be known as the people of Israel, and the land that they claim as their own will bear that same name.

The story of Jacob's struggle took place near the Jabbok River. He called the site Peniel.[2] The explanation of this name is given in the story: "For I have seen God face to face, and yet my life is preserved" (v. 30). Though Peniel alone means "face of God," the phrase "yet my life is preserved" refers to the belief that a mere human being cannot see God and live (see Exod 33:20). This meaning has led many to conclude that Jacob was indeed wrestling with God rather than with a lesser numinous being. The fact that the name indicates a struggle with God illustrates how elements of an ancient folktale have been reinterpreted by the biblical author and given theological meaning.

Finally, the thigh muscle on the hip socket that Jacob injured while wrestling refers to the sciatic nerve. Some believe that there was an early taboo against eating this muscle because of its proximity to the reproductive organs. The explanation in this passage provides a religious reason for the dietary prohibition.

Reconciliation (Gen 33:1-20)

Jacob prepares to meet Esau. He divides his family into three groups, in the order of his affection for them. In this way, Jacob's favorites will have some degree of protection. Jacob himself leads the company, thus displaying his willingness to ward off any possible attack. As he moves forward, he bows seven times until he is face-to-face with his brother. Bowing when one approaches another is the customary Near Eastern political form of greeting. Jacob does not merely bow; rather, he prostrates himself, a sign of great respect. Moreover, Jacob performs this act of obeisance seven times. Ancient Egyptian correspondence contains records of such

---

2. פְּנוּאֵל (Penuel) is the standard name of the site; פְּנִיאֵל (Peniel) is a variant of it.

sevenfold reverence shown to the pharaoh. Jacob's behavior is extraordinary for two reasons. First, Esau is not Jacob's superior. If anything, they are political equals, yet Jacob acts toward Esau as if he were of greater importance. Furthermore, such submissiveness does not correspond with the prayer that accompanied the blessing Jacob received from his father Isaac: "and may your mother's sons bow down to you" (27:29).

Esau's reaction to seeing Jacob is startling. While Jacob's manner of greeting is formal and deferential, Esau's is familial and affectionate. Crediting God with his success, Jacob presents himself as a humble and grateful man. This portrayal is reinforced by his insistence on identifying himself as "your servant" when addressing his brother (v. 5). With that, the members of Jacob's family come forward and prostrate themselves before Esau. Thus Jacob's entire family pays obeisance to Esau.

Jacob admits that the droves of animals offered to Esau are more than the customary gift required by Near Eastern courtesy. They are intended as a peace offering, a way of gaining Esau's favor. Once again Jacob ends his remark with an address of respect, referring to Esau as "my lord" (v. 8). Acknowledging the need to find favor with Esau is as close as Jacob gets to explicitly admitting that he wronged him in the past. Though Esau has greeted him as a long-lost brother, Jacob is taking nothing for granted. He continues with the prescribed protocol of respect. Esau's refusal to accept a gift also follows this protocol, for it was inappropriate to appear too eager. Esau declines by stating that he does not need the animals; he has plenty of his own. This admission on Esau's part is evidence that he has prospered. Despite having been deprived by Jacob of his birthright and the blessing intended for the firstborn, Esau has had a good life in Edom.

Again, following protocol, Jacob insists that Esau accept the gifts. Jacob's wish flows not only from Near Eastern custom, however, but also from his need for signs that Esau has forgiven him his duplicity. Jacob does not consider his gift a favor to Esau. Rather, he sees Esau's acceptance as evidence that he has found favor with his brother. Esau might not need this favor, but Jacob does. Jacob is not simply reverting to Near Eastern exaggeration when he says that seeing Esau's face is like seeing the face of God. He is really claiming that the affability he sees in his brother's face signals the fact of their reconciliation, and he perceives this reconciliation as a blessing from God. In the end, Esau concedes.

This narrative clearly demonstrates the steps to be taken in the movement from alienation to reconciliation. Jacob perpetrated a transgression that victimized Esau. The story shows that Jacob is clearly repentant of his wrongdoing. His repentance, however, is not enough. In fact, there is no genuine reconciliation until the victim forgives the perpetrator. True, there must be a willingness to reconcile on the part of both. Nevertheless, reconciliation really begins with forgiveness, not with repentance.[3] Once the brothers are reconciled, Esau returns to Seir, and Jacob sets out for Succoth.

It is at Succoth that Jacob builds a house for himself and booths to shelter his cattle. This is the only place in the ancestral accounts where one of the ancestors is said to have constructed a dwelling. To this point, the Israelites have lived in tents. While building a house might suggest the beginning of settled existence after generations of nomadic life, it could also reflect a way of life that included both a pastoral existence of herding small livestock and an off-season life in villages and towns. There is archaeological evidence that many ancient Near Eastern groups led such lives.

Jacob pitched his tent near the city of Shechem. At long last he has returned to Canaan, the land of his birth. His successful flight from Laban in Paddan-aram, the realization of the pact of nonaggression made with his uncle, and the reconciliation with his brother Esau all confirm God's protective care of him and his household. Like Abraham before him (23:16), he purchases a plot of land. Mention of Hamor and Shechem anticipates the following story about the family of Shechem and Jacob's daughter Dinah.

Nothing is said about the intended purpose of the land that Jacob purchases. He sets up an altar there and dedicates it to the God of Israel. This action suggests that worship of the God of Israel (Jacob) replaces worship of the Canaanite deities.

Contemporary Reading: The Women and Children Are Safe

So often the violence between men engulfs women and children as well. Such is the case in this set of narratives. Jacob does not come alone to meet his brother. He brings his entire household—women, children, and servants. Though he went ahead of his retinue, those who followed

---

3. Contemporary Truth and Reconciliation Commissions in countries such as South Africa, Bosnia, and Rwanda attest to this.

were vulnerable as well, beginning with the least-loved maidservants who came directly behind him. Had Esau not been willing to reconcile with his brother, these people would that been victims of war. As so often happens in war, many women would have been raped, then killed or taken as prisoners, only to face further violation. It is no wonder that women often swell the ranks of antiwar movements.

The women and children were safe, not because Jacob now repented his offense against his brother, but because Esau the victim was ready to forgive. Thus, a second important theme surfaces, that of reconciliation. Women who have been victimized might be challenged to heroic virtue by the process of genuine reconciliation, for, as this passage demonstrates, reconciliation begins with the forgiveness extended by the one victimized. This is not the same as acceptance of one's victimization in fear or weakness. On the contrary, forgiveness of one's perpetrator requires great inner strength. It signals the victim's refusal to remain a victim, which means that the perpetrator no longer exercises dominance. Reconciliation does not mean forgive and forget. Quite the opposite. It insists on remembering. This remembering is done not out of vengeance, however, but out of vigilance, lest one be victimized again.[4]

---

4. The ultimate example of the victim forgiving the perpetrator is seen in Jesus: "Forgive them, they know not what they do" (Luke 23:34).

Chapter 14

"An Outrage in Israel"
(Gen 34:1–36:43)

The present set of stories opens with an account of the violation of Jacob's daughter Dinah and the avenging behavior of her brothers. Though the focus of the account is on the young woman, she does not enjoy a major role in this drama. Instead, in this androcentric narrative, the men treat her as they might treat a piece of property. Because of the cruel reprisal devised and executed by her brothers, the entire family leaves the area. Later, Jacob's joy at the birth of Benjamin is mitigated by the death of his beloved Rachel. The final listing of Jacob's sons follows the ranking of their respective mothers, his wives and concubines, a departure from the standard male-focused genealogy.

A Sister Is Violated (Gen 34:1-12)

This is the only story in the ancestral tradition in which a daughter is featured. Even the report of the birth of a daughter is seldom included in the collection of stories, unless that daughter figures prominently in a subsequent episode. Many commentators believe that the story and its placement here are meant to point out the dangers inherent in living among the Canaanites.

The story opens with the identification of Dinah as Jacob's daughter by Leah. Thus the reader is alerted to the side of the family to which she belongs, a point that may prove to be important later. Though her age is not given, she is old enough to leave her mother's tent (see 31:33) in order to visit the women of the region. Since Dinah comes from a group of nomadic herders, the sedentary character of city life and women's involvement in that life seem to have intrigued her, and she may have decided to meet her new neighbors. Earlier narratives show that the young Near Eastern girls were not confined to the tents as were married women. (The unmarried Rebekah spoke freely with Abraham's servant [24:17-27], and the youthful Rachel tended her father's flock [29:6].) Consequently, Dinah's venturing out into an unfamiliar situation was not frowned on by custom.

The Hivites, the people to whom Shechem belonged, were a Canaanite tribe (10:15-17) that occupied the hill country as far north as Mount Hermon. Shechem is the son of Hamor, the chief of the country, whose name in Hebrew means "he-ass," a hint at the lack of esteem in which the men of Israel held the Hivites. Jacob has already had financial dealings with this chieftain, purchasing land from his descendants on which he pitched his tent (33:19). Therefore, Jacob has no reason to suspect any form of treachery.

The description of the girl's abduction and rape is brief and to the point: "[he] saw her, he seized her and lay with her by force" (v. 2). In a most unusual turn of events, Shechem falls in love with his victim and wants to marry her. Knowledge of several cultural issues is presumed here. First, the young woman is the victim of rape, yet neither Shechem nor Hamor is concerned with her victimization. Though the hoped-for marriage is to be arranged by the respective fathers, as is the custom in patriarchal families, it stems from the man's desire; the woman is not consulted. Furthermore, the girl is no longer a virgin, the implications of which significantly diminish the value of the bridewealth. Finally, no thought is given by the Hivites to the affront to the honor of the girl's family, an honor that, in patriarchal societies, is a most cherished possession of the men of the family. It seems that the only factor that matters here is Shechem's desire for Dinah.

Jacob's silence should not be seen as evidence of his loss of leadership and power in his tribe or clan. Dinah is the daughter of Leah, the wife whom Jacob does not love. Therefore, favoritism for Rachel and her son could explain Jacob's lack of interest in Leah's daughter. It is Jacob's sons, particularly Dinah's full brothers Simeon and Levi, who are enraged by this crime. Yet even here, it seems that they are angry because of the affront against their honor as a tribe, not because of the violation of their sister.

Still oblivious of their offensive behavior, Shechem and Hamor propose a marriage agreement. The conditions of this agreement show that this story weaves together an episode in the history of Jacob's family and details of a legal relationship between two peoples; Shechem wants Dinah as his wife, and Hamor proposes the exchange of Jacob's daughter for all the daughters of his people. In addition, Hamor offers Jacob free access to his land: "You shall live with us; and the land shall be open to you; live and trade in it, and get property in it" (v. 10). Hamor's offer sounds quite generous, an offer that is in keeping with marriage practices of the day. Or Hamor's extravagance of gifts might be an attempt to appease the man his son has wronged. After all, he is only asking for the marriage of the young woman his son loves, a young woman who, because she is no longer a virgin, will probably not be able to command a sizeable bridewealth. While Hamor's offer of land might persuade Jacob to turn from the nomadic to the sedentary life, however, Hamor is not aware of this people's resistance to exogamous marriage and the intercultural and religious assimilation that often follows it.

After Hamor makes his appeal and offers his proposal, it is Shechem's turn to plead his cause. His marriage offer mirrors a directive found in the much later Mosaic Law: "When a man seduces a virgin who is not engaged to be married, and lies with her, he shall give the bride price for her and make her his wife. But if her father refuses to give her to him, he shall pay an amount equal to the bride price for virgins" (Exod 22:16-17). It is clear from this directive that Shechem's offer is merely the prescribed penalty that he must pay for his transgression.

Dinah's Honor Avenged (Gen 34:13-31)

It is Dinah's brothers, not her father, who respond to Hamor's offer and Shechem's plea. Cultic piety is the reason they give for their negative response. They allege that they cannot agree to a marriage between their sister and an uncircumcised man, claiming that such a union would cause them to lose honor. Presumably, they are concerned about the religious identity associated with circumcision, not with the bridewealth that Shechem is willing to provide. In fact, the brothers are using circumcision, a requirement for the male descendants of Abraham (17:10), as a ploy in their plan to seek revenge for the violation of their sister.

On the condition that all the males of the city be circumcised, the sons of Jacob agree to all of Hamor's offers: to give their daughters in marriage and to marry the daughters of Hamor's people; to settle among the inhabitants of this city and eventually merge with them as one people. What begins as an agreement between the two families is now broadened into a pact between two peoples. Little does Hamor know that the brothers have no intention of giving their sister in marriage. Instead, they have devised a ploy that will enable them to avenge their family honor that was defiled by Shechem's violation of Dinah.

Shechem is so eager to marry Dinah that he is circumcised immediately. Though Hamor and Shechem are held in high regard by the people of the city, they do not have the authority to force circumcision on the entire population. Nor can they arbitrarily decide on matters of broader public interest, such as inviting strangers to settle in land that is held in common or agreeing to future marriage arrangements for all the young women of the city. Therefore, they bring the brothers' proposition to the men of the city, who have assembled at the city gate where all important business is transacted.

Hamor and Shechem might have been quite candid with the sons of Jacob, but they are not as straightforward with their fellow townsmen. They never mention the episode of rape and the hoped-for marriage that, in point of fact, precipitated this entire state of affairs. Instead, they present the brothers' proposition as the condition for an advantageous business venture. All the men gathered at the city gate agree to be circumcised. While they are indisposed as a result of the procedure, Simeon and Levi enter the city and kill them. The other sons of Jacob then plunder the city, taking flocks and herds and whatever is in the city and the fields, along with their wealth and their wives and their children. It is only when Hamor and Shechem have been put to the sword that the brothers are able to rescue their sister from Shechem's house, where she has been.

Jacob takes a stand once this massacre is over. His opposition to the behavior of his sons has nothing to do, however, with the suffering endured by the slaughtered people. He is concerned with the possibility of negative repercussions that he himself and his entire household might have to face because of his sons' violent actions. He reprimands them, claiming that their actions have made him "odious to the inhabitants of the land" (v. 30). He is afraid that the more numerous Canaanites might gather against him and destroy him and his household.

Jacob's sons argue that their actions are a justified response to the violation of their sister. Their defense is probably less a concern for Dinah, however, than it is for their own honor. In patriarchal societies men are duty bound to protect the integrity of the women of the household, for they carry reproductive potential within them. If the women are left unprotected, the men are judged incompetent and suffer the loss of honor. If Dinah were considered a whore, the men in her family would suffer personal disgrace. These young nomadic herders are no longer satisfied with peaceful negotiations as were their predecessors. Instead, they are quick to resort to nationalistic revenge when they believe that their honor is under attack.

Return to Bethel (Gen 35:1-15)

God spoke to Jacob, telling him, "Arise, go up to Bethel and settle there" (v. 1). "Arise" indicates that Jacob's journey is not yet complete. "Go up" usually refers to a pilgrimage. These words suggest that Jacob's movement into the land of Canaan has religious significance and that Bethel is the destination of this pilgrimage. "Settle" indicates that the very place from which Jacob launched his travels so many years ago (28:10, 19) is the place where he is to construct an altar and then set up his abode.

Although Jacob was on the sidelines in the previous story, he resumes leadership here. He gives orders to all in his company to prepare themselves to enter the sacred precincts of a shrine. They are to rid themselves of anything connected with foreign gods. As mentioned earlier, the people are probably henotheistic (allegiance to one god without denial of the existence of other gods) and they practice monolatry (worship of only one god). The reference to foreign gods would include the *teraphim* that Rachel stole from her father Laban, as well as any idols, sacred images, or amulets that were confiscated in the looting of the city of Shechem.

The people are told to perform rites of purification. These include ritual bathing, which denotes the cleansing of their offenses, and a change of clothing, which symbolizes their transformation into new people. Jacob collects any paraphernalia that has any cultic or religious significance and buries it under a tree near Shechem, thus depriving the foreign gods of any power they might otherwise exercise. Actually, Jacob has nothing to fear from the people of the land, for they are overcome with a terror of

God. This is yet another sign that God is with Jacob. The account of God's revelation to Jacob at the shrine at Bethel is interrupted by the report of the death of Rebekah's nurse Deborah (v. 8). Planting a tree over a burial site, as Jacob did over Deborah's grave, was a common practice. It might have developed from an animistic belief that the souls of the dead could then live in the trees. The name of the tree planted here is very fitting for the occasion, אַלּוֹן בָּכוּת (*Allon-bacuth*; the oak of the weeping).

After Jacob had wrestled all night with the mysterious stranger, he was given a new name, Israel. Here God confirms that change of name (v. 10) and reaffirms the promises made to the ancestors. This blessing begins with the same commission given to the first man and woman at the time of creation: "Be fruitful and multiply" (1:28). That earlier charge alluded to the increase of the entire human race. This charge refers to the increase of the descendants of Jacob. In many ways, this blessing draws a parallel between Jacob and Abraham. Both have name changes (v. 10; 17:4); to both, God is self-disclosed as אֵל שַׁדַּי (God Almighty; v. 11; 17:1); God promises both men that nations and kings will stem from them (v. 11; 17:6); and finally, the promise of land is made to both (v. 12; 13:15). The ancestral period that began with Abraham now closes with Jacob. What follows are stories of various sons of Jacob, the ones who will move God's promise forward into history, the precursors of the tribes of Israel.

Finally, this passage reports the fulfillment of the vow that Jacob had made to God on the occasion of his first revelatory experience at Bethel. At that time, Jacob promised, "If God will be with me, and will keep me in this way that I go . . . so that I come again to my father's house in peace, then YHWH shall be my God" (28:20-21). God has been faithful to that promise, and now Jacob is faithful to his vow. He repeats the cultic rite of consecration, setting up a memorial stone and pouring out oil (v. 14; 28:18). His life has now come full circle. The future is in the hands of his descendants.

Wives and Concubines (Gen 35:16-29)

No exact chronology is given for the continuing movements of Jacob and his caravan, so there is no way of knowing when Rachel becomes pregnant. It is while they are en route that she is overcome by labor pains, however, and the company is forced to stop near Ephrath. What follows is a very difficult birth. The midwife tries to console Rachel by assuring her that she is bringing forth another son, a reference to Rachel's own wish made at the birth of Joseph, her first son: "May YHWH add to me another son" (30:24). The biblical text identifies Ephrath as Bethlehem (v. 19), a city that is about five miles south of Jerusalem. Later passages, however, place Rachel's tomb closer to Bethel in the north, at Ramah (see Jer 31:15) in the territory that will eventually be occupied by the tribe of Benjamin (1 Sam 10:2).

The story of Rachel's death and burial underscores a tragic but common reality that people in the ancient world were forced to face, that is, that the survival of the group is always precarious. While it is impossible to gauge the percentage of pregnancies that were brought to term, records indicate that there was a high incidence of infant mortality. Add to this the ever-present risk of the mother dying in childbirth and it is easy to understand why ancient societies put so much importance on a woman's ability to bear children. Without multiple pregnancies and births, extinction of the group was a real possibility. Rachel had been desolate because she had been unable to perform this essential duty. She experienced utter joy, however, at the birth of each of her sons. Now, the price of this new life was the life of the mother. Rachel dies, but not before naming her second son בֶּן־אוֹנִי (*Ben-oni*), which means "son of my suffering or misfortune."

Jacob will not allow his son to be the constant reminder of the agony endured by his favorite wife, and so he renames the boy בִּנְיָמִן (Benjamin), which means "son of the right side," the side of honor or of good fortune. Though the name itself is a touching reminder of how Jacob cherishes the child that Rachel bore, this renaming serves to blot out Rachel's last words. Following this, in a move that must have been heartrending, he buries his beloved wife on the side of the road, and the caravan continues its journey. Before they move on, however, Jacob marks her grave with a memorial stone (a burial custom that is observed around the world today). The importance of this stone becomes apparent in the fact that it is long remembered. The biblical author, who undoubtedly lived many years after this event, states, "[It] is there to this day" (v. 20).

Jacob next pitches his tent just beyond Migdal-eder (tower of the flocks). Shepherds often built towers from which they could watch their flocks. These gave them a much better vantage point for perceiving any approaching danger. The site itself is not important to the story. Rather, it is what happens there that is significant; Reuben, Jacob's firstborn son and, presumably, the heir to the promise, has intercourse with Bilhah,

Rachel's maidservant and Jacob's concubine (v. 22). Such an act is a blatant attempt to usurp the power of the leader. A later Levitical law will
condemn such behavior: "The man who lies with his father's wife has
uncovered his father's nakedness; both of them shall be put to death"
(Lev 20:11). Acts of adultery are generally perpetrated by the man. Yet
this law states that both the man and the woman should be punished,
because the man has violated the property of another man and because,
having been violated, the woman no longer has value in the eyes of her
husband. The gender bias here is obvious.

Reuben's act shames Jacob because it implies that his father has lost
control over the members of his household. More than this, it is an act
of treason, for assuming sexual dominance over the wives of the leader
of the group is a sign of the commandeering of political power (see 2
Sam 3:7; 16:21-22). At this point Reuben is not punished. Justice for this
heinous act will, however, be served later at Jacob's deathbed pronounce-
ment (49:4).

The sons of Jacob are listed according to their birthmothers, not their
chronological births (vv. 23-26): first Leah's sons and then Rachel's; next
the sons of Rachel's maidservant, Bilhah; and finally those of Leah's maidservant, Zilpah. No daughter (Dinah) is mentioned. The placement of this
list follows the pattern chosen by the biblical editor to provide a listing of
sons just before the death of the patriarch is reported. This arrangement
is probably meant as a literary device that ensures continuation of the
bloodline. It is not clear why the present passage lists the sons according
to Jacob's wives. Perhaps it is meant to alert the reader to the internecine
struggles that the sons of various mothers will pursue.

Jacob's journey ends in Mamre, the home of his father Isaac. The
family has come full circle. Though the text does not explicitly state that
Isaac is buried in the family tomb there, it is implied. Just as the estranged
brothers, Isaac and Ishmael, buried their father Abraham in the cave of
Machpelah (25:9), so now the once-alienated brothers, Jacob and Esau,
come together to bury their father (v. 29). Isaac is gathered to his people
(v. 29), a phrase meaning that he lived a full and successful life.

The Edomites (Gen 36:1-43)

With the death of Isaac, the focus of the narrative turns to the lines
that stem from Esau. Little can be said about the historical accuracy of

the lists. Scholars agree that a variety of sources were used in their composition. The first genealogy (vv. 1-5) is structured around Esau's three Canaanite wives. His decision to marry Canaanite women demonstrates his disregard for his family's practice of endogamous marriage. His choice of settlement outside of the land of promise distanced him further from his family of origin. The biblical text suggests that his move was precipitated by economic matters. The land was not able to support both his flocks and those of his brother Jacob (v. 7). Thus Esau, here identified as Edom, settles in the hill country of Seir (v. 8). The second listing is a segmented genealogy (vv. 9-14), for it moves the lines of descent through Esau's wives and sons to his grandsons. As is typical in biblical genealogies, daughters are not included.

Another genealogical listing (vv. 20-30) traces the descendants of the clans that had inhabited the land of Seir before Esau and his family settled there. It is probably included here because these people and their descendants were eventually included in the nation of Edom. This is followed by the listing of the kings who reigned in Edom before any monarchy was established in Israel (vv. 31-39). The Edomite kingdom did not have a permanent capital, but various kings established their own capital cities. The statement that Edomite monarchies predated the monarchy in Israel indicates that the biblical author was acquainted with Israelite royal rule. This detail has been utilized by many commentators to date these genealogies near the time of David. Later in Israel's national story, David is reported to have set up Israelite garrisons in the land of Edom, thus making Edom a part of Israel (2 Sam 8:14). This fact is another example of how "the elder [Esau/Edom] shall serve the younger [Jacob/Israel]" (25:23). The final designation of Esau as the father of Edom (v. 43), brings to an end the family history of Esau/Edom.

Contemporary Reading: Honor and Shame

The accounts of the rape of Dinah and the revenge of her brothers are stories of honor and shame. But whose honor and whose shame? As the stories are told, they suggest that the shame of the woman causes the loss of the men's honor. These are read, however, from a totally different point of view today. All the men are now seen to be shameful, while the woman, despite the fact that she was violated and tyrannized, retains her dignity and honor. This difference in understanding stems from the radical change today from ancient social mores. This is to say not that rape and exploitation no longer occur but that these are no longer considered acceptable behavior.

From ancient Israel's point of view, the story illustrates the crass character of the hated Canaanites (Shechem). This characterization is an example of the very common human inclination to demonize enemies or those with whom there is disagreement. Such unfavorable depiction is found not only in literature but also in various forms of humor, whenever the one characterized is often portrayed as naïve or dim-witted, as seen in the portrayal of the Shechemite men.

Joseph
(Gen 37:1–50:26)

The Joseph cycle is unique among the ancestral traditions. It is not a collection of legends, as are the other cycles. Rather, it is a well-organized composition belonging to the literary category of short story. With the exception of the story of Tamar (chap. 38) and Jacob's last testament (chap. 49), the account of Joseph's life unfolds smoothly, one episode flowing into the next. The character of the tradition is also unique. Absent are the theophanies or manifestations of God so prevalent in the earlier cycles. The focus here is humanistic, exhibiting great interest in the emotional state of the characters. God is silent, working through human events rather than directly. Joseph learns from experience, not from divine revelation. This feature has led some commentators to ascribe a wisdom influence to this cycle of narratives.

Perhaps the most significant difference between this cycle and those that precede it is the lack of attention to the promises made to the ancestors. There is no concern for occupation of the land. In fact, the dominant context of the stories is the people's journey to and from Egypt and their final settlement in that land, not in the land of Canaan. Though the cycle ends with Jacob's testament to his sons, there is no preoccupation with descendants in the stories themselves. These differences suggest that this cycle of stories has a purpose different from that of the other ancestral cycles. It does not continue the thread of promise. Rather, it links the ancestral traditions with the people's settlement in Egypt. It explains why, having been promised land in Canaan, Abraham's descendants journeyed to Egypt and remained there.

Chapter 15

"Family History"
(Gen 37:1–38:30)

The Dreamer (Gen 37:1-11)

Jacob, his wives, and his children are settled in Canaan, where his sons shepherd flocks. This suggests a very common lifestyle practiced at the time, the life of nomadic people who lived on the fringes of settled society while shepherding flocks or herds of small cattle. Though Joseph assists his elder brothers with the herding, he reports their poor work habits back to their father. This talebearing certainly does not endear him to his brothers.

Though not named, the brothers are identified as the sons of Bilhah and Zilpah, the maidservants of Rachel and Leah, respectively. This identification calls to mind the rivalry among Jacob's wives and concubines, family rivalries that were present even before the brothers were born. Furthermore, these are sons of concubines, not of primary wives. The inferior social status of these women augments the tension between their sons and Joseph, the son of Jacob's favorite wife, Rachel.

Jacob gives Joseph a tunic described as "flat of the hand," suggesting that it is long, with sleeves that extend to the palm of the hand. It is unlike the cloaks that men usually wrap around themselves. The Aramaic word (כְּתֹנֶת; *kuttōnet*) describing the tunic appears in only one other place in the Bible, and there it refers to the garb worn by young royalty (2 Sam 13:18). In other words, this tunic is clearly a luxury, not something that one wears while engaging in shepherding flocks. The gift from his father openly sets Joseph apart from his hardworking brothers.

With very few words, the author traces the consequences of Jacob's preferential love. The contention among the women brought on by Jacob's well-known preference for Rachel spills over into the next generation and is refueled by Jacob's obvious favoritism toward Rachel's son. Every aspect of this exclusive father-son relationship simply adds to the brothers' resentment of Joseph. This resentment engenders hatred of him, hatred so deep that the brothers cannot even be civil toward him.

Many traditional societies prize dreams as vehicles of divine revelation. Joseph's dreams are of a different nature. They contain glimpses into the future, not directives from God. His first dream depicts a scene from agriculture, which is strange because the people are pastoralists. Perhaps the image foreshadows Joseph's future role as the one responsible for distributing the grain that Egypt is able to amass (41:39). Joseph's brothers mock his description of the dream, refusing to accept the possibility that he might indeed rule over them some day. What they see as effrontery on Joseph's part only makes them hate him more.

The second dream contains astral imagery. At first Jacob berates Joseph, challenging the respect that the dream implies will be given his favorite son. In the end, however, Jacob ponders the dream's meaning. Throughout these events, nothing is said about Joseph's attitude of mind. Is he naïve, unaware of how his father's favoritism has turned his brothers against him? Or is he as arrogant as his family accuses him of being? Whatever the case may be, the hatred of his brothers is almost palpable.

Human Trafficking (Gen 37:12-36)

Both Jacob and Joseph seem oblivious of the antagonism that both Joseph's visit to his brothers and the sight of his garment breed in them. This insensitivity only intensifies the antagonism. It is actually Jacob's blindness to the ill feelings among the brothers that puts Joseph in jeopardy. As soon as the brothers see Joseph, their anger is enflamed, and they decide to rid themselves of him. Their first plan is to kill him and throw his body into a pit. As the eldest brother, Reuben assumes the authority that is ascribed to this position in the family. He objects to the plan and suggests that they simply cast Joseph into the pit. The brothers undoubtedly see this as a way of eliminating Joseph without being guilty of shedding his blood. The verbs employed describe their attack on Joseph as swift and decisive: "they stripped him . . . took him and threw him into a pit" (vv. 23-24). The pit or cistern is dry, indicating that this event occurred during the dry season. Reuben sees the pit as a hiding place until he can rescue Joseph and return him to their father; the other brothers see it as the place of Joseph's death.

The callousness of the brothers is striking. They have just manhandled their younger brother, cast him into a pit where they presume he will die, and then sit down for a meal. The caravan that they see is probably following the ancient trade route that ran from Damascus to Gilead, across the Jordan River south of Carmel, along the east coast of the Mediterranean Sea to Egypt. Dothan, where they are shepherding the flocks, is on that route. The caravan, bound for Egypt, is carrying various spices obtained from Gilead, spices used as healing agents, for cosmetics, and for worship.

The caravan presents a change of plans. Unlike Reuben who is concerned for his brother's safety and his father's peace of mind, Judah proposes a way of acquiring financial gain while at the same time avoiding guilt for their brother's death: "let us sell him" (v. 27). The twenty pieces of silver for which they sell their brother was the standard price of a slave as stated in the *Code of Hammurabi* and in the later Israelite law; it was the amount of ransom required for a young man under the age of twenty (Lev 27:5). The brothers not only sell Joseph into slavery but also turn a profit by means of their villainous deed of human trafficking.

The brothers may have rid themselves of their troublesome sibling, but now they wonder what they are to tell their father. The scheme that they devise bears striking similarity to the ruse that Jacob himself contrived against his father Isaac (Gen 27). In both cases, a father who dotes on one son is tricked by offspring who are less favored; in both cases, the father's favored son is the victim of the ruse; in both cases, clothing and the product of a kid are used to fool the father. Jacob now experiences the grief he once inflicted on his own father. It seems that the sins of his youth have now been visited upon him.

Jacob is devastated at the news of the loss of Joseph. His words are heartrending, and his grief is profound. Engaging in traditional mourning rites, he tears his garments and girds himself in sackcloth, material that was probably made of coarse black goat hair. His other children try to console him but to no avail. In fact, he claims that he will mourn the death of this favored son until his own death.

Ancient Israel had no clear concept of an afterlife. Nevertheless, neither did these people believe in total annihilation at death. Rather, they held that both the righteous and the wicked went to Sheol, a shadowy place where the dead were gathered. Throughout the older biblical traditions, Sheol is described as a tomb, dark, dusty, but without suffering. Occasionally, the word simply refers to death. As Jacob mourns the presumed death of his beloved son, that very son is being sold to an Egyptian dignitary. The human trafficking continues. Mention of Potiphar foreshadows Joseph's future access to the pharaoh.

A Widow in Her Father's House (Gen 38:1-11)

This narrative about Tamar and Judah interrupts the complex of stories about Joseph. The only connection this narrative has with those surrounding it is its focus on Judah, the brother who sought to preserve Joseph in order to benefit financially from his sale to the Midianites. In that narrative, Judah's concern did not spring from fraternal loyalty. In other words, he has already shown his true colors. He is a man whose decisions stem more from self-interest than from concern for others.

Judah has settled in the Shephelah, the lowlands west of the hill country. There he marries outside of the tribal structure (exogamy). The Canaanite woman he marries bears him three sons. The fact that her own name is not given—she is identified simply as the daughter the Canaanite Shua—indicates that her sole importance rests in the sons that she bears Judah.

The story demonstrates the levirate law. "Levirate" comes from the Latin word *levir*, which means "husband's brother." It stipulated that if a man died without leaving an heir, his brother was to take his widow as wife. The first child born of that second union was considered the legal heir of the dead man. This practice ensured that the property of the deceased man would remain within the family or clan, for if the widow married outside of her husband's family, his property might be lost to it. It also ensured the widow a secure place within her deceased husband's kinship structure, with all of the benefits that it provided. Finally, the levirate law provided a way for the deceased man's name to be remembered in future generations.

In this account, Judah himself arranges for the marriage between Tamar and his firstborn son. This son dies without leaving an heir, and so Tamar is given as wife to the next son, who also dies childless. Tamar is then directed by Judah to live in her father's household until Judah's youngest son is able to take her as his wife.[1] Judah is, however, apprehensive. He fears that the same fate will befall his youngest and sole surviving son. His anxiety indicates that he blames the deaths of his sons on Tamar. This presumption calls to mind a common narrative motif in which the embrace of a beautiful young woman brings death (see Tob 7:8). Gender bias can be seen in Judah's ascribing blame to the woman, for the text clearly states that both sons died because they offended YHWH. The Rabbinic interpretation of this story directs any blame for these deaths away from Tamar and levels it toward the sons of Judah, arguing that their very names portend their future.

The transgression of Er, the firstborn, is not mentioned. The sin of Onan, the second son, is. Whenever he has intercourse with Tamar, he withdraws prematurely, so that no conception can take place. Onanism, the word that has been coined to describe this behavior, implies that Onan's offense was the spilling of his seed. That is not, however, what the biblical account says. It states very clearly that Onan's sin is greed. He does not want to father a child who will be the legal heir of his dead brother and thereby inherit property and possessions that he himself might have been able to claim. This was the behavior that so displeased YHWH that Onan was struck dead.

On the Road to Timnah (Gen 38:12-30)

Tamar returns to her father's household where, though she is betrothed to Judah's youngest son Shelah, she lives as a widow. As such, she is something of a burden to her own family, for she has no other prospects for marriage. As the years pass, she comes to realize that Judah has no intention of fulfilling his levirate responsibility, a responsibility first to his deceased firstborn son and only then to her.

After Judah's wife dies and he fulfills the customary rites of mourning, he and his Canaanite friend Hirah go to the place where his sheep are being sheared. Tamar sees this as an opportunity to redress the wrong that has been done to her, and she decides to take matters into her own

---

1. The names of the sons are significant: Er (עֵר) means childless, Onan (אוֹנָן) means afflicted, and Shelah (שֵׁלָה) corresponds to the Aramaic for neglected.

hands. Tamar is prevented by one law (family control of her reproductive potential) from enjoying the rights provided by another law (the levirate). She can simply accept Judah's disregard of her rights and remain in her father's household, relying on the care given to a widow. Instead, despite the risk and possible misunderstanding involved, she musters the necessary ingenuity and courage needed to act.

It is now Tamar's turn to engage in the family tradition of disguise and trickery. She sets aside her widow's garb and stations herself at the side of the road where Judah is certain to see her. Though it is not clear which guise Tamar has chosen, Judah mistakes her for a prostitute (v. 15). It should be noted that she is later referred to as a temple prostitute (vv. 21, 22). Perhaps she is judged in this way because her dress resembles elements of local cultic custom, elements that are unfamiliar to Judah. Tamar places herself in jeopardy in order to secure her dead husband's rights, which were guaranteed by levirate marriage practice.

Judah's inability to recognize Tamar might be due to factors other than her disguise. After all, she has been living in her father's household for several years and her appearance may have changed. Or it might be because Judah is returning from shearing, an event that was typically accompanied by festivities and drinking. In any event, Tamar successfully hides her identity from her father-in-law, and he engages her services. The biblical author does not condemn Judah for this sexual liaison. Having relations with a prostitute might not have been proper, but at this time it does not seem to have been condemned. Besides, his wife is dead, and so he is not violating any marital commitment.

The fact that Judah offered to provide, in the future, a kid from his flock in payment for sexual favors reinforces the perception that Tamar is considered a temple prostitute, for the kid was the animal frequently offered in sacrifice. Tamar demands a pledge in the face of deferred payment. Judah agrees, not realizing that his daughter-in-law intends to use this pledge later to prove his culpability. She asks for his signet ring, which might have been used as a seal; for the cord on which this signet hangs; and for his staff. Judah willingly relinquishes these items, confident that they will be returned to him when he supplies the kid from his flock.

Tamar's pregnancy soon becomes obvious. Though she is living in her father's household, her reproductive potential really belongs to the family of Judah. Since she is still betrothed to Judah's son Shelah, this pregnancy is considered an act of adultery. Judah prepares to have her burnt as punishment for her sin. It is only then that Tamar reveals Judah's signet, cord, and staff, evidence that she is not guilty of adultery but that she was forced to resort to subterfuge in order to secure the rights both of her deceased husband and of herself, rights guaranteed by the levirate law. Realizing the truth in her words, Judah acknowledges, "She is more in the right than I, since I did not give her to my son Shelah" (v. 26).[2]

Regardless of how it might appear, Tamar is not a woman who tricks a man with sex in order to get what she wants; she is a woman who willingly places herself at risk in order to overcome whatever obstacles might prevent her from achieving her legitimate goal. This goal is not merely personal; she is not set on simply having a child of her own. She seeks to secure justice for her deceased husband and to ensure that his inheritance will be passed down to his descendants. She has gone to great lengths for the sake of justice.

Tamar delivers twins (v. 27). The report of their births recalls the account of the births of Esau and Jacob (25:24). In the earlier narrative, the younger Jacob grips the heel of the older Esau, as if he were trying to hold him back. Here, the hand of one child appears. The midwife ties a crimson thread around it so that the twins will be able to be distinguished later. The child withdraws his hand, however, and the other child is then born. He is called Perez, which means "breakthrough." The consequence that results from these unusual births is another example of the second son usurping the prerogative of the first (25:23). Perez's preeminence becomes evident only much later in Israel's history, for he will be an ancestor of David (Ruth 4:18-20), who is the ancestor of Jesus. Of all of the ancestors who might have been memorialized in Matthew's genealogy of Jesus, Tamar is one of the few women included (Matt 1:3).

Contemporary Reading: Human Exploitation

These stories tell of human exploitation of a man and of a woman. In his own way, Joseph was an innocent victim, first of his father and then of

---

2. Phyllis Bird, "The Harlot as Heroine: Narrative Art and Social Presupposition in Three Old Testament Texts," *Semeia* 46 (1989), 124; Mary E. Shields, " 'More Righteous Than I': The Comeuppance of the Trickster in Genesis 38," in *Are We Amused? Humor about Women in the Biblical Worlds*, Journal for the Study of the Old Testament Supplement Series 383 (New York: T & T Clark, 2003), 31–51.

his brothers. Jacob did him no favor by treating him as he did. He should have learned from the hostility generated among his wives by his preference for Rachel that his favoritism of Joseph would spawn resentment among his other sons. This is an example of love gone awry.

Human trafficking is always exploitation of the vulnerable by the powerful. Though today victims are usually women and children forced into sexual slavery, often men are brutalized in order to break their spirits. Very few countries today can claim that their history is innocent of this sordid practice. Though Joseph will eventually maintain that his having been sold into slavery was part of God's plan, victims today do not see it that way. Nor should the rest of society. The human dignity of all must be respected by all.

Tamar, like so many vulnerable women, suffers from the gender biased restrictions of social custom. Nevertheless, this does not confine her. She achieves her rights even though she is forced to employ untraditional and unorthodox methods. While she is certainly quite shrewd, her actions are deemed more than wise; Judah, the very man she duped, calls her righteous.

Chapter 16

"This Is Its Interpretation"
(Gen 39:1–41:57)

Joseph's ability to interpret dreams, which contributed to his having been sold into slavery in the first place, now enables him to rise to power in the court of Pharaoh. His rise illustrates several prominent biblical themes: God's care for those who are vulnerable, integrity under fire, the foreigner as agent of blessing for others, the victim as the initiator of reconciliation.

In the House of Potiphar (Gen 39:1-20)

Once again, Joseph is the victim of human trafficking. Purchased by Potiphar, a court official of the pharaoh, however, Joseph moves quickly from the status of slave to a position of prominence. His appointment to the household of his master is a sign of great trust and responsibility. He is soon made Potiphar's personal attendant, in charge of all of the Egyptian's possessions. The story of Joseph in Egypt continues the pattern of his rise and fall. Preferred by his father, he was betrayed by his brothers, only to rise again in Potiphar's favor.

The biblical author goes to great lengths to show that YHWH is working behind the scenes in Joseph's life rather than instructing him directly through divine manifestations, as was the case with his ancestors. Despite this change in the manner of divine involvement in human affairs, God's faithfulness to the promises made to the ancestors is evident: "I will be

165

with you, and will bless you" (26:3, 24; 28:15; 31:3). Furthermore, God rewards those who show kindness to Joseph: "I will bless those who bless you" (12:3). It is clear that the power of God is not circumscribed by the boundaries of Canaan. Rather, God's protection and care of Joseph is operative in Egypt, a land believed to be under the jurisdiction of Egyptian deities.

Joseph's meteoric rise in importance and his physical appearance set the stage for the next episode. He is truly his mother's son. Just as Rachel was known for her physical attractiveness (29:17) so is Joseph (39:6); they are both described as beautiful in form and appearance. While physical beauty served as an advantage for Rachel, it is a factor in Joseph's fall from favor. Potiphar's wife becomes obsessed with the young man and tries to seduce him. The theme of an aggressive woman and her sexual desires is quite common in various male-biased literatures. This bias against women is meant to underscore the integrity of the men.

Though the story about Joseph and Potiphar's wife describes the encounter between a woman and a man, other major dynamics are also at play. Bias grounded in ethnic origin and social class erupts as the story unfolds. Joseph is a foreigner; the woman is an Egyptian, if not by blood at least through marriage. Though Joseph is given charge of Potiphar's household and all of his possessions, he is still a servant; she is the wife of the master of the house. Contrary to what some commentators claim, this story is not primarily meant to underscore the licentiousness or desperation of the woman, though that is certainly an important theme. Nor is it a commentary on the fickle character of Egyptians. Rather, it is intended to underscore the righteousness of Joseph. His sexual attractiveness provides the occasion for Joseph to demonstrate the quality of his loyalty to Potiphar and to God.

Joseph offers three reasons for not succumbing to the woman's enticements (v. 9). He appeals first to the trust that Potiphar has placed in him. It is unthinkable that he should violate that trust. He then describes adultery as an act of great wickedness. In ancient patriarchal societies, adultery was considered a violation of the man's rights to the reproductive potential of his wife rather than an assault on the emotional bond between husband and wife. The wife belonged to the husband, and other men were required to respect that right. Finally, Joseph adds a religious reason for his self-restraint. He maintains that the behavior the woman is proposing is a sin against God.

Once again clothing is featured in the story of Joseph. In an earlier episode, the long robe that signaled Jacob's preference of Joseph was used as a ploy to persuade his father of Joseph's tragic demise (37:33). Here, the woman strips Joseph of the clothing he is wearing in order to use it as evidence of his alleged sexual assault of her. Her allegation is not only false but also compounded with ethnic bias. She refers to Joseph as a Hebrew[1] to show the difference between him and the men of her Egyptian household.

Potiphar's wife's xenophobic accusation implies that Hebrews cannot be trusted, and she actually faults her husband for falling prey to Joseph's charismatic personality. When her husband returns home, the spurned woman repeats her allegation and produces Joseph's confiscated clothing as evidence of his guilt. Either Potiphar is not completely convinced by his wife's account of the incident or his appreciation of Joseph's loyalty to him and of his expert management of Potiphar's household has softened his anger, for he does not impose on Joseph the customary harsh punishment of death meted out to convicted rapists.

Once again Joseph's situation is dramatically altered. His rise to prominence in the household of Potiphar is reversed. He not only falls out of favor but also is reduced to the status of prisoner. He is sent to a royal prison where those who are guilty of offenses against Pharaoh or members of his court are confined. Having been unfairly sold by his brothers, he is now unfairly imprisoned. As unusual as it seems, this move opens the path Joseph will take to the house of Pharaoh himself.

The Interpreter of Dreams (Gen 39:21–40:23)

Joseph's rise to prominence in the prison resembles his rise to importance in the household of Potiphar. Like Potiphar before him, the chief jailer becomes very impressed with Joseph's ability and entrusts him with responsibility, placing him in charge of all the other prisoners. In fact, Joseph manages the entire prison, "and whatever was done there, he was the one who did it" (v. 22). Here too Joseph's success is credited to God:

---

1. עִבְרִ (Hebrew) has often been linked to the Habiru or Apiru, a loosely organized amalgam of nomadic people. When Abram is identified as a Hebrew, however, it refers to his descent from Er (14:13). The word should be understood in this ethnic sense in the Joseph story.

"because the LORD was with him; and whatever he did, the LORD made it prosper" (v. 23; see v. 21).

The official cupbearer and the chief baker occupy very important and trusted positions, because they are responsible for ensuring the safety of Pharaoh's drink and food. Most likely, their offense has something to do with negligence in these matters. Their importance in the court signals the complexity of the hierarchal structure of Egyptian government, a type of government organization seldom found in tribal groups such as the one to which Joseph originally belonged. Having placed Joseph in charge of the management of the entire jail, the chief jailer assigns these two men to his supervision.

Ancient people were more than fascinated with dreams. Because they were not able to force a dream or to determine its content, they concluded that dreams were controlled by a supernatural power. The mysterious and often fanciful character of dreams made them very difficult to understand. This led to the sophisticated practice of dream interpretation. Believing that dreams contained a message from beyond this world, ancient people were very careful about engaging in this practice. Both Mesopotamian and Egyptian artifacts include manuals or books of magic containing principles for and methods of dream interpretation. Individuals with exceptional insight and religious sensitivity developed skills in this area. It is against this background that Joseph's ability to interpret dreams should be understood.

Pharaoh's cupbearer and baker both have dreams that they are unable to interpret. Though these dreams contain details that relate to the responsibilities they once held in the royal court, their present imprisonment and the uncertainty regarding their fate make them very anxious about the meaning of these dreams. Joseph perceives that anxiety and inquires about its cause. Their replies indicate that their apprehension stems from the absence of a dream interpreter, not from the dreams themselves. Joseph has already demonstrated his facility in dream interpretation (37:5-10). He offers his services, but he takes no credit for his competence. Rather, he insists that the ability to interpret comes from God, not from any occult practice he might have learned.

Aspects of the dream of the cupbearer are both realistic and allegorical. He probably did tend the vine that produced grapes that were crushed into drink that was handed to Pharaoh, so he would certainly understand much of Joseph's interpretation. Still, how is he to understand the three branches? Joseph insists that the three branches stand for the three days within which the cupbearer's fate will be determined. At that time, "Pharaoh will lift up your head" (v. 13). This phrase suggests a throne room scene in which the suppliant cupbearer with bowed head kneels before his ruler. The phrase means that Pharaoh will show him favor, will restore him to his former office with all of the responsibilities and privileges this entails.

The only compensation Joseph asks of the cupbearer is that, once he has been reinstated in the good graces of Pharaoh, he might intercede on Joseph's behalf. He explains that though he is a foreigner, and the trustworthiness of foreigners is usually suspect, he is a victim of human trafficking. Furthermore, the accusations made against him while in the service of Potiphar are false. The trust the chief jailer placed in him and his own willingness and ability to provide an interpretation of the cupbearer's dream should be evidence of his innocence and goodwill.

The baker is encouraged by the positive interpretation of the cupbearer's dream, and so he relates his own dream to Joseph. His dream contains many elements similar to those of the cupbearer, some realistic and others figurative. The final detail of the dream suggests negligence and should have alerted the baker to a possible unfavorable interpretation.

Joseph uses the very words he used previously (vv. 18-19a; see vv. 12-13a). In fact, he also tells the baker that "Pharaoh will lift up your head." This time, however, the phrase has almost the opposite meaning. Instead of implying that Pharaoh will show the baker favor, it means that the baker will be executed. The gravity of the baker's offense is implied by the announcement of the violation of his corpse. This detail of the interpretation must have been particularly disturbing, since Egyptians usually took great pains to show honor to corpses, believing that mistreatment of a corpse would deny the person peace in the afterlife. For this reason they mummified the dead.

Joseph's interpretation proves accurate, for on the third day Pharaoh assembles his servants for a feast celebrating his birthday. On such occasions, it was quite customary for rulers to grant amnesty to those guilty of certain crimes. Pharaoh does just that. Precisely as Joseph announced, Pharaoh restores the cupbearer to his former place of importance, but he condemns the baker to a horrible death. One might expect that Joseph's skill in dream interpretation would be rewarded. But it is not to be—at least not yet. In his joy at having been reinstated, the cupbearer completely forgets about Joseph, and so Joseph remains in prison.

Pharaoh's Dream (Gen 41:1-32)

After two years Joseph's ability to interpret dreams is called upon once again. This time it is Pharaoh who requires his assistance. This third instance of Joseph's ability to interpret dreams makes clear a certain pattern in such narratives. In each case, the dreams corresponded to their specific context: Joseph's dreams are related to his status within his family; the court officials' dreams pertain to their authorized duties; Pharaoh's dreams deal with the welfare of his kingdom.

The magicians and wise men of Pharaoh's court are unable to interpret the dreams satisfactorily. Either these men lack the insight needed to understand the dreams or they are afraid to propose a negative interpretation for fear of being punished for bringing bad news. The cupbearer now recalls the apprehension he himself experienced when he was unable to understand his own earlier dreams, and he remembers Joseph's extraordinary ability. Admitting his negligence in not bringing Joseph's competence to the attention of Pharaoh at that time, he explains what took place in the past. Impressed by what he hears, Pharaoh sends for Joseph.

Before Joseph can appear before Pharaoh, he must be made presentable. In keeping with the Egyptian penchant for neatness, his face is shaved, his hair is cut short, and he is dressed in clean clothes. Once again, clothing plays an important role in Joseph's story. Following court protocol, Pharaoh speaks first, stating that he has heard of Joseph's ability. Joseph corrects Pharaoh, insisting that it is God and not human, mantic skill that interprets dreams. This is a bold act, because the Egyptians considered Pharaoh divine, and one does not correct a deity. Speaking in this way, Joseph is probably arguing that his God, not some deity worshiped by the Egyptians, is exercising power in Pharaoh's land.

Surprisingly, Pharaoh takes no offense at this bold statement of a foreign prisoner. Instead, he recounts his dreams. The symbolism in the first dream is striking. The Nile was not only the river along which Egyptian civilization developed but also believed to be the womb from which the nation was born. Cattle were to the land of Egypt what sheep were to the land from which Joseph came. Besides this, the cow was a sacred animal associated with the goddess Hathor and considered a major symbol of fertility. Seven is universally a significant number, implying fullness of blessing. Most likely, the rise of the fat, sleek cows from the Nile has something to do with fertility coming from the river.

It is the meaning of the ugly, thin cows that devour the fat, sleek ones that perplexes Pharaoh.

The second dream is no less intriguing. The underlying theme in both dreams is the same, though their details differ. Here too the number seven plays an important role. The ears of grain reflect Egypt's importance as the breadbasket of its geographic region. The regular rising and receding of the Nile left the land adjacent to it rich for farming. Despite the richness of the land, there is always the threat of a hot, dry, dust-laden wind that originates in the desert. On occasion, this wind is able to produce sandstorms that can obliterate an entire crop. Pharaoh would certainly know this, but he might still question why the thin ears of grain devour the full ones.

Since Pharaoh brought Joseph into his presence precisely for the purpose of interpreting his dreams, Joseph shows no hesitation in doing so. After interpreting the two dreams, he makes a dangerously bold statement, claiming that it is God, and not Pharaoh, who is determining the future of Egypt. He declares this three times (vv. 25, 28, 32). The seriousness of such a theological claim cannot be overstated. It challenges Pharaoh's pretensions of divinity. Despite the audacity of the statement, Joseph is not punished. Rather, Pharaoh continues to listen to his interpretation.

Joseph's ability to interpret Pharaoh's dreams corresponds to a story common to many cultures in which a person of low rank is called upon to solve a problem that the wise men of the nation are unable to solve; he fearlessly does so and is rewarded by being raised to a position of prominence. Such a rags-to-riches story fascinated the ancients, and it continues to do so in each succeeding age.

Second in the Land (Gen 41:33-57)

Joseph is manifestly bold in stepping forward and interpreting Pharaoh's dreams even though he is not a skilled, professional interpreter. Now he fearlessly suggests a comprehensive plan whereby food is collected and conserved for later distribution on a national, and even international, scale. His insight in this matter is remarkable, for he is neither a practiced agriculturalist nor an experienced organizer or manager of a nationwide program such as he is advocating. He comes from a family of tribal sheepherders who live relatively independent lives on the outskirts of villages or small towns. His only managerial experience was as majordomo of Potiphar's household and overseer of a royal prison. His plan is daunting, but Pharaoh recognizes its merits.

This is the third time that Joseph's extraordinary talent impresses the one who exercises authority over him; first there was Potiphar, then the chief jailer, and now Pharaoh. In the first two instances, Joseph was rewarded by being promoted to the highest position possible without any change to his basic circumstances. He remained a servant of Potiphar but was put in charge of his entire household; he remained a prisoner but became the overseer of all the other prisoners. Here, Pharaoh not only installs Joseph as the second most important person in the entire land of Egypt but also releases him from prison.

Ancient Egyptian history contains several reports of Asiatic slaves rising to power in the land of Egypt. One of the best-known instances occurred during the Eighteenth Dynasty of Egypt, in the reign of Akhenaten, a man who was believed to have Semitic background. Akhenaten is frequently called the heretic pharaoh, because he closed the major shrines in the land, forbidding the worship of all gods but Aten, the sun-disc god whom Akhenaten himself worshiped. At his death, the governing structure he established was destroyed by those who wished to rid Egypt of any remnant of Akhenaten's rule. Some commentators believe that the entire land was purged of foreign—including Semitic—influence. This period of Egyptian history might serve as a backdrop for the story of Joseph, his rise to power, and the eventual oppression of his family after his death.

Joseph's installation as vizier of the land follows the customary Egyptian protocol. A signet ring was usually a sign of victory. Because it was used to validate important documents, it served as a kind of signature of the wearer. When Pharaoh places his ring on Joseph's finger, he is granting Joseph the authority of his own signature, to use as Joseph sees fit. Egyptian officials dressed in high-quality linen. In fact, the word "linen" is actually an Egyptian word. Here again, clothing plays a key role in Joseph's life. Like the robe given him by his father, this garment with which Pharaoh clothes him sets Joseph apart from the others. Now, even from afar, Joseph can be recognized as an important person in the land. This investiture ceremony indicates that Joseph is a new man.

Even today a gold chain, sometimes with a medal, frequently serves as a reward for distinction in social or government endeavors, military service, or athletic competition. Joseph is rewarded for his exemplary service to Pharaoh in interpreting his dreams and to the entire nation of Egypt for proposing a plan that will save the whole people during the time of famine. Finally, he is awarded a chariot. Though chariots were also instruments of war, here it signifies Joseph's status as second in the land, for heralds are assigned to run ahead of him and summon the people to pay him homage. Having ceremonially installed Joseph, Pharaoh then solemnly proclaims the young man's new position and the extent of his authority.

Joseph's installation is a public event, one that makes clear the role that he is to play in the lives of the people. He is given a new Egyptian name and a new Egyptian wife. His new name, צָפְנַת פַּעְנֵחַ (Zaphenath-paneah), means "God speaks; he lives." It refers to the role that Joseph has played in the affairs of the Egyptian nation. His wife's name is אָסְנַת (Asenath), which means "belonging to the Egyptian goddess Neit." She is the daughter of On, a highly respected Egyptian priest. Marriage to her reinforces Joseph's status in the land.

The marriage practices in Egypt are as gender-biased as are those in Mesopotamia and Canaan. The daughter of the priest of On is given to Joseph as reward for his success in dream interpretation and national economic planning, in the same way as the signet ring, the chain, and the chariot are given to him. Though of higher standing, she is still considered a possession. There is no ethnic concern here for purity of bloodline, as there was in the case of Rebekah and Isaac (24:27). Nor is there a relationship of love, as there was between Rachel and Jacob (29:18). Rather, Joseph is given a wife with social standing derived from the prominence of her father, a sociopolitical gesture.

A change in name is always a sign of a change in identity, as was the case with his ancestors Abram, Sarai, and Jacob. Though Joseph's new name is Egyptian in origin, its meaning is grounded in his faith in the God who appeared to his ancestors. It is that God who, through Joseph, now directs the fortunes of Egypt. Joseph is far removed from his original family and from its customs. He is now an official in the hierarchal structure of Egyptian governance, and in that position he most likely participates in the official state cult; he has been given an Egyptian name and has entered into an exogamous marriage with the daughter of a priest of the Egyptian god Re. For all practical purposes, Joseph is now an Egyptian.

The sons that Joseph fathers are named מְנַשֶּׁה (Manasseh), which means "making to forget," and אֶפְרַיִם (Ephraim), which means "fertile land." These names exemplify Joseph's detachment from his former life in Canaan. He has forgotten his father's household and the hardships he endured because of his brothers' betrayal, and he is now firmly ensconced in a new and fertile land. The sons are mentioned here because they foreshadow their much later importance in the story of Joseph's family of origin.

The famine that often accompanies climate change was always a threatening possibility in the ancient Near East. A shift in rainfall could be very destabilizing. In Egypt, if the Nile did not rise at its customary time or to its normal height, crops would not be planted on time or might wither for lack of water, and harvests would not supply the food needed for a large population. If a nation like Egypt, which normally produced an extensive crop, would suffer in this way, how much more would the smaller neighboring nations suffer? The biblical story has already noted how such famines affected the ancestors and their families. Abram moved to Egypt for a time, because of famine in the land (12:10); Isaac suffered a similar fate (26:1). Egyptian records report that Egypt frequently provided food for its starving neighbors. Therefore, the biblical reports of travel to Egypt to acquire food during times of famine are well-founded in ancient history. Here, such a situation sets the stage for a family reunion.

Despite the hardships that Joseph has faced, God has been with him throughout, protecting him and providing good fortune to those who have been kind to him. Thus, the fortunes of Egypt unfold just as Joseph predicted they would. It has taken a long time for the first part of his own earlier dream to materialize: "Suddenly my sheaf rose and stood upright" (37:7a). It will take a famine before the second part of that dream unfolds: "then your sheaves gathered around it, and bowed down to my sheaf" (37:7b).

Contemporary Reading: God Lifts Up

With the exception of the episode with the wife of Potiphar, these stories focus exclusively on Joseph and the men with whom he interacts. They do contain themes, however, that impact the lives of women as well. Chief among them is a theme that seems to run through the entire complex of stories, a theme that shows that those who are vulnerable and underprivileged are often lifted up by God and granted security and good fortune. A second theme, closely related to this yet quite distinct, cautions against ethnic or racial bias, demonstrating that it might be the disdained individual who becomes the agent of God's blessing for others.

Chapter 17

"God Sent Me Here ahead of You"
(Gen 42:1–45:28)

The story of Joseph's revelation of his true identity weaves together several important themes. The most obvious one is the apparent abuse of power. Taking full advantage of his administrative position in Egypt, Joseph places his brothers in various situations that jeopardize either their freedom or their safety. He does so in order to test the depth and character of their commitment to their father Jacob and the strength of the fraternal ties that bind them to each other. This plan raises some questions: Is such testing legitimate? Is it really an abuse? Or is it a necessary ploy meant to test his brothers' sincerity? Under the circumstances, do the ends justify the means? Could Joseph have discovered their trustworthiness in any other way? Only after the brothers have proven that they finally have achieved some level of integrity does Joseph reveal himself and initiate the process of reconciliation, the prominent theme of the story.

The Trip to Egypt (Gen 42:1-24)

Once again Jacob becomes an important character in the story. He sends ten of his sons to procure grain from Egypt. Only Benjamin, the youngest, the son of Rachel and the full brother of Joseph, stays behind. Sending ten sons is a wise move on Jacob's part, for this means that the bags of ten sons will be filled with grain rather than the bags of only one. Jacob's reluctance to send Benjamin is clearly stated. He is afraid that some disaster will sweep this son away as had been the case with Joseph. Evidently he has not learned from sad experience that showing favoritism to one son can enrage the others.

It is unexpected that Joseph, a man of such stature in the land of Egypt, is personally involved in the distribution of food. Such a job presumably would be performed by someone less important, perhaps one of the appointed overseers. The grain stored in various granaries throughout the land is probably limited to the needs of the local population, while people coming from outside of Egypt are required to present their petitions directly to Joseph. This arrangement could very well be a way of ensuring equitable distribution. Whatever the reason, Joseph's personal involvement makes possible his encounter with his brothers.

Joseph immediately recognizes his brothers. Perhaps their manner of dress identifies them as inhabitants of Canaan; perhaps their personal characteristics reveal who they are. He recognizes them, but they do not recognize him. After all, he is clean shaven with short hair, and he is dressed like an Egyptian. Furthermore, they are prostrate on the ground before Joseph, having come in a humbled state to ask for food, and so they are not likely to stare at him directly. Near Eastern protocol forbids such behavior. Their very first act is one that brings to realization the second part of the dream Joseph had so many years ago: "your sheaves . . . bowed down to my sheaf" (37:7b). Finally, Joseph speaks to them through an interpreter, and so they do not hear his voice. The brother they sold into slavery so many years ago is the last person they would expect to find in the guise of an Egyptian official.

Joseph speaks to them in a commanding voice, immediately establishing the nature of the power relationship that is operative. He accuses them of being spies, an accusation that is not incomprehensible, since the northeast border of Egypt, the point at which inhabitants of Canaan enter the country, is dangerous. It is not inconceivable that spies might infiltrate Egypt from that direction. The brothers protest their innocence, addressing Joseph with the honorific title "my lord" and referring to themselves as his servants (v. 10). In the process of defending themselves, they reveal that they have a brother at home with their father, and in the past they had yet another brother who is now gone. Joseph knows they are referring to him. At no time do the brothers or Joseph make mention of their sister Dinah. It is almost as if the only importance she has in the story of Jacob is simply as the victim of the lust of Shechem (Gen 34).

Joseph uses the information about Benjamin as the reason for the test he will put to them: "As Pharaoh lives, you shall not leave this place unless your youngest brother comes here!" (v. 15). Joseph does not trust his brothers because of his earlier experience with them. After all, they had no love for him when he was his father's favorite. What proof does he have that they treat Benjamin differently? The brothers conclude that the predicament in which they find themselves is just recompense for the vile manner in which they treated Joseph in the past. Unbeknownst to them, Joseph understands what they are saying, and he is overcome with emotion. He demands that one of the brothers remain in his custody as surety. Simeon, the second son of Leah, is held in exchange for Benjamin, the second son of Rachel. It then falls to Reuben, the eldest of the family, to tell Jacob of the Egyptian official's demand.

Return to Canaan (Gen 42:25-38)

Joseph orders that the brothers' bags be filled with grain and, without informing them of his intentions, that the money paid for the grain be secretly placed in their bags. This action can hardly be seen as a demonstration of unqualified goodwill on Joseph's part, for he has already intimidated his brothers with his accusations of their spying. Discovery of the money can only compound their anxiety; having already been falsely accused of treachery, possession of the money will appear to be evidence of thievery. This ploy on the part of Joseph is meant to uncover the genuine character of his brothers.

A complex dilemma presents itself when the money is discovered. Should the brothers retrace their steps and return the money to Joseph, thus demonstrating innocence of any attempt to cheat him? But Joseph has already accused them of spying, though he had no corroborating evidence to support this accusation. How can they possibly expect him to believe that they are innocent of theft when the money in question is clearly in their possession? They decide that their best option is to continue on to Canaan and clarify this matter when they return to Egypt with Benjamin. They have already recognized the parallel between the circumstances in which they have found themselves in Egypt and those surrounding their earlier treatment of Joseph, and they judge the distress they are experiencing to be well-deserved.

On returning to Canaan, they tell Jacob what has transpired and what is expected of them in the future. They do not, however, tell their father that their own lives are in jeopardy if they do not follow Joseph's demand for Benjamin. Beside himself with grief, Jacob accuses his sons of afflicting him with the loss of yet another son. First Joseph is gone, then Simeon, and now Benjamin is in danger. When he refuses to surrender Benjamin, Reuben promises his father, on the life of his own two sons—a very serious pledge in a patriarchal society in which sons represented future prosperity—that he will protect Benjamin and will bring him home safely to his father. The other brothers know that earlier Reuben stood alone against them in defense of Joseph, and they are desperate that he will act courageously in Benjamin's defense now. Jacob does not know this, however, and he will not concede to the plan laid before him.

As far as Jacob is concerned, he loved only two sons, Joseph and Benjamin, the sons of his beloved Rachel. He has never come to see that it was his own favoritism that precipitated the envy of his other sons in the first place. Now he is willing to sacrifice Simeon for the sake of Benjamin. Jacob has not changed, but have the brothers? Do they harbor the same envy toward Benjamin as they did toward Joseph, even though Benjamin's favored status did not compare with the excesses lavished upon Joseph?

A Second Trip to Egypt (Gen 43:1-34)

The famine persists, the rations are soon consumed, and all the while, Simeon languishes in prison. Once again Jacob directs his sons to journey to Egypt for grain. This time the situation they face is far more complex. They are not simply foreigners dependent on the generosity of another nation. They are suspected spies, at least that is what they believe, and they have been warned not to return to Egypt without their brother Benjamin. Is Jacob willing to forfeit all of his sons for the sake of Benjamin? Judah declares that without Benjamin they will not return to Egypt. This is a most unusual statement, for in a patriarchal society, the word of the head of the household is considered the law.

Joseph's questioning, which sprang from his heartfelt desire to know how Jacob and Benjamin fared, is interpreted by Jacob and his other sons as a form of sinister interrogation. Judah insists that it is no longer simply a question of a choice between Benjamin and his brothers. There are now other people involved, other children who face the possibility of starvation if grain is not procured. Will Jacob choose Benjamin over the entire family, over the very future of the family? It is now Judah who sees the larger picture, not Jacob; it is now Judah who insists on the only course of action open to them. Jacob finally comes to his senses and concedes.

When Joseph sees that Benjamin is with the other brothers, he makes provisions for a sumptuous banquet to be held in Joseph's own house. His brothers become understandably apprehensive, for during their earlier trip Joseph treated them quite severely, accusing them of spying and taking one of their brothers into custody. Furthermore, they must presume that he is aware of the confusion regarding the money. Why this change of behavior? Is he really planning a banquet? Or is this a ploy to separate them from other travelers only to punish them more severely? Joseph's house manager reassures his brothers that they have no reason to fear him. He did indeed receive their initial payment. As for finding the money in their bags, he credits their God for having reimbursed them, a statement that once again points to the belief that God indirectly regulates the unfolding of history by acting through human beings.

The famine that struck this part of the world has made the sons of Jacob dependent on Egyptian generosity. Despite this, they are shown the kind of Near Eastern hospitality accorded guests of honor. Their personal needs are met, and their animals are tended. This apparent cordiality is dispelled when Joseph appears, however, for his brothers prostrate themselves before him in humble obeisance as they offer him the gifts their father sent with them. Without realizing it, they once again actualize Joseph's earlier dream of them bowing before him (37:5-9). Joseph asks about their father, who is also his father. Is he well? This is probably not an idle question. Joseph must have known that Simeon's detainment and his own demand for Benjamin's presence caused Jacob great consternation. Therefore, Joseph's interest is probably genuine. His brothers assure him of Jacob's good health and then they prostrate themselves once more.

Joseph certainly knows who Benjamin is, but he inquires as to the young man's identity. When he utters a prayer for Benjamin's good fortune, he is again overcome with emotion. He quickly leaves the room, lest his brothers become aware of his emotional state. When he regains his composure, he returns and orders that the meal be served. Proper protocol is observed. Since Egyptians generally considered it beneath their dignity to eat with foreigners, Joseph eats separate from his guests. By his orders, the brothers sit according to seniority, a fact that amazes them, for they wonder how Joseph has come to the knowledge of such intimate family matters.

As the meal progresses, it becomes clear that Benjamin is being treated as the guest of honor, for much more food is given to him than to any of the others. This is an example of reversal of social custom, for the senior member is usually the one to whom deference is shown.

The Test (Gen 44:1-34)

The brothers are ready to leave Egypt and Joseph instructs his steward to fill their bags with far more grain than was requested, along with the money paid for the purchase. Joseph once again conspires against his brothers by placing his own silver cup in Benjamin's bag. This cup is valuable, not only because it is made of precious metal, but also because it is used as a divining cup. Such a method of divination was quite common in the ancient Near East. The practice consisted of the addition of a few drops of oil into a cup of wine. The configurations that resulted from this mixture were then read in order to discover the future.

At the command of Joseph, one of his stewards demands, "Why have you stolen *my* silver cup?" (v. 4b). Confident of their own innocence, the brothers insist that the guilty one should be put to death and, because of their association with him, the others should be made Joseph's slaves. The severity of the punishment suggested is meant to support their claim of innocence. Speaking in Joseph's name, the steward tempers the sentence. Only the guilty one will be punished, and the punishment will be slavery, not death. The others will be exonerated. Jacob's sons are relieved by this resolution, for they know that they are not guilty of the offense. They willingly and eagerly open their bags of grain in order to prove their innocence. Following Near Eastern protocol, the search begins with the eldest and moves to the youngest. The men are in disbelief when the cup is found in Benjamin's bag. Stricken with grief and in fraternal solidarity, they rend their garments, a sign of profound mourning. They return to Egypt to face Joseph.

Just as Judah acted as spokesperson for the others in convincing Jacob to allow Benjamin to travel with them to Egypt, so now he acts as their spokesperson before Joseph. The brothers throw themselves down before

Joseph in complete submission. Protocol dictates, however, that Joseph, the dignitary, speak first. He begins his remarks not with the issue of justice but with the question of reasonableness. They should have known that their offense would be discovered, particularly since Joseph possesses powers of divination. With this allusion to his extraordinary abilities, Joseph reinforces his stature.

Judah does not protest their innocence, as the brothers had when apprehended by Joseph's steward. Instead, he seems to surrender to what he considers to be God's will. Judah concedes that all the brothers are guilty, and the dilemma in which they find themselves is proof that God has now uncovered that guilt. Therefore, if the one in whose possession the cup was found must face a life of slavery, all the brothers deserve the same punishment. The day of reckoning has now dawned, and they have no defense in the light of it.

Listening to Judah, who now acknowledges his own culpability and that of his brothers, Joseph must have remembered how Judah had previously conspired with the others to sell him to the Ishmaelites who were traveling to Egypt (37:26-27). The similarity between that incident and the present situation is striking. In both instances, Jacob's favorite son is innocent yet he faces slavery in Egypt. This is precisely the scenario Joseph has planned, for in it he hopes to discover whether or not his brothers have changed. In order to achieve this, he insists that only the one in whose bag the cup was found will be committed to slavery.

Judah's speech (vv. 18-34) is the longest and most impassioned speech in the entire book of Genesis. Though he is arguing against Joseph's stated plan, he does so with the greatest respect, consistently acknowledging that Joseph's nobility surpasses all but that of Pharaoh. He speaks of their father with great affection and concern. He is an old man who has already lost one of the beloved sons of his favorite wife. The death of that son broke their father's heart, and they cannot bear to submit him to such anguish a second time. He acknowledges that their father favors the sons of a wife who is not their mother. Years ago, this admission would have enraged Judah and his brothers. Now, the very same circumstances elicit devotion. Rather than allow the favored son to suffer, Judah pleads for his safety.

This is the first time that Joseph has heard of the anguish his father suffered when he thought that Joseph, his beloved son, had lost his life. He realizes that losing Benjamin would put Jacob through the same suffering, and perhaps the old man is not strong enough to endure it a second time.

The brothers might not have been moved by Jacob's earlier grief, but they certainly are concerned about their father now. Judah begs Joseph, for the sake of their father, to take him as a slave rather than their brother. This willingness to sacrifice himself for his brother is the Bible's first example of vicarious suffering, the suffering of one person in the place of another. It is very clear that Judah's principal concern is the comfort of their father.

The Truth Is Revealed (Gen 45:1-28)

Joseph is at last convinced that his brothers have truly changed. Though innocent of any transgression in this case, they submit to Joseph's accusation and offer themselves as ransom for their younger brother. In the face of this unselfishness, Joseph is once again overcome with emotion. He orders all of his attendants to leave the room. Then, alone with his brothers, he reveals his true identity: "I am Joseph." This is immediately followed by a heartfelt inquiry: "Is my father still alive?" (v.3). The brothers are paralyzed with disbelief, and so Joseph repeats his self-identification; this time he adds a detail that only the real Joseph would have known: "Joseph, whom you sold into Egypt" (v. 4). It has been more than twenty years since they have seen their younger brother. Now this clean-shaven, short-haired, chief official of the Egyptian government claims to be their own flesh and blood. The guilt of their offense against him crashes down upon them.

The scene that unfolds contains one of the most touching demonstrations of reconciliation found in the Bible. Like the wronged Esau before him (33:4), Joseph initiates the process of reconciliation. Though the brothers acknowledge their culpability, the process begins with the forgiveness by the victim, not the repentance of the perpetrator. Not yet understanding Joseph's benevolence, the brothers fear possible reprisals. Joseph is not, however, intent on revenge. In fact, he seeks to quell their fears. He insists that their earlier betrayal of him was really part of God's plan. He makes this claim in four different ways: God sent him ahead of them so that he might save lives; that they themselves might be delivered; they have sold him, but it was really God who sent him to Egypt; God made him lord over all of the land (vv. 5-8). Each example shows that Joseph perceives himself as God's agent; he believes God was working through him for the benefit of others, making it clear that Joseph too has changed and matured since they were together in Canaan.

Throughout Joseph's speech, his brothers have been standing thunderstruck. At its conclusion, Joseph embraces his full brother Benjamin and both men weep. In a final gesture of forgiveness, he kisses all of the brothers as they weep. Only then are the others able to speak. Their devotion to their father and their concern for Benjamin have demonstrated their change of heart. Acknowledgment of guilt in their mistreatment of Joseph and their willingness to accept severe treatment at the hand of the Egyptian official as just punishment for that earlier crime are evidence of their repentance. It is Joseph's openheartedness, however, that makes reconciliation possible.

The designation "father of Pharaoh" might seem curious today, but it was not uncommon in the ancient world. It simply means one who gives counsel to Pharaoh. The title certainly corresponds to Joseph's position, for, as minister of state, he advises Pharaoh, makes decisions in his name, and oversees their execution. Joseph is indeed "lord of all his house and ruler over all the land of Egypt" (v. 8).

Pharaoh has known Joseph's ethnic background and slave status from the very beginning (41:12). Therefore, he and his courtiers are pleased when word comes to them that Joseph's brothers have come to Egypt. Since all in the land are indebted to Joseph, Pharaoh is moved to extend extraordinary favor toward Joseph's family of origin. He provides enough wagons to transport Jacob's entire family from Canaan to Egypt. He also assigns them the best land in Egypt where they will be near Joseph and will be able to thrive. Since, as Joseph predicted, the famine will last for five more years, this move will put an end to their need to journey to Egypt for grain.

Joseph furnishes his brothers with a change of fresh clothing, but he presents Benjamin with five sets of garments. Here again, clothing plays a significant role in the Joseph story. He also gives him a huge amount of silver. While Joseph's preference for Benjamin is certainly behind his exceptional generosity, this largesse might also reflect the need for some form of compensation. After all, Benjamin was an innocent victim in Joseph's ruse. His brother had demanded that he come down to Egypt and had then taken advantage of his vulnerability. Frequently, in the ancient world, one received double blessing as an external expression of one's vindication. It was considered evidence of the original innocence of that person who had been wrongly considered guilty (see Job 42:10).

The final scene brings the entire account of the trip to its conclusion. At first, Jacob does not believe the report his sons bring to him. This is understandable, considering the fact that they are frequently the bearers of bad news. They are the ones who led him to believe that Joseph had been torn to pieces by wild animals (37:32-33); they are the ones who told him that Benjamin's presence in Egypt was demanded (42:34). How can Jacob be expected to believe a story that seems so preposterous? When they recount everything that happened, however, and when Jacob sees the riches they brought back with them, his spirit revives and he announces, "I must go and see him before I die" (v. 28). Though in this account, Jacob appears to be an old man, broken by the loss of one beloved son and the possible loss of another, it was always in response to his directives that his sons traveled to Egypt for grain (42:2; 43:2). Here again, it is Jacob who decides on the trip.

Contemporary Reading: Suspicion

Since Joseph had been betrayed and exploited by his brothers, it is understandable that he would be suspicious of their motives when they met again. Many people today know what this is like. When those they should have been able to trust take advantage of them, they often put up barriers so that they will not be hurt again. At other times, unwilling to presume that someone can be trusted, they devise tests meant to demonstrate that person's trustworthiness. Women and men alike have become aware of and guard themselves against possible pitfalls of blind acceptance. This enables them eventually to be open to others.

Chapter 18

"They Came into Egypt"
(Gen 46:1–47:27)

The story underscores the importance of land management for the purpose of human survival. Joseph's initial plan to set aside a portion of the produce of the land during the years of abundant harvest demonstrates wise guardianship. His later plan of crop distribution, however, enacted when Egypt itself was stricken with famine, demonstrates how people's dependence on the fruits of the land can be used against them by those in power. Joseph's initial generosity in sharing with the needy is replaced by greed in the service of personal enrichment for Pharaoh and his family.

The Family in Egypt (Gen 46:1–47:12)

Once again Jacob takes center stage. Gone is the hidden involvement of God, directing the events of life through human agency. Instead, the narrative reverts to the experience of divine revelation through a dream. On the way to Egypt, Jacob stops to offer sacrifices at Beer-sheba, the place where God spoke to his father Isaac (26:23-25). Jacob's experience of God at this holy place is very similar to that of his father. In both instances: the deity is identified as the patron God of the ancestors; God makes the promise that is repeated again and again throughout the tradition: "I will make of you a great nation" (46:3; see 12:2; 18:18; 21:18). There is, however, a significant difference here. The earlier promise of greatness was meant to be fulfilled in the land of Canaan. Here, God promises that Jacob will be a great nation in Egypt.

Jacob's journey to Egypt is more than a trip. It is a major migration. He intends to settle in that land. The seriousness of this move cannot be overemphasized. For two generations Jacob's family has been promised a land of their own; little by little, they have acquired sections of that land. Moving out of that land now, without divine approval, could be considered a serious transgression against God. Nonetheless, God assures Jacob in a dream that this move is acceptable and that, in fact, God will go down to Egypt with him. Once again, the unique character of this God becomes clear, for every deity was thought to be bound to one place and one land. Such is not the case with this God, who is bound to a people, not to a parcel of land. Wherever the people travel, their God moves with them. In his vision, Jacob is assured that, though he will die peacefully in Egypt with Joseph closing his eyes, he will be buried with his ancestors in the land of promise.

The record of the names of the members of Jacob's family is simply a listing, not a true genealogy. While the names of Jacob's children are well-known and found in several other places (29:31–30:24; Exod 1:1-5), the names of some of the grandchildren are unique. Since names often refer to events that occur at the time of birth, some grandchildren bear the names of animals or places. Other names are theophonic in character, including a shortened form of a divine title. Though daughters and granddaughters are said to be included in the caravan (v. 7), only Jacob's daughter Dinah and his granddaughter Serah are explicitly named (vv. 15, 17). This listing admits its own male bias when it states that, in counting the number of people involved, it does not include the wives of Jacob's sons (v. 26). This is another example of the culture's disregard of the important roles played by women.

The reunion of Jacob and his long-lost son Joseph is quite moving. Since it was Judah who earlier acted as spokesperson before Joseph and offered himself as surety for Benjamin, he is now sent to Joseph by their father to announce the arrival of the family. Although he is the second most important man in all of Egypt, Joseph shows great honor to his father by going out to meet him. Such a show of deference was uncommon in Egyptian culture. When father and son see each other, they embrace and weep. Jacob's words are telling: "I can die now, having seen for myself that you are still alive" (v. 30). To the end, Jacob's favoritism is evident.

Once his family has arrived in Egypt, Joseph plans to go to Pharaoh in order to actualize the promises of land made to them. Before he does so, he directs his family in how to respond to the questions that Pharaoh will put to them. Since they come from Canaan, the bordering land from which treacherous people frequently entered Egypt, it is important that they not appear to be dangerous. They must assure Pharaoh that they have not come to infiltrate the land. Nor do they have any desire to rise in prominence in Egypt, as Joseph had, and thereby threaten to take over the total administration of the land. Nor should they appear to be simple squatters, living off the land of Egypt or dependent on the generosity of Pharaoh. Rather, they should identify themselves as self-sufficient shepherds with their own flocks and herds, people who plan to continue that livelihood in Goshen, a land not fit for the agriculture the Egyptians prefer but well suited for the grazing necessary for herding.

As custom dictates, Pharaoh opens the exchange, asking the brothers about their occupation. According Pharaoh the honor that is his due, Joseph's brothers acknowledge their status as resident aliens, neither citizens of the land nor foreigners merely passing through. Thus they appeal to the generosity of Pharaoh for food, a place to settle, and an opportunity to herd their livestock. Pharaoh outdoes himself in generosity. He not only makes the previously decided upon land available to Joseph's family but also suggests that if any of Joseph's brothers prove themselves to be extraordinary herders, he will put them in charge of Pharaoh's own livestock.

Joseph then presents his father Jacob to Pharaoh. The text says that Jacob blessed Pharaoh. Since blessing is both a way of greeting and a way of saying farewell, and since Jacob blesses Pharaoh both at the beginning of their conversation (v. 7) and at its end (v. 10), Jacob's blessing is simply an expression of respect. Pharaoh's earlier questions to the brothers dealt with their livelihood and their plans for the entire family. The question he puts to Jacob is personal: "How many are the years of your life?" (v. 8). The number given—130—probably means many years rather than his exact age. Jacob explains that they have been difficult years, for he and his ancestors before him have lived as resident aliens in the land of Canaan. Though he does not explicitly say it, perhaps he cannot help but think that, despite Pharaoh's benevolence, his family will continue to live as resident aliens, now in the land of Egypt.

Egypt's Agrarian Policy (Gen 47:13-27)

Most commentators agree that the section describing the agrarian policy put into effect in Egypt by Joseph is an etiological legend explaining how most of the land in Egypt came to be under the control of Pharaoh. They relate this policy to the conditions that prevailed in the fourteenth or thirteenth century BCE, during Egypt's Nineteenth Dynasty. The phrase "to this day" (v. 26) indicates that the policy was still in force at the time of the editor who appended it to the well-known story of Joseph. State-owned land must have appeared strange to those acquainted with life in Canaan, where the land was not under the authority of one ruler. Debt slavery was not unknown in the ancient world. In Mesopotamia and those lands under its rule, however, debt slaves were a part of the population and generally were freed after six years, a practice later observed in Israel as well (Deut 15:12).

Though harsh, Joseph's agrarian policy saved the people of Egypt from starvation. The narrative that recounts this policy portrays Joseph as a hero. In fact, it serves as an ethnic boast: a former Hebrew slave with no agrarian experience is shrewder than any of the Egyptian sages who, most likely, were acquainted with farming practices. An apparent injustice existed in the overall policy, however, and this injustice raises questions about Joseph's use and abuse of power.

The story states that there is no food in the land and, consequently, Egypt and Canaan are both languishing from the famine (v. 13). The people come to Joseph for some of the reserve food that was stored during the seven years of abundance. According to the earlier policy, however, 20 percent of their crop was contributed to the general reserve (41:34-35). The people are required now to buy back what they themselves had earlier saved and contributed to this reserve. Even if that food were originally a free gift, the present policy is taking advantage of the vulnerability of the people. The people's desperate need for food forces them to pay for their own reserves. Eventually this empties their pockets of money but fills the treasury of Pharaoh.

The famine continues, as does the people's need for food. Having depleted their finances, they are now forced to barter away their livestock. As a result, Pharaoh acquires countless flocks of sheep and herds of horses, cattle, and donkeys. The provisions obtained in this way last for only a year, and so the people are forced to return to Joseph once again. Now all they have to offer are their lands and themselves, and so they agree to enter into debt bondage.

Joseph provides the people with seed to sow in order to prevent the land from becoming desolate and the people from starving. The land that was once theirs now belongs to Pharaoh, however, and working on it makes them Pharaoh's indentured slaves. To add even more to their financial burden and to Pharaoh's windfall, they are required to surrender 20 percent of their harvest to him. Some commentators consider this a sign of generosity, since people were often required to submit as much as 40 percent of their crop to landowners.

Joseph's shrewd management certainly does save the people from starvation. On the other hand, it also enables Pharaoh to benefit from their plight. Several points should be highlighted here. The earlier statement about stockpiling the surfeit of grain during the years of plenty (41:34-35) challenges the justice of a policy that requires people to purchase their own reserves. Moreover, even without questioning this blatant injustice, the policy itself is biased. Not only does it disadvantage the majority of the people and bring about their financial enslavement, but their very disadvantage benefits those in power.

Furthermore, not all of the inhabitants of the land suffer from the famine or are forced into debt bondage. Jacob and his family have settled in Goshen where "they gained possessions in it, and were fruitful and multiplied exceedingly" (v. 27). It is only appropriate that Joseph cares for his family and that the story of Jacob's life ends on a positive note. Still, under the circumstances described in the broader story, the nepotism shown here favors foreigners while Egyptians are made to endure terrible hardship. The fairness of such a situation is questionable. In fact, this fruitfulness and extraordinary increase are later given as reasons for the Egyptians' antipathy toward Jacob's descendants and for their eventual enslavement in that land (Exod 1:7). Once again, favoritism plays an important role in the history of this family, and members of the family will eventually suffer because of it. The Egyptian priests are also exempt from this policy. They live off a fixed allowance supplied by Pharaoh and so their lands are not confiscated. Though not stated, they certainly also benefit from the sacrifices offered by the people in the temples where the priests officiate.

The account ends on a curious and troublesome note. The people are said to be grateful to Joseph for having saved their lives. They do not seem to realize that they are the victims not only of natural disaster but also of a burdensome, unjust administrative policy. As is so often the case with unjust systems, those who are disadvantaged often interiorize their oppression and do not see the injustice in it. They accept the circumstances as the way things are. As for Joseph, he has become part of the system. In fact, he is the architect and administrator of its oppressive agrarian policy. He is hardly a hero.

Contemporary Reading: Management or Exploitation?

There is something wrong with an economic system that benefits those in charge at the expense of the workers. That is precisely the situation in Egypt under the management of Joseph. This story might have been very popular in ancient Israel because it shows the shrewdness of an Israelite as compared to the gullibility of the Egyptians. Nevertheless, it still depicts social and economic exploitation.

In addition to his exploitative managerial approach, Joseph appears to have inherited his father's propensity for favoritism, a trait that will eventually cause great hardship to his own family whom he favors. Joseph, who has advanced to a prominent position in Egypt by exploiting others, should hardly be held up as a model to be emulated.

Chapter 19

"I Am about to Be Gathered to My People"
(Gen 47:28–50:26)

The stories of the ancestors of Israel come to a close with the account of the death and burial of Jacob, the one whose new name, Israel, will come to identify the people of God. The book of Genesis closes with the family living in relative peace in Egypt, enjoying a degree of prosperity. The stage is set for the next chapter in the drama.

Adoption and Blessing (Gen 47:28–48:22)

Jacob's frail condition prompts Joseph to visit his father and to bring his sons Manasseh and Ephraim with him. Jacob rallies at the news of the impending visit. He knows that what Joseph probably considers a family responsibility, namely, visiting an elderly parent, will actually be the occasion of a radical and permanent change in the makeup of the family, for Jacob intends to adopt Joseph's sons and make them his own legal heirs.

The ancestors to whom God made the promises all observed the custom of endogamous marriage. Thus, the promises were handed down through the appropriate bloodline, the legitimacy of the heirs dependent on the ethnic origin of the mother. Joseph married Asenath, the daughter of an Egyptian priest (41:45), however, and now Jacob wishes to make the offspring of an Egyptian woman his heirs on a par with his firstborn sons, Reuben and Simeon. This is certainly a significant move.

Jacob informs Joseph that, though God gave him many sons through Leah, Zilpah, and Bilhah, his beloved Rachel died giving birth to Benjamin.

Therefore, in order to increase Rachel's offspring, Jacob has decided to make Joseph's two sons, who are Rachel's grandsons, his own legitimate heirs. Any children born of Joseph after this, however, will be considered Joseph's offspring and will not share in the inheritance enjoyed by Manasseh and Ephraim. As head of the household, Jacob has the authority to make this momentous decision and to enact it. Still, he searches for some form of divine authentication of this move.

The deathbed scene is reminiscent of a much earlier event in Jacob's own life, when he received the blessing of his father Isaac (chap. 27). Like the earlier occasion, the present situation involves an aged father who suffers from failing eyesight, two brothers, and the transmission of a divine promise. Here, however, there is no deception. In fact, Jacob, the elderly father, is in full control of what is about to take place. In expressions of profound emotion, Jacob receives Joseph's sons and then kisses and embraces them. Having once again seen Joseph, Jacob is convinced that his life has been completely fulfilled, and he is ready to die.

The adoption consists of a rite of incorporation and a blessing. Such adoption took place at the knees of the one who was adopting. A man would take a child on his knee and, thereby, claim parental rights and responsibilities. Adult adoptees probably knelt at or stood next to the knees of the one adopting. When this rite is completed, Joseph stations his sons next to Jacob in order to receive the blessing, Manasseh on his right and Ephraim on his left. Laying hands on them signifies the transfer of Jacob's spirit onto them. Jacob then crosses his arms so that his right hand rests on the head of Ephraim, the younger of the two, and his left hand rests on the head of the older, Manasseh. Since the right hand is considered the hand of privilege, the gesture indicates that Ephraim is favored over Manasseh. Thinking that his father has made a mistake, Joseph attempts to correct Jacob's error. Jacob assures him that his action is deliberate, however, and his choice is intentional. This is yet another instance of the younger being preferred over the older.

Though the fruits of the blessing are meant for Ephraim and Manasseh, the blessing itself is directed toward Joseph. God is identified as the God of Jacob's ancestors, thus the blessing joins the present generation with those of the past. It holds a threefold promise: that the same God who protected Jacob will now protect his newly adopted sons; that these sons will remember his name and the names of his ancestors, a responsibility of sons in patriarchal societies; finally, and perhaps most important, that

God's promise of many descendants will be fulfilled in them. The tribes that stem from these newly adopted sons of Jacob will eventually form the core of the northern kingdom. In fact, that political entity will often be referred to as Ephraim.

Jacob's impending death adds solemnity to the occasion, for many ancient peoples believed that the dying had extraordinary insight into the future. Furthermore, a deathbed blessing was considered a last will and testament and, as such, was legally binding. The words spoken have performative force and, therefore, are irreversible. Jacob's blessing is not simply a pious wish that God might accomplish that for which he prays. The force of performative verbs indicates that his very words begin the actualization of what they describe. In other words, they not only describe what will take place in the future but actually begin the process that brings it about as well.

Jacob's final words are a comfort to both Joseph and to Jacob himself. He assures his favorite son that in the end, he, Joseph, will finally return to the land of Canaan. This promise recalls a similar promise that God made to Jacob, that his descendants would inherit the land promised to Abraham and Isaac (35:11). This promise was fulfilled when Jacob returned to the land after spending so many years in Paddan-aram. Here the same promise is made to Joseph, and it will be fulfilled when Jacob's sons return after spending many years in Egypt. Jacob then bequeaths to Joseph a portion of land that he earlier claimed as his own. Though the Hebrew is uncertain, most commentators identify it as Shechem, the place where Joseph's bones will eventually be buried (Josh 24:32). The city of Shechem is in the central part of Israel, the area where the Rachel tribes of Ephraim, Manasseh, and Benjamin eventually settle.

Last Testament (Gen 49:1-28)

Jacob's final words are really a collection of tribal sayings collected and arranged in the form of a last testament (see the Blessing of Moses in Deut 33). Though these sayings identify and describe Jacob's twelve sons, their content suggests that they really point to characteristics of the later Israelite tribes known by the names of these brothers. In ancient Israel, inheritance is transferred through the male line, and the later tribal federation assumes an exclusively male structure. This might explain why Dinah is not even mentioned in Jacob's last testament.

As firstborn, רְאוּבֵן (Reuben) is considered the fruit of his father's youthful sexual vigor. More than this, he is the heir of the birthright, a double portion of his father's possessions. Reuben is guilty, however, of one of the most heinous crimes a son can commit against his father. He had intercourse with Bilhah, one of Jacob's concubines (35:22). This act of contempt implied that Jacob had lost his sexual prowess and, therefore, was not fit to rule. In this patriarchal society, the reproductive potential of a man's wife or concubine was considered his possession. The personal concerns of the woman are not considered. Reuben appropriated what belonged to his father, and as punishment, the birthright and the other privileges of the firstborn are taken from him.

Simeon (שִׁמְעוֹן) and Levi (לֵוִי) also face recriminations. They are described as violent, bloodthirsty, and unscrupulous. They are called brothers, but this means more than being siblings of each other. They are also brothers of Dinah, and the reference here probably recalls their vengeful reaction to her rape at the hands of Shechem (Gen 34). As discussed earlier, their concern was less for Dinah's welfare than for the honor of their family and, therefore, their own reputation as protectors of the women of their household. Jacob earlier reprimanded them for behavior that actually threatened the safety of the entire family (34:30). Here he declares that they will be scattered throughout the land, thereby losing the cohesiveness needed for their survival as independent tribes.

The description of Judah is composed of three independent sayings. There is a play on the sounds of the name יְהוּדָה (Judah), the verb יוֹדוּךָ (yôdûkā; they praise you), and יָדְךָ (yādekā; hand), the image of rule or domination. The first word links the name with Leah's cry of joy at Judah's birth: "'This time I will praise YHWH'; therefore she named him Judah" (29:35). "Your hand" reinforces the notion of Judah's rule over his brothers. The three metaphors that characterize Judah all point to his royal character. This is reinforced by mention of the scepter and the staff, symbols of royalty. Finally, the foal and the donkey's colt are royal mounts, signifying peace, unlike the warlike horse. This description of Judah is very positive and totally disregards his shameful and unjust treatment of Tamar, his daughter-in-law. Neither his misconduct nor her bravery is remembered here.

Though Zebulun is not the next born, the saying describing him follows. The references to the sea are difficult to understand because the area of Canaan in which the tribes settled is landlocked. Sidon was a

Phoenician city on the northeastern shore of the Mediterranean Sea. Since the name זְבוּלוּן (Zebulun) is associated with זְבֻל (*zᵉbūl*; high dwelling), it might simply refer to a geographic designation. Like the strong-boned donkey, יִשָּׂשכָר (Isaachar) lacks initiative, "lying down between the sheepfolds" (v. 14). Only when he feels secure is he willing to act as a beast of burden. He pays for this security, however, with his freedom. Dan is described by means of a play on his name and an animal metaphor. The name דָּן (Dan) is derived from the verb דִּין (*dîn*; to judge). When Dan was born, Rachel declared that God had vindicated her barrenness by giving her a son through Bilhah, her maidservant (30:6). Though a small tribe, Dan is forceful and furtive, like a viper or horned adder whose attack is sudden and deadly.

The name גָּד (Gad) is derived from the verb גָּדַד (*gādad*; to invade). The saying merely points to Gad's experience of warding off raids of desert nomads. Asher's destiny is also a play on his name אָשֵׁר, which comes from the word "happy." At his birth, Leah exclaimed, "Happy am I! For the women will call me happy" (30:13). Asher is promised a happy and prosperous life. Naphtali is described as an agile and free-running hind, suggesting that the tribe loves peace and enjoys a relatively tranquil existence.

Joseph's blessing is the longest, evidence once again of Jacob's preference for this son יוֹסֵף (Joseph), who is first characterized as a fruitful bough. A promise follows: he will be victorious over the misfortunes that he must face because God is his defense. A series of divine epithets not only names God but also characterizes God's protection of Joseph. The simplest and most familiar is the title "God of your father" (v. 25), a general term that identifies God as the patron deity of any one of the ancestors. More specifically, God is also well-known as the Mighty One of Jacob (v. 24b). Having protected his father Jacob, this God will surely protect Joseph. (This title will be used widely in the future; see Ps 132:2, 5; Isa 49:26; etc.) In his earlier adoption blessing, Jacob already referred to God as a caring Shepherd. The title Rock of Israel, however, is found in only one other place (2 Sam 23:3). It suggests strength and stability, a power that is dependable. Finally, God is called the "Almighty," the title revealed by God to Abraham when God initiated the covenant with that ancestor (17:1). God was also called upon by this name when Isaac blessed Jacob as he left for Paddan-aram in search of a wife (28:3), at Luz/Bethel when God changed Jacob's name to Israel (35:11), and when Jacob gave his permission for Benjamin to travel to Egypt (43:14). This is the God who now watches over Joseph, the one who is personally involved in his life, who cares for him, and who is all-powerful.

Numerous and varied blessings of fertility are in store for Joseph: the fertility of the land, the blessings of the beasts, a multitude of descendants. Jacob claims that the blessing he now bestows on Joseph will far surpass any of these earlier promises. The eternal mountains and the everlasting hills represent abundance and endurance; Joseph's blessings will surpass even these. Finally, the reference to Joseph's head and brow points to the ritual act of placing one's hands on the head of the one receiving the blessing. This gesture signifies the transmission of power from one to another. With this gesture, power is transferred from Jacob to Joseph.

The final saying describes Benjamin as a ravenous wolf known for its cunning, prowess, and courage. This portrayal is in sharp contrast to the picture of the silent, younger brother depicted in the Joseph narrative. Formerly, he was the one about whom everyone is concerned; here, he is a military threat to his enemies. Jacob's last testament closes with an editorial comment that identifies the recipients of the sayings as both the individual sons of Jacob and the tribes of Israel.

Death and Burial (Gen 49:29–50:26)

Aware of his impending death, Jacob makes his sons take an oath that they will bury him in Canaan, in the cave at Machpelah that Abraham bought from Ephron the Hittite (23:8-11), because to be buried in a foreign land was considered a great misfortune. Jacob chooses to be buried with his ancestors, Abraham and Sarah, Isaac and Rebekah, rather than with his beloved wife Rachel (see 35:19-20). The phrase "gathered to his people" is a typical way of saying that he had a peaceful death after a fulfilling life (see the deaths of Abraham [25:8], Ishmael [25:7], and Isaac [35:29]).

The period for mourning Jacob's death lasts for seventy days, forty of which are required for the embalming process, which was considered essential if the spirit (Egyptian *ka*) and soul (Egyptian *ba*) were to find peace. Since the traditional period of mourning an Egyptian king was seventy-two days, the length of this period illustrates the high regard in which Jacob was held. At the completion of this period, Joseph requests permission from Pharaoh to honor the oath he made to his father, to bury Jacob with his ancestors in Canaan. Normal protocol requires that

Joseph make any request to Pharaoh in person. Funereal mourning customs usually make an exception to such protocol, however, for to appear before Pharaoh in mourning garb would be most inappropriate. Joseph promises to return to Egypt when this family responsibility is completed, and so Pharaoh grants Joseph's request.

The elaborate funeral arrangements made for Jacob rival those of Egyptian royalty. In addition to the dignity of embalming, the funeral cortege consists of Joseph's household, his brothers, and Jacob's household. Curiously, the text says that the children are left behind with the flocks and herds. Since they would not be left alone, one can presume that the women are also left behind. This means that here women and children are not considered part of the household, evidence of a very troublesome bias. The male cortege is accompanied by members of Pharaoh's own household as well as various other Egyptian officials. They are also given a military escort, which is further evidence of the importance of Joseph's father and an obvious guarantee of protection for the cortege during the long journey to Canaan.

They travel around the southern tip of the Dead Sea and stop just east of the Jordan River at the threshing floor at Atad. Though a more direct route would have taken them north into Canaan and then east to Mamre, the itinerary sketched foreshadows the route that Jacob's descendants will take much later when they escape Egypt and return to the land promised by God to their ancestors. A solemn memorial service is conducted there. The mourning lasts for the typical seven-day period. The Canaanite inhabitants are so impressed by the grief that they have witnessed that they call the site אָבֵל מִצְרַיִם (Abel-Mizraim), which means "mourning of the Egyptians." The cortege then continues its journey until it reaches the appointed burial place. God's final promise to Jacob has now been fulfilled: "I will also bring you up again" (46:4). After Jacob's body is placed in the cave, they all return to Egypt.

The brothers are worried that Joseph's earlier reconciliation with them was merely a gesture to satisfy their father's concern. With Jacob dead, they fear that Joseph's true feelings toward them will surface and they will be made to suffer the consequences of their earlier treachery. Hence, they beg for his forgiveness. In a threefold manner, they confess their culpability: they are guilty of פֶּשַׁע (*pesha*; crime), of חַטָּאת (*ḥaṭṭā't*; wrong), and of רָעָה (*rā'â*; harm). The brothers throw themselves down at his feet, actualizing yet again Joseph's earlier dream: "Suddenly my sheaf rose and stood upright; then your sheaves gathered around it, and bowed down to my sheaf" (37:7).

Joseph is quick to allay their fears. He assures them that his show of reconciliation is genuine. He reiterates his conviction that, though they intended harm, God intended good, and this good would benefit many, even the brothers themselves. Joseph describes what God promised so many years ago to Abram: "In you all the families of the earth shall be blessed" (12:3). Joseph not only forgives his brothers but also promises to provide for them and for their children, just as he did when their father was alive.

Joseph lives the remainder of his life in Egypt. He is 110 years old at his death, an ideal number in ancient Egyptian thought rather than a precise age. In most ancient cultures, a long life is considered a blessing from God. This age signifies that Joseph has been truly blessed. This belief is reinforced by the claim that he lives to see his great-grandchildren. Furthermore, just as his father Jacob adopted his own two sons, so Joseph adopts one of his grandsons. This statement about adopting Machir is probably more etiological than historical, providing an explanation for the appearance of this name along with those of other tribes (Judg 5:14).

Before he dies, Joseph assures his brothers that their sojourn in Egypt will not be permanent. Instead, God will bring them out of this land and will lead them into the land promised to Abraham, Isaac, and Jacob. The story of the ancestors opened with this promise: "Go from your country and your kindred and your father's house to the land that I will show you" (12:1). It now closes with the same promise.

Joseph lived his entire adult life as an Egyptian. When he comes to die, however, he makes his brothers swear that they will take his remains with them when they return to Canaan so that he too might be buried in the land of his ancestors. This wish demonstrates his undying loyalties to his family and to his land of origin. The account describing his presence and that of his family in Goshen links this first chapter in the history of Israel with the tradition of their sojourn in Egypt, which will unfold in the book of Exodus. While this episode is the end of the beginning, it points to the future of Joseph's descendants.

Contemporary Reading: Left Out

The reports of the last days of Jacob and those of his death and burial are both elaborate, demonstrating the high regard in which he was held by all, and troublesome, because of the patent gender bias of both the reports and the events described. The fact that deathbed blessings were given only to sons, though problematic today, was acceptable as a patrilineal practice in ancient Israel. The fact that wives and daughters were not included in the burial and that, in this report, women and children were not considered part of the household, however, is outrageous. It is an extreme example of how, even today, women are often prevented from full participation in situations that touch their very lives.

In a way, this last section of the book of Genesis summarizes the state of affairs of people depicted in the entire book. It also highlights the predicament of those reading the book. While the biblical portrayal of those in society who are vulnerable (women, children, foreigners) cannot be changed, contemporary readers need not and should not allow themselves to be constrained by the biased details of a story. The revelatory value of the story is in its religious message, not in the character of its cultural telling.

Works Consulted

Bach, Alice. *Women in the Bible*. New York: Routledge, 1999.

Bach, Alice, ed. "A Story of Reading the Story of Genesis 39." In *Women, Seduction, and Betrayal in Biblical Narrative*. Cambridge: Cambridge University Press, 1997.

Bagnall, Roger S. "The Environment." In *Egypt in Antiquity*. Princeton, NJ: Princeton University Press, 1993.

Bal, Mieke. *Lethal Love: Feminist Literary Readings of Biblical Love Stories*. Bloomington: Indiana University Press, 1987.

Bal, Mieke, ed. *In Anti-Covenant: Counter-Reading Women's Lives in the Hebrew Bible*. Journal for the Study of the Old Testament Supplement Series #81. Sheffield, UK: Almond Press, 1989.

Bauckham, Richard. *The Bible and Ecology: Rediscovering the Community of Creation*. Waco, TX: Baylor University Press, 2010.

Bellis, Alice Ogden. *Helpmates, Harlots, Heroes: Women's Stories in the Hebrew Bible*. Louisville, KY: Westminster/John Knox, 1994.

Binz, Stephen J. *Women of the Torah: Matriarchs and Heroes of Israel*. Grand Rapids, MI: Brazos Press, 2011.

Bird, Phyllis A. "The Harlot as Heroine: Narrative Art and Social Presupposition in Three Old Testament Texts." *Semeia* 46 (1989): 124.

———. *Missing Persons and Mistaken Identities: Women and Gender in Ancient Israel*. Minneapolis, MN: Fortress Press, 1997.

———. "'Male and Female He Created Them': Gen 1:27b in the Context of the Priestly Account of Creation." *Harvard Theological Review* 74 (1981): 129–59.

Brenner, Athalya. *I Am . . . Biblical Women Tell Their Own Stories*. Minneapolis, MN: Fortress Press, 2005.

————. *The Israelite Woman: Social Role and Literary Type in Biblical Narrative*. Sheffield, UK: JSOT Press, 1985.

Brenner, Athalya, ed. *A Feminist Companion to Genesis*. Sheffield, UK: Sheffield Academic Press, 1997.

Brenner, Athalya, Archie Chi Chung Lee, and Gale A. Yee, eds. *Genesis*. Minneapolis, MN: Fortress Press, 2010.

Brenner, Athalya, and Carole Fontaine, eds. *A Feminist Companion Reading of the Bible: Approaches, Methods and Strategies*. Sheffield, UK: Sheffield Academic Press, 1997.

Brett, Mark G. *Genesis: Procreation and the Politics of Identity*. New York: Routledge, 2000.

Bronner, Leila Leah. *From Eve to Esther: Rabbinic Reconstructions of Biblical Women*. Louisville, KY: Westminster/John Knox, 1994.

————. *Stories of Biblical Mothers: Maternal Power in the Hebrew Bible*. Lanhan: MD: University Press of America, 2004.

Büchmann, Christina, and Celia Spiegel, eds. *Out of the Garden: Women Writers on the Bible*. New York: Faucett Columbine, 1994.

Campbell, Antony F., and Mark A. O'Brien. *Sources of the Pentateuch: Texts, Introduction, Annotations*. Minneapolis, MN: Fortress Press, 1993.

Clines, David J. A. "The Significance of the 'Sons of God' Episode (Genesis 6:1-4) in the Context of the 'Primeval History' (Genesis 1–11)." *Journal for the Study of the Old Testament* 13 (1979): 33–46.

Cotte, Robert B., and David Robert Ord. *In the Beginning: Creation and the Priestly History*. Minneapolis, MN: Fortress Press, 1991.

Darr, Katheryn Pfisterer. *More Precious than Jewels: Perspectives on Biblical Women*. Louisville, KY: Westminster/John Knox, 1991.

Davies, Philip R., and John Rogerson. "Geography and Ecology of Ancient Palestine." In *The Old Testament World*. 2nd ed. Louisville, KY: Westminster/John Knox, 2005.

Day, Linda, and Carolyn Pressler, eds. *Engaging the Bible in a Gendered World: An Introduction to Feminist Biblical Interpretation in Honor of Katharine Doob Sakenfeld*. Louisville, KY: Westminster/John Knox, 2006.

Dennis, Trevor. *Sarah Laughed: Women's Voices in the Old Testament*. Nashville, TN: Abingdon, 1994.

Davies, Eryl W. *The Dissenting Reader: Feminist Approaches to the Hebrew Bible*. Burlington, VT: Ashgate, 2003.

Dreshner, Samuel H. *Rachel*. Minneapolis, MN: Fortress Press, 1994.

———. "Rachel and Leah: Sibling Tragedy or the Triumph of Piety and Compassion?" *Biblical Review* 23 (1990): 20–27, 40–42.

Ebling, Jennie R. "Marriage." In *Women's Lives in Biblical Times*. London: T & T Clark, 2010.

Exum, J. Cheryl. ""Who's Afraid of 'The Endangered Ancestress'?" In *The New Literary Criticism and the Hebrew Bible*. Sheffield, UK: JSOT Press, 1993.

Fewell, Danna Nolan, and David M. Gunn. *Gender, Power, and Promise: The Subject of the Bible's First Story*. Nashville, TN: Abingdon Press, 1993.

Fischer, Irmtraud. *Women Who Wrestled with God: Biblical Stories of Israel's Beginnings*. Collegeville, MN: Liturgical Press, 2005.

Fretheim, Terence E. *Creation Untamed: The Bible, God, and Nature Disasters*. Grand Rapids, MI: Baker Academic, 2010.

Friedman, Mordechai. "Tamar, a Symbol of Life: The 'Killer Wife' Superstition in the Bible and Jewish Tradition." *Association of Jewish Studies* 15 (1990): 23–61.

Fuchs, Esther. *Sexual Politics in the Biblical Narrative: Reading the Hebrew Bible as a Woman*. Sheffield, UK: Sheffield Academic Press, 2003.

Fung, Yiu-Wing. *Victim and Victimizer: Joseph's Interpretation of His Destiny*. Sheffield, UK: Academic Press, 2000.

Gerstenberger, Erhard S. *Yahweh the Patriarch: Ancient Images of God and Feminist Theology*. Minneapolis, MN: Fortress Press, 1996.

Green, Barbara. *Remembering the Story of Joseph*. Lanham, MD: University Press of America, 1996.

Habel, Norman C., and Peter Trudinger, eds. *Exploring Ecological Hermeneutics*. Atlanta, GA: Society of Biblical Literature, 2008.

Habel, Norman C., and Shirley Wurst, eds. *The Earth Story in Genesis*. Sheffield, UK: The Pilgrim Press, 2000.

Hamilton, Victor P. *The Book of Genesis: Chapters 1–17*. The New International Commentary on the Old Testament. Grand Rapids, MI: Eerdmans, 1990.

Hiebert, Theodore. *The Yahwist's Landscape: Nature and Religion in Early Israel*. New York: Oxford University Press, 1996.

Higgins, Jean. "The Myth of Eve: The Temptress." *Journal of the American Academy of Religion* 44, no. 4 (1976): 639–47.

Hillel, Daniel. *The Natural History of the Bible: An Environmental Exploration of the Hebrew Scriptures.* New York: Columbia University Press, 2006.

Jeansonne, Sharon Pace. *The Women of Genesis: From Sarah to Potiphar's Wife.* Minneapolis, MN: Fortress Press, 1990.

Jeremiah, Anderson. "Reclaiming 'Her' Right: Rereading the Story of Tamar (Genesis 38:1-27) from Dalit Women Perspective." *Bangalore Theological Forum* 38 (2006): 145–56.

Kaminski, Carol M. "Beautiful Women or False Judgment? Interpreting Genesis 6:2 in the Context of the Primeval History." *Journal for the Study of the Old Testament* (2008): 457–73.

King, Philip J., and Lawrence E. Stager. *Life in Biblical Israel.* Louisville, KY: Westminster/John Knox, 2001.

Kramer, Samuel Noah. *The Sumerians: Their History, Culture and Character.* Chicago, IL: University of Chicago Press, 1963.

Kvam, Kristen E., Linda S. Schearing, and Valarie H. Ziegler, eds. *Eve & Adam: Jewish, Christian, and Muslim Readings on Genesis and Gender.* Bloomington: Indiana University Press, 1999.

LaCocque, André. *Onslaught against Innocence: Cain, Abel, and the Yahwist.* Eugene, OR: Cascade Books, 2008.

Lapsley, Jacqueline E. *Whispering the Word: Hearing Women's Stories in the Old Testament.* Louisville, KY: Westminster/John Knox, 2005.

Legrand, Lucien. "Israel and Canaan." In *The Bible on Culture.* Maryknoll, NY: Orbis Books, 2000.

Lerner, Gerda. *The Creation of Patriarchy.* New York: Oxford University Press, 1986.

Levison, John R., and Priscilla Pope-Levison, eds. *Return to Babel: Global Perspectives on the Bible.* Louisville, KY: Westminster/John Knox, 1999.

McKay, Heather. "Confronting Redundancy as Middle Manager and Wife: The Feisty Woman of Genesis 39." In *The Social World of the Hebrew Bible: Twenty-Five Years of the Social Sciences in the Academy,* 221–24. Semeia Series 87. Atlanta, GA: Society of Biblical Literature, 1999.

Mathews, Kenneth A. *Genesis 1–11:26.* The New American Commentary: An Exegetical and Theological Exposition of Holy Scripture. Vol. 1A. Nashville, TN: Broadman & Holman Publishers, 1996.

Matthews, Victor H. "Ancestral Period." In *Manners and Customs in the Bible: An Illustrated Guide to Daily Life in Biblical Times*. 3rd ed. Peabody, MA: Hendrickson Publishers, 2006.

———. "The Anthropology of Clothing in the Joseph Narrative." In *Journal for the Study of the Old Testament* 65 (1995): 25–36.

Mbuwayesango, Dora R. "Childlessness and Woman-to-Woman Relationships in Genesis and in African Patriarchal Society: Sarah and Hagar from a Zimbabwean Woman's Perspective (Gen 16:1-16; 21:8-21)." *Semeia* 78 (1997): 27–36.

Meyers, Carol. *Discovering Eve: Ancient Israelite Women in Context*. New York: Oxford University Press, 1988.

———. "The Family in Early Israel." In *Families in Ancient Israel*, edited by Leo G. Perdue, Joseph Blenkinsopp, John J. Collins, and Carol Meyers, chap. 1. Louisville, KY: Westminster/John Knox, 1997.

———. "'To Her Mother's House': Considering a Counterpart to the Israelite *Bêt 'āb*." In *The Bible and the Politics of Exegesis*, edited by David Jobling, Peggy Lynne Day, and Gerald T. Sheppard. Cleveland, OH: The Pilgrim Press, 1991.

Meyers, Carol, ed. *Women in Scripture: A Dictionary of Named and Unnamed Women in the Hebrew Bible, The Apocryphal/Deuterocanonical Books, and the New Testament*. Boston: Houghton Mifflin Company, 2000.

Millett, Craig Ballard. *Archetypes of Women in Scripture*. San Diego: LuraMedia, 1991.

Neuser, Jacob. *Genesis Rabbah: The Jewish Commentary to the Book of Genesis*. Vol. 1. Atlanta, GA: Scholars Press, 1985.

Newsom, Carol A., and Sharon H. Ringe, eds. *Women's Bible Commentary*. 3rd ed. Louisville, KY: Westminster/John Knox, 2012.

Ngan, Lai Ling Elizabeth. "Neither Here nor There: Boundary and Identity in the Hagar Story." In *Ways of Being, Ways of Reading: Asian American Biblical Interpretation*, edited by Mary F. Foskett and Jeffrey Kah-Jin Kuan. St. Louis, MO: Chalice Press, 2006.

Nowell, Irene. *Women in the Old Testament*. Collegeville, MN: Liturgical Press, 1997.

Oduyoye, Modupẹ. *The Sons of the Gods and the Daughters of Men: An Afro-Asiatic Interpretation of Genesis 1–11*. Maryknoll, NY: Orbis Books, 1984.

Pardes, Ilana. *Countertraditions in the Bible: A Feminist Approach.* Cambridge, MA: Harvard University Press, 1992.

Park, William. "Why Eve?" *St. Vladimir's Theological Quarterly* 35 (1991).

Perdue, Leo G., Joseph Blenkinsopp, John J. Collins, and Carol Meyers. *Families in Ancient Israel.* Louisville, KY: Westminster/John Knox, 1997.

Petersen, John. *Reading Women's Stories: Female Characters in the Hebrew Bible.* Minneapolis, MN: Fortress Press, 2004.

Primavesi, Anne. *From Apocalypse to Genesis: Ecology, Feminism and Christianity.* Minneapolis, MN: Fortress Press, 1991.

Räisänen, Heikki. *Reading the Bible in the Global Village: Helsinki.* Atlanta, GA: Society of Biblical Literature, 2000.

Rashkow, Ilona N. "Daughters and Fathers in Genesis . . . Or, What's Wrong With This Picture?" In *The New Literary Criticism and the Hebrew Bible*, edited by J. Cherly Exum and David J.A. Clines. Sheffield, UK: JSOT Press, 1993.

———. *The Phallacy of Genesis: A Feminist-Psychoanalytic Approach.* Louisville, KY: Westminster/John Knox, 1993.

Redford, Donald B. "Joseph." In *Egypt, Canaan, and Israel in Ancient Times.* Princeton, NJ: Princeton University Press, 1992.

Reisenberge, A. T. "The Creation of Adam as Hermaphrodite—and Its Implications for Feminist Theology." *Judaica* 42 (1993): 447–52.

Richards, Phillip. "The 'Joseph Story' as Slave Narrative: On Genesis and Exodus as Prototypes for Early Black Anglophone Writing." In *African Americans and the Bible: Sacred Texts and Social Textures*, edited by Vincent L. Wimbush. New York: Continuum, 2000.

Sakenfeld, Katharine Doob. *Just Wives? Stories of Power and Survival in the Old Testament and Today.* Louisville, KY: Westminster/John Knox, 2003.

Schneider, Tammi J. *Mothers of Promise: Women in the Book of Genesis.* Grand Rapids, MI: Baker Academic, 2008.

———. *Sarah: Mother of Nation.* New York: Continuum, 2004.

Scholz, Suzanne. *Introducing the Women's Hebrew Bible.* London: T & T Clarke, 2007.

Schottroff, Luise, Silvia Schroer, and Marie-Therese Wacker. *Feminist Interpretation: The Bible in Women's Perspective.* Translated by Martin and Barbara Rumscheidt. Minneapolis, MN: Fortress Press, 1998.

Schreiter, Robert J. *Reconciliation: Mission and Ministry in a Changing Social Order.* Maryknoll, NY: Orbis Books, 1992.

———. *The Ministry of Reconciliation: Spirituality and Strategies.* Maryknoll, NY: Orbis Books, 1998.

Schroeder, Joy A. *Dinah's Lament: The Biblical Legacy of Sexual Violence in Christian Interpretation.* Minneapolis, MN: Fortress Press, 2007.

———. *Sarah: Mother of Nations.* New York: Continuum, 2004.

Schwantes, Milton. "Do Not Extend Your Hand against the Child." In *Subversive Scriptures: Revolutionary Readings of the Christian Bible in Latin America,* edited and translated by Leif Vaage. Valley Forge, PA: Trinity Press International, 1997.

Shanks, Hershel, ed. *Feminist Approaches to the Bible.* Washington, DC: Biblical Archaeology Society, 1995.

Sheres, Ita. *Dinah's Rebellion: A Biblical Parable for Our Time.* New York: Crossroad, 1990.

Shields, Mary E. "'More Righteous Than I': The Comeuppance of the Trickster in Genesis 38." In *Are We Amused? Humor about Women in the Biblical Worlds.* Journal for the Study of the Old Testament Supplement Series 383. New York: T & T Clark, 2003.

Simopoulos, Nicole M. "Who Was Hagar? Mistress, Divorcee, Exile, or Exploited Worker; An Analysis of Contemporary Grassroots Readings of Genesis 16 by Caucasian, Latina, and Black South African Women." In *Reading Other-Wise,* edited by Gerald O. West. Atlanta, GA: Society of Biblical Literature, 2007.

Spanier, Kitziah. "Rachel's Theft of the Teraphim: Her Struggle for Family Primacy [Gen 31]." *Vetus Testamentum* 42 (1992): 404–12.

Stratton, Beverly J. *Out of Eden: Reading, Rhetoric, and Ideology in Genesis 2–3.* Sheffield, UK: Sheffield Academic Press, 1995.

Teubal, Savina J. *Hagar the Egyptian: The Lost Tradition of the Matriarchs.* San Francisco: Harper & Row, 1990.

———. *Sarah the Priestess: The First Matriarch of Genesis.* Athens: Ohio University Press, 1984.

Trible, Phyllis. "Genesis 22: The Sacrifice of Sarah." In *Not in Heaven: Coherence and Complexity in Biblical Narrative,* edited by Jason P. Rosenblatt and Joseph C. Sitterson. Bloomington: Indiana University Press, 1991.

———. *God and the Rhetoric of Sexuality.* Overtures to Biblical Theology. Philadelphia, PA: Fortress Press, 1978.

———. *Texts of Terror: Literary-Feminist Readings of Biblical Narratives.* Overtures to Biblical Theology. Philadelphia, PA: Fortress Press, 1984.

Trible, Phyllis, and Letty M. Russell, eds. *Hagar, Sarah, and Their Children: Jewish, Christian, and Muslim Perspectives.* Louisville, KY: Westminster/John Knox, 2006.

Harold D. Washington, Susan Lochrie Graham, and Pamela Thimmes, eds. *Escaping Eden: New Feminist Perspectives on the Bible.* New York: New University Press, 1999.

Waters, John W. "Who Was Hagar?" In *Stony the Road We Trod: African American Biblical Interpretation,* edited by Cain Hope Felder. Minneapolis, MN: Fortress Press, 1991.

Weems, Renita J. *Just a Sister Away: A Womanist Vision of Women's Relationships in the Bible.* San Diego: LuraMedia, 1988.

———. "Two Modes of Reading the Cain and Abel Story." In *Biblical Hermeneutics of Liberation: Modes of Reading the Bible in the South African Context.* Maryknoll, NY: Orbis Books, 1991.

Wenham, Gordon J. *Genesis 1–15.* Word Biblical Commentary. Waco, TX: Word Books Publication, 1987.

West, Gerald O. "Difference and Dialogue: Reading the Joseph Story with Poor and Marginalized Communities in South Africa." *Biblical Interpretation* 2 (1994): 152–70.

———. "Two Modes of Reading the Cain and Abel Story." *Biblical Hermeneutics of Liberation: Modes of Reading the Bible in the South African Context.* Maryknoll, NY: Orbis Books, 1991.

West, Gerald O., and Musa W. Dube, eds. *The Bible in Africa: Transactions, Trajectories and Trends.* Boston: Brill Publishers, Inc., 2000.

Westermann, Claus. *Genesis 1–11: A Commentary.* Minneapolis, MN: Augsburg Publishing House, 1984.

———. *Joseph: Eleven Biblical Studies on Genesis.* Minneapolis, MN: Fortress Press, 1996.

Winter, Miriam Therese. *The Chronicles of Noah and Her Sisters: Genesis and Exodus according to Women.* New York: Crossroad, 1995.

Wray, T. J. *Good Girls, Bad Girls: The Enduring Lessons of Twelve Women of the Old Testament.* Lanham, MD: Rowman, Littlefield Publishers, Inc., 2008.

Yamauchi, Edwin M. "The Curse of Ham." In *Africa and the Bible,* chap. 1. Grand Rapids, MI: Baker Academic, 2004.

Yee, Gale A. *Poor Banished Children of Eve: Women as Evil in the Hebrew Bible*. Minneapolis, MN: Fortress Press, 2003.

Subject Index